D0768925

# AS I REMEMBER

# ARTHUR BLISS

## As I Remember

London
FABER AND FABER

*First published in 1970*
*by Faber and Faber Limited*
*24 Russell Square London WC1*
*Printed in Great Britain by*
*Western Printing Services Ltd Bristol*
*All rights reserved*

*SBN 571 09282 9*

© *1970 by Arthur Bliss*

To My Wife and Dear Companion
during forty-five years

# Illustrations

# Acknowledgements

Grateful acknowledgements are due to the following for their kind permission to reproduce letters: Howard Bliss, Nickolas Bridges Adams (for his father's letters), Mrs. Carice Elgar Blake (for her mother's and father's letters), Benjamin Britten (for the extracts from his letter used on the jacket), Thurston Dart, J. B. Priestley, Kathleen Raine, the Executors of Dame Edith Sitwell, the Society of Authors as Agents for the estates of James Joyce, John Masefield and Bernard Shaw, Professor G. P. Wells (for his father's letter), Ursula Vaughan Williams (for the letter of Ralph Vaughan Williams), and Kenneth Wright.

# Foreword

It has proved, from the distance of old age, more difficult than I had expected to portray clearly the child, the growing boy and the young man that I once was. It is not so much memory that fails as the ability to convey in vivid enough words the sensations felt in those early days. Time gradually dulls the poignancy of feelings, and what is called the serenity of age is only perhaps a euphemism for the fading power to feel the sudden shock of joy or sorrow.

For instance, I can clearly see myself at the age of eight, left for the first time at a boarding school, a small, miserable, bewildered figure; what I cannot express is what I then felt as the familiar world of home crumbled in an instant before my eyes. Nor can I succeed in conjuring up the rapture of the first falling in love. I remember how my heart would beat at the postman's knock, and, if no letter came, how long and sullen was the day that followed, but the pain and ecstasy of those days now belong to a stranger.

That they still have a hidden life is proved by their continuing to supply the emotional content of my music long afterwards, but I cannot today depict with the right immediacy the diamond-clear images which the years between have softened and blurred. It needs a Tolstoy to perform that miracle.

In these reminiscences I have not entered the Confessional box; I know it is a customary practice nowadays for a biographer to strip his victim naked and explore whatever malformations he may find, but I must leave this sort of dissection to some future investigator, if there should be one who feels there is something worth discovering.

An omission more due for an apology is the absence of the names of a great number of friends. I could have filled many pages about those met in the course of the years who contributed to the colour and gaiety of life, but I have confined myself to mentioning only those, and they are not necessarily the most famous, who have in some way or other directly or indirectly shaped my career.

I wish first to thank my wife and my brother Howard for having helped me with their keen memories to reconstruct many scenes

13

of the past; without their aid some of these would have vanished beyond recall.

Then I owe special gratitude both to Eric Crozier for being the first to read, check, and comment on each chapter as it was written and sent to him, and to John Waterhouse without whose professional skill the amorphous mass of material might never have got itself shaped into anything like a readable book.

Finally, two personal friends of mine, Betty Lammin and Elizabeth Travis made themselves responsible for deciphering my almost illegible pencilled pages and converting them into clear typescript; I am indeed greatly indebted to them both for their long task.

# Chapter I

## 1891–1914

ONE PREDILECTION OF PROUST I certainly share and that is a love for the hawthorn and especially for that deep red variety which reminds a child of his or her first sweet strawberry ice. This vivid colour may have been the first that caught my gaze as I lay in my 'pram' beneath its display, in the garden of the house where I was born.

The site of this house (it suffered destruction in the last war) was in Queen's Drive, bordering on Barnes Common, and its name 'Hawthornden' derived from the splendid hawthorn planted in the small circular drive that led to the house. I owe, also, my third Christian name to this tree, for my mother christened me Drummond in the hope, perhaps, of my becoming a poet.

My mother ardently loved music and must have been a good amateur pianist, if the volumes of her music that I have, all marked with her phrasing and fingering, are sufficient proof. Although she died when I was only four years old, I like to imagine that the first sounds of music that I ever heard came from her fingers as she practised in our drawing-room in Hawthornden.

Early childhood memories that sink for many years below the surface of consciousness are apt to rise slowly and clearly again in old age.

My first experience of drama! One night the gorse bushes on Barnes Common caught fire and the blaze quickly spread in a strong wind. Awakened by shouts and cries I went to my bedroom window and watched with frightened fascination dark shapes leaping around with brooms as they beat out the flames which had rapidly approached our road; a vision of Walpurgisnight, if I had known *Faust* in those days.

I am told that as a very small child I was entranced by watches, clocks or by any object that chimed and tolled the hour, and that at children's parties I would wander away from the others at their games and stand transfixed in front of any new clock that the strange house could provide. This obsession of mine must have caused my father

15

some anxiety, for temporarily all clocks in our home were removed or covered up. I expect this simple solution was more successful than any that a future psychologist could have devised. I had forgotten how retentive a child's first enthusiasms could be until some thirty years later when the curtain rose on a performance of Ravel's opera *L'Heure Espagnole*. As the contrapuntal chiming and ticking of the clocks filled the clockmaker's shop with sound, suddenly a hand seemed to draw aside the covering of all these years, and I felt once more the inexplicable warmth of pleasure that as a child I found in these rhythmically pulsating inventions.

Sometimes on Sundays my father, my two younger brothers, and I would drive over to Mortlake to have tea with my grandmother. Her house held a number of delights. It ran down to the river, and on Boat Race days we were invited to come and catch a glimpse of the scene on the Thames. A charming way of knowing which boat had won was to wait until disks of coloured paper (dark or light blue) were seen floating down over the garden—thrown, I always imagined, from a balloon high over the finishing point.

Over and above the delicious variety of food to be eaten at tea, there was the added attraction of my Uncle Kennard who, after retirement, lived with his mother. His retirement had been from China where he had lived for many years, and for his work there he was reputed to have been given the title of Mandarin. He certainly seemed to us to have the inscrutability of one who knew the mysteries of Pekin; perhaps this was accentuated by a present he once gave us.

This was a Chinese vase some two feet in height topped with a lid, and a key in one of its sides. When it was wound up, music would issue from the inside, the lid would slowly rise, and up would come—yes, a mandarin, in green silk with long drooping moustaches, who, slowly turning his head from side to side, would then raise a cup of tea to his lips: after more salutations in which his long moustaches would quiver, he would gracefully withdraw again and the lid would close over him. My brother Howard, who has a phenomenal memory for the past, can still remember and play this long-vanished music.

After my mother's death my father moved to a house in Holland Park, Bayswater. It was in this house (No 21) that I was to live, with my father and my brothers, for the next twenty-seven years. After Hawthornden it seemed very big and magnificent. My father had taken a cruise round the world, and had sent back treasures to furnish it. He was a man who loved fine things and was a discriminating collector. The influence of beautiful things daily before my eyes proved an imperceptible but abiding form of education. I was supremely lucky not only in having such a father, to whom indeed I owe all that I may have myself achieved, but also in having one who by his own ability and hard work was able to give me the perfect environment in which to spend the years of my youth.

He was born in Springfield, Massachusetts, and for many years his ancestors had come from New England. When in 1923 I went with my father to America, and visited the places whence this branch of our family derived, I felt very strongly the dual allegiance that I had inherited.

My first memory of the great outside world that existed alongside my own childish one was of seeing the Diamond Jubilee of Queen Victoria. I was six at the time, and my father had obtained seats in a stand in Regent Street. After what seemed an interminable wait a wave of cheering and clapping announced the approach of the Queen, a little old woman in black bowing from an open carriage, escorted, surely, by Indian lancers. Whether accurate or not, the impression of glittering splendour surrounding a lonely blob of black is what is etched on the retina of memory.

About this time I must also have been taken by my father to see Sousa conducting his famous band; as an American he rightly thought we should support this concert. Was it the immaculate white kid gloves that Sousa drew on before raising his baton, with something of a Beecham panache, which attracted me most or the drilled precision with which various groups of his band, cornets, trombones, woodwind, acknowledged in turn the applause? I forget, but I wish I could re-hear how he performed those marches of his, marches which Constant Lambert declared the best ever written.

Until the age of eight, I went to a school (since demolished by a bomb) tucked away in the north-west corner of Orme Square, off the Bayswater Road. My memories today are not of certain boys destined later to become very important persons indeed, but of one boy whose name and face I can no longer identify. He lives for me through his talent for drawing, and for sketches, mostly in ink, of a precise character. They were copies of warriors as commonly seen on Greek pottery, and as my father was in the habit, when taking us for walks, of retelling stories from the Homeric tales, these boyish sketches brought to life the heroes fighting on the plains of Troy and around the Grecian ships. Again I should have completely forgotten this image from my first school, if it had not pressed its attention on me when I was composing my choral symphony, *Morning Heroes*, thirty years later, and setting the passage from Chapman's *Iliad* in which the arming of Achilles is described.

At about this time my brothers and I underwent dancing instruction in the school of a Mrs. Wordsworth, who, Dame Ninette de Valois told me years later, was just as formidable a figure as she then appeared to us. An occasional black patch over one eye and a commanding voice gave her a personality to be much respected, and when she shouted at me 'Point your toes, little boy', emphasising this with a bang of her stick on the polished floor, I pointed. Mirrors all around the room showed my efforts to overcome ineptitude, and also, I expect, the smiles of the little girls to whom all poses came so easily. This ordeal seemed to be the necessary introduction to whatever pleasure there might be in going to dances. The only ones I really enjoyed were at the house of my two cousins, Nellie and Betty Davis, in Roehampton; at less friendly houses the etiquette of those days could be completely off-putting—the white gloves to wear, the introductions, the dance programmes with the dangling pencil in which one wrote the name of the little girl introduced, but not comprehended; one simply scrawled 'Dance No. 3 girl in yellow'. Alas! when Dance No. 3 came, there were at least three girls in yellow. I had not the courage to make the choice of Paris. To my shame I admit that I temporarily vanished. Compensation came with the symphonic rendering of *The Lancers* or with such excellent speed-boat dances as the *Washington Post* or the *Galop*. As I write the names of these forgotten dances, the whole era before the onslaught of the twentieth century seems as faint as the tinkle of a spinet.

I was nine years old when the present century launched itself, and had been for a term at the preparatory school, Bilton Grange. This lay a few miles from Rugby School, to which many of the boys including myself and my brothers were destined to go. In my time at Bilton Grange there were still a few Dickens-like horrors persisting, but there were happy moments as well. I shall always be grateful to the self-effacing and dedicated music master there who introduced me to the Beethoven Sonatas, and who on my leaving presented me with the piano works of Schubert. I still have these two volumes in constant use and love their old-style printing and binding.

For many years I have made it a habit to pencil an exclamation mark into the margin of music whenever I come across a bar or passage which surprises and so delights me (lately I find myself saying 'wonderful!' instead). I find the two Schubert volumes liberally sprinkled with these signs, and there are few that are later rubbed out as not being on second thoughts worthy of the accolade. I read somewhere that Petrarch used to write letters to the great dead whom he particularly admired. There are composers too lofty for such correspondence, but I should have liked to have written to Schubert, if I had thought of Petrarch's engaging fantasy.

My introduction to Beethoven through practising his *Andante con Variazioni*, Op 26, and then through hearing in London his *Coriolan Overture* and Fifth Symphony fired me with a longing to find out all there was to know about his personality and life. The image of this tragic figure became so vivid to me that it resulted in a recurrent dream the scene of which has not left me till this day. I was to have a lesson from Beethoven himself. I dreamt that he was living in some broken-down hut on the Thames, such a hovel as would have suited Quilp's Wharf (I must have been dipping into *The Old Curiosity Shop* at the time). I knew I was late as I started to run, music case in hand, through the ever poorer and poorer streets of London towards the waterside. As I desperately hurried, suddenly the sound of what was then called a German band brought me to a stop. There was something threatening and sinister in the music, and I turned aside in fear down a parallel street. Again the strident and forbidding sounds halted me. Frightened I darted hither and thither to avoid the very sight of those players, till at last almost distraught I flung myself through the danger, and panting and dishevelled hurled myself up the steps of the poverty-stricken house where Beethoven was waiting for me. I had no sooner hammered on the door than a veiled figure appeared at the entrance and in a low voice said 'The master is dead'.

It was at Bilton Grange that I realised that my first ambition, to become a famous pianist, was without any doubt a vain one. From an early age I had taken piano lessons from a succession of teachers, but I was not an apt pupil. I had quickness and facility, but not the faculty of concentration: the next page of any score was always more interesting than the one in front of me, with its instant difficulties to be overcome. I preferred to skim like a humming-bird moth from piece to piece rather than remain a caterpillar meticulously devouring a single leaf.

The vision of a soloist sitting on the platform at his concert grand with a breathlessly expectant audience filling the large hall around him was an enticing one, but its realisation demanded gifts I certainly did not possess. My moment of decision came at a school concert at which I was to play Handel's Variations in E (popularly called *The Harmonious Blacksmith*). As I dilly-dallied with my piano stool, my mind went blank, and the simple statement of the tune on which the Variations are based completely eluded me. After an anguished moment of indecision I plunged recklessly into a later variation. Recollections of early failures cast long shadows, and today, even when conducting my own music, which I should know intimately, I keep a score before me in case a similar lapse of memory should harass me.

At thirteen or so I duly went on to Rugby where I remained the statutory five years. I did not see the school again for forty-seven

19

years, not until in 1962 I accepted an invitation to conduct a performance of my cantata *The Beatitudes* in the Speech Room which I had last seen at its ceremonial opening by King Edward VII. I naturally found that an immense improvement in the attitude to musical training had taken place. In my time any boy who showed a determination to become a musician was *rara avis*, to be treated with a good deal of condescension, if not worse. All teaching and practising had to be squeezed in after school hours and in very inadequate premises. On this later visit I found a finely equipped department, with music being assessed at its true value as a force in education.

Basil Johnson was the organist and music master in 1905, and he fought hard and with enthusiasm for increased opportunities. I owe him many happy hours of a Sunday at his house playing on two pianos with friends and gaining in this way knowledge of classical symphonies. Mrs. Basil Johnson was always a kind hostess and an original personality too: if I remember rightly there was a good-sized tree growing in one of her rooms, she having refused to have it cut down when the building was proceeding.

It was in this house that I first heard a chamber work of mine performed. Somewhat unusual, it was a quartet for piano, clarinet, cello and timpani, written for my brother Kennard and myself with the addition of two friends who played the cello and drums in the school orchestra. Still under the spell of Beethoven it consisted of variations in the sombre key of C minor. The small invited audience recoiled each time the timpani were thwacked and finally could not restrain their laughter: perhaps a good preparatory lesson against some future audience reactions. Further expansion in musical knowledge came from a young master temporarily filling the post of a sick colleague. He vehemently claimed that the so-called classics were now completely outmoded, and should be regarded as so much dead matter, and that the only music worth studying was that written in our own time. He illustrated this shock opinion by giving me some piano pieces by Debussy and Ravel. How often since then have I heard similar denunciations of dead composers in favour of those living!—and indeed I must have delivered some myself, for in a published letter to the *Daily Telegraph* by Walter Damrosch, dated 1921, in answer to something I had said, I find:

Mr. Arthur Bliss wonders why I still place Beethoven and Brahms on my symphony programmes. I have not yet lost my admiration for these masters; and, to judge from the acclaim which your public still gives them, I fancy there must be many in England who feel as I do. I have never heard any of the compositions of Mr. Bliss, and therefore do not know whether I should class him as a disciple of that 'ugliness in music' which some of the younger school seem to worship.

At fifteen years of age I was immediately captivated by the French masters. I loved the delicious sounds and poetry of Debussy and the cool elegant music of Ravel—no beetling brows and gloomy looks here, but a keen and slightly quizzical look at the world.

When, in 1919, I met Ravel in Paris I told him that his was the first 'modern' music I had ever known, and his slight answering shrug perhaps conveyed an ironic comment on my choice of words, the reaction against his works in favour of the 'circus music' of his juniors being very apparent at the time. My first affection for his music has never wavered. Some of his work may consist of trifles, but they are trifles fashioned with all the imagination and finish of a Fabergé ornament.

What great events were taking place in the world during the years 1905–10 while I was at Rugby? Who was in power, who was dethroned? Who had conquered, who had lost? Without looking at a history of the period, I could not now give any account of those global matters. The small but infinitely dramatic and hazardous doings in the microcosm of Rugby absorbed me entirely, and then—there were the holidays with their special joys. The first decade of this century seems in retrospect to glow with a succession of golden years.

The holidays were all stamped with characteristic variety; Christmas in London, Easter by the sea, generally near Swanage, and for the summer months my father used to rent some house in the beautiful counties of Worcestershire, Shropshire, or Herefordshire. I have mentioned my bachelor uncle Kennard before, and he it was who marked Christmastide by taking all his nephews and nieces to the opening matinée of the yearly pantomime at Drury Lane.

He always managed to get the front row of the dress circle, and from that vantage point, after far too heavy a lunch at the Trocadero Restaurant, we saw the famous fairy tales embellished by the comic genius of Dan Leno and Herbert Campbell—*The Sleeping Beauty, Bluebeard, Mother Goose, Humpty Dumpty*, all enjoyed in successive years before my thirteenth birthday. If I remember rightly these performances, before judicious cutting, were enormously protracted, and the pantomime was then followed by the traditional harlequinade, ending with the splitting open of a gigantic cracker from which Joey and his fellow characters hurled presents into the stalls and neighbouring boxes.

In my later years at Rugby my father took us in two winter holidays to Territet, where we had our first thrill of real ice and snow, as we stumbled about on the slopes at Caux and Les Avants. It was on one of these visits that I suffered a well-remembered musical humiliation. Staying in our hotel was a French flautist, who to celebrate Christmas organised a performance of the *Toy Symphony*, cajoling as many of his acquaintances to take part as he could find. I think we must have quickly offered our own services, expecting to play the instruments that we naturally thought were our due. Affronted that we were only allotted the toys, I, at least, was unwilling to spend time indoors at rehearsals. Others possibly felt the same reluctance, for we were rather a haphazard lot when we finally sat together to enliven the evening for the hotel's guests—I had some kind of bird to play, and needed only to count my bars, put the toy to my lips and blow. To my astonishment no sound came forth, and blew I ever so lustily no sound ever *did* come forth. The French conductor was rightly annoyed, and gave me to understand that I had no right to push myself forward without even knowing how to play a toy instrument. It was only later, deeply ashamed, that I discovered that my little bird needed a fill of water before consenting to trill.

But it was the summer holidays in England that promised the most rewarding joys. These old rectories or country houses with their gardens were perfect repositories for happiness. Names like Clungunford House, Street Court, Yatton Court, Cradley Rectory sound like magical incantations in my ears. At Cradley where we spent five summers the church was just through the rectory garden gate, and I could drop in and play the organ if I could get a friend to act as 'blower' for me. It was here too that I became enamoured of a hobby, remote from music, microscopy. The resident curate was a keen naturalist, and filled me with enthusiasm for the beauty of tiny objects such as flower pollen, fern spores, butterfly scales, as seen through the lens of a microscope. He made beautiful slides himself, and, when I knew him, was making a study of the hair structure of animals. I write as an amateur in these matters, but I think he said, following the example of his contemporary Sherlock Holmes, that a single hair viewed through the microscope was sufficient to determine the species of animal from which it came.

In course of time my father gave me a microscope of my own, and many rewarding but expensive visits I paid to the alluring optician's shop in High Holborn in search of stronger lenses and more slides. I seem to remember a prismatic lens that created wonderful beauties. Any trained young scientist would have smiled at my amateur results, but the fact remains that I held on to my microscope and collections until I left for America in 1923, and I have always regretted the abandoning of so entrancing a hobby. This miniature and magic world of beauty provided the perfect anodyne for the frustrations and failures of creative efforts.

My musical life during the years at Rugby was enriched by a growing love for the music of Elgar. I had heard the *Enigma Variations* on several occasions, and in my last year at Rugby I took part in a performance of *Gerontius*, which put the seal on my fervent admiration. The summers we spent so close to the Malvern Hills made much of his music seem an intimate utterance of our own pleasures.

In some mysterious way a countryside, the look of a landscape can reveal the secret of a composer's attraction. During a walk many years later along the shore of the Lake of Constance I felt I was penetrating the charm of some of Liszt's 'pictorial' music, and a visit to the Benedictine Abbey of Melk seemed to offer a clue to the appreciation of Bruckner: neither of these composers had hitherto meant much to me. Perhaps seeing with one's own eyes what they must have seen gives rise to a sympathetic understanding. Certainly in Elgar's case it is his own loved countryside that provides the key to much of his music.

My appeal to Elgar for an autographed photo met with a chilly printed refusal, and it was not till 1912 that through the kindness of a mutual friend I was allowed to meet Lady Elgar and then the composer himself. The Elgars were living at Severn House in Frognal, and I received an invitation to tea. I toiled up Netherhall Gardens and asked a passerby where the house was. 'Oh! the composer man,' was the reply, 'big house at the top on the right.' I nervously rang the bell, and wondered what I could possibly say to Elgar that would interest him. Luckily he had his own subject and I was at once put at my ease. *His* subject was *Falstaff*, the Symphonic Study at which he had long been working.

After tea in the imposing music-room, he took me into his study, where books on *Henry IV*, essays on Falstaff and histories of the period were strewn about everywhere. Obviously during the composition of this complex work he had been completely absorbed in the study of Shakespeare's world.

The Elgars were very sympathetic friends to me during the following years. When the war came she wrote to me to France:

*Severn House,*
*Hampstead,*
*N.W.*

Dear Mr. Bliss, *Nov. 15th 1915*

I must send you a few lines to tell you I had a great pleasure on Friday as I was able to hear your Quartet. I did so wish you could have been present too as it was, at least it seemed to me, beautifully played and was received with much warmth of applause. An unknown lady sitting behind me asked if I could tell her what other works you had written and seemed thrilled when I told her you were in the trenches.

I much wished Sir Edward could have heard it, but he was engaged that afternoon. The music seemed to me so full of eager life and exhilarating energy and hope, and the writing for the instruments so interesting, and producing delightful effect, some beautiful cello sounds in the 1st movement for instance. I shall hope to hear it again. Sir Edward is very occupied and I hope you will hear some wonderful new things some day.

I hope your leave will really come before long and we hope you will let us know and come and see us as soon as possible.

All best wishes for your health and safety. May God keep you and all our splendid men.

Sir E. does not know I am writing just now or he would send all messages. Your letters interest him greatly.

Yours most sincerely

C. ALICE ELGAR

One of my treasured possessions is a signed miniature score of *Cockaigne*, with his inscription 'Good luck' scrawled across it. This reached me during the first week of the Battle of the Somme, and now, elegantly bound, still carries the mud marks of the trenches on its pages. Elgar's handwriting like the shape of his themes was very characteristic: the pen drew incisive strokes, the words rising boldly in sharply angular lines.

I was welcomed to Severn House on two other occasions, the first of these being in 1917 when I was waiting to be redrafted to France. As I entered the corridors of his home I heard the piano being played, one phrase repeated slowly over and over again: it was some minutes before Elgar joined his wife and myself. Afterwards I discovered that this phrase came from an 'occasional piece', *Le Drapeau Belge*, which, with recited words by E. Cammaerts, was performed later that spring.

The second invitation, just after the war had ended, was to hear a play-through of his newly-written violin sonata. W. H. Reed played the violin with Elgar at the piano—I had the privilege of turning over the pages of the score for Elgar. Some of his oldest friends were present. Landon Ronald and the Bernard Shaws among them, but all I can recall now was a certain embarrassment as to what I ought to say as the sonata ended. Was my disappointment due to the far from brilliant performance or to the belief that its musical substance had little in common with the genius of his earlier masterpieces? I hope I sat quiet, as if absorbed.

I have always thought the popular image of Elgar, in his last decade, as a typical country squire or retired colonel wholly ridiculous. He was really a shy and proud man given to great extremes of emotion. He could laugh uproariously or weep: he had a biting tongue, which on one occasion hurt me much. That he liked being photographed with a couple of dogs and a shooting stick, or that he overemphasised his interest in racing probably arose from his need for a decoy to lure the inquisitive away from private preserves. I have known many artists, especially British ones, employ a similar stratagem.

I have somewhat outrun the chronology of these memoirs, and I must now return to 1909, to my final year at Rugby. These last terms were made wholly exceptional by the presence of Robert Whitelaw, Rupert Brooke's godfather. He was an inspired teacher, and to have seen his small tense figure quivering with excitement as he declaimed famous passages from *King Lear* and *Oedipus Rex* is to have had a vision of what teaching could be.

I used to go to his house for the correcting of Greek or Latin verse, and there happily found a convincing proof of the belief that eccentricity accompanies great learning. Whitelaw had no ear whatsoever for music, but he loved the sound of barrel organs as he worked. So, outside in his drive there was usually one hired, or, if he was lucky, two, grinding out tunes from the Italian operas. I have known several painters who have found music (any music) a help while they work, and who have enjoyed the soft seep of sound that flows continuously from a radio, but I have never met anyone except Whitelaw who could handle words, especially Greek or Latin, under a sound barrage. I am sure that in the Hillmorton Road I never heard a thing he said to me and certain Verdi tunes are now debarred from my enjoyment.

I had continued piano lessons through all these Rugby days with one teacher or another, and one holiday I thought it would be of value to me to know something of a stringed instrument. My elder half-brother had taken lessons from a German violinist, Wilhelm Sachse, and I decided to learn the viola with him. There are as many different types of teachers as there are species of birds. Some drive you too hard and are discouraging, others are too lenient and you stay *in statu quo*, some are talkers and reminisce, others are silent and preoccupied; the majority of course *must* be very good, or we should not have the brilliant players of today. Now Professor Sachse liked to play himself, during a lesson, on his fine violin. I had hardly got the viola under my chin, and was bowing a slow scale, when, knowing that I was a fair pianist, he stalked to the piano, opened it, and muttered 'What about ending with a little Brahms?' We would then

25

play happily together for three quarters of the hour. I willingly forgive him his preference, for I learnt the Brahms Sonatas, but years later I learnt more about the viola by writing a large-scale work for Lionel Tertis than I should have done in a year's tuition from this performing teacher.

Cambridge, like Rugby, has greatly developed its musical resources since my time, but even in the years 1910–13 there were many opportunities for taking an active part. I studied counterpoint and fugue with Charles Wood, a gifted musician whose complete lack of ambition prevented his own music from gaining much of a hearing, though a stirring setting of Whitman's poem *Ethiopia saluting the Colours* was then widely popular.

He taught counterpoint by the old-fashioned system of Rockstro's 'Species', and though I revolted against what seemed unmusical drudgery I nevertheless gained some facility. He took his composition pupils at his home, and there, standing with his back to the fire and teetering sideways from one foot to the other with his eyes fixed on the second button of my waistcoat—he seldom stared you in the face—he would utter irreverent comments on the styles of the day. I grew to like him very much, and just before I left Cambridge I invited him to come to a Queen's Hall concert to hear Henry Wood give the first performance in England of Schoenberg's *Five Pieces for Orchestra*. We had front seats in the dress circle, and during the Schoenberg his irreverence passed so beyond the bounds of discretion that I pretended I had no connection with my laughing neighbour.

To us musicians in Cambridge Vaughan Williams was the magical name; his *Songs of Travel* were on all pianos, and under the direction of Cyril Rootham the Cambridge University Musical Society prepared one of the earliest performances of his *Sea Symphony*. I do not remember now whether the composer came to conduct or not, but he certainly was present at a memorable concert, given by the Cambridge Music Club in the customary rooms over the fish shop in Petty Cury, to hear the first performance of his song cycle *On Wenlock Edge*. Steuart Wilson was the singer, and Denis Browne played the piano: alas, I have forgotten the names of the string players, my attention being riveted on Vaughan Williams himself as he sat in front, dressed in tweeds, smoking a pipe, a massive man with a magnificent head. Epstein is said to have remarked while moulding a bust of him that studying his head gave him strength, and it is an impression that many who knew Vaughan Williams must have shared. His creative life was a long and varied one, in growth and grandeur like some great English oak, and his finest music will surely survive as long as that of a predecessor whose character was perhaps not dissimilar, William Byrd.

26

The experience gained by singing in such works as the *Sea Symphony*, the B Minor Mass of Bach, and the Choral Symphony of Beethoven (the last under Henry Wood) made me realise what a world of difference lies between active music making and just passive listening. The present great increase in children's orchestras and school choirs, and the willingness of today's composers to write special works for their needs, provide the surest way to this country's musical future.

In the pre-war years at Cambridge Edward Dent was the most stimulating influence, bringing into a somewhat provincial backwater a keen breeze from musical Europe. He gave generously of his time to young musicians, and a visit to his house might lead to playing through an act of a Mozart opera, with Dent singing most of the parts in Italian, or to a heated discussion about contemporary music.

He was a close friend of Busoni, and I found myself by this lucky coincidence taking piano lessons from a teacher who had acquired knowledge of his theories. Busoni's own playing made an overpowering impression on me: I first heard him in 1910 during what might be called his 'bearded period'.

As in the case of Liszt, it was the combination of performer and creative artist that gave his interpretations their authority and confident justification. He had his detractors, for his vision was a very personal one, and indeed may not have at all suited the composers themselves. His interpretation of Chopin, for instance, was very masculine, the long Bellini-like cantabiles being played a full mezzo-forte: I have heard him say he wanted them to sound as firm and legato as if played on a clarinet. The twenty-four Preludes which he performed without a break emerged almost as if 'realised' by Busoni. He had a controlled command of dynamics from *ppp* to *fff* and to take one example, in Bach's Chromatic Fantasy and Fugue he would play the Fugue on a long continuous crescendo, which was as exciting as it was unorthodox.

Another personal characteristic was his use of the pedal. In the Fantasy of the same work his arrangement allowed of a mysterious blurring of colours, far more orchestral in sound than the keys of the piano seemed capable of giving. He was a unique phenomenon among the great players I have heard, and I am grateful that even at second hand I had a chance to glimpse something of his ideals.

Most events that took place forty years ago in Cambridge have now coalesced into a kaleidoscopic 'montage'. There was the society formed by friends and myself modestly called 'The Gods', which regularly met to read and play each other's works in a mood of mutual admiration. There were the occasional extravaganzas to enliven such serious mental concentration; the hiring of a bus for the evening in which we dined in formal dress, driving in our mobile restaurant slowly through Cambridge, the challenging of a girls' team to hockey, our handicap being to wear long skirts. I still have a photo of this weird-looking team, which was soundly and painfully beaten by the amazons.

There were long afternoons spent reading in punts, long evenings with heated discussions about everything and nothing, country excursions on an ancient motor-bike, always an object of fear to me; for only by running alongside until the monster fired, and then risking the jump, could I start on my project. There was also, of course, as a climax to each year the approach of May Week and the anxiety over the current charmer.

What I discern in these 'flash-backs' is, with the days, the weeks, the months imperceptibly slipping by, a sporadic and undirected excitement, and a reluctance to concentrate, except haphazardly, on the central core of my being, my music. Life with a very large capital L was too delicious just to breathe in, and I think that I mortgaged the immediate future by this dilettantism, just when I should have closed the doors on a good slice of life and locked myself in with my work. I am well aware that this is an old man moralising, an easy wisdom in retrospect.

After leaving Cambridge, I entered the Royal College of Music and stayed there for a year almost up to the outbreak of war in the August of 1914. It was an age of brilliant students—Herbert Howells, Eugene Goossens, Arthur Benjamin, Ivor Gurney among them. Of these Howells had the outstanding talent. His quickly written scores, showing a beautifully resolute calligraphy, with their technical maturity simply disheartened me. I had to learn one of the most painful lessons in life, that there are others who are born with more gifts than oneself; no amount of self-confidence can at heart convince one to the contrary.

Howells, Goossens and Benjamin became close friends of mine, and it added greatly to the zest of evenings at the Diaghilev ballets and operas to have them alongside me in the gallery at Drury Lane or His Majesty's Theatre. These evenings were shot through with unexpected excitements, as the curtain went up on a Bakst design or the opening notes of a Stravinsky score were heard. On a return home from such a feast we seemed to board the bus with the dash of a Nijinsky leap.

Parry was then director of the R.C.M., and though I never came much in contact with him, I vividly remember a lecture he gave on early programme music, illustrating it from a keyboard sonata by Johann Kuhnau (*The Fight between David and Goliath*). It was an imaginative talk, and I wish now I had had the opportunity of harvesting the rich experience of Parry's mind. I prefer to forget the hours I spent with Stanford: they were not many and from the first moment when he scrawled on my manuscript 'He who cannot write anything beautiful falls back on the bizarre', I felt the lack of sympathy between us. He was a good teacher when in the mood: I felt that instinctively, and certain of his maxims, such as 'Let in air to your score', linger in the mind as truisms to be followed, but his own disappointments as a composer perhaps affected his outlook and he had a devitalising effect on me. Also at twenty-two I was too old to conform, and like my brother Kennard, a hero-worshipper of Berlioz, I regarded the defiant attitude of the great Hector towards the Paris Conservatoire as the only right one for a student.

During these terms I worked in a top room over a carpet shop in Church Street, Kensington. My father kept too large a staff at our house in Holland Park to ensure my working undisturbed. I wish I had the concentration of my friend Darius Milhaud, who could work in Paris with friends chattering around him in the room and despite the noise of the Place Clichy blaring in at the window. I must not only *be* alone, but *feel* that I am. A personal reason, *not* conducive to steady work, also determined the choice of Church Street. The charmer of the time lived close by and could be depended upon to take her poodle for an outing in Kensington Gardens most mornings. Frequent glances from the window gave warning of her approach, and quickly descending the stairs I would nonchalantly wander out to intercept her. This manoeuvre proved as barren of results as the similar one employed by Marcel to win the good graces of Madame de Guermantes.

# Chapter II

## 1914–1917

MANY YEARS AFTER THE First World War I looked for some poems to set which would in some measure convey the emotions of those first months of the summer of 1914. The only lines I could find that had any relation to the feeling of that time came from Walt Whitman's *Drum Taps* in the poem *The City Arming* in which he describes New York at the opening of the Civil War. Neither in 1861 nor in 1914 would the word 'war' have carried the terrible significance that it has acquired since. No war had ever come near me: the South African War, fought in my childhood, was but a distant vague rumbling, and I bought the buttons carrying the little portraits of the various Generals as I might have worn the dark or light blue favours on a Boat Race Day. The crash of a European War on our very beaches sucked me into its undertow without my ever probing the consequences. My action was purely automatic, sparked off by a feeling of outrage at the cause of the war, of a debt owed, and added to this was the spirit of adventure and the heady excitement which the actions of my own contemporaries engendered. Since then the ever-deepening horrors of wars have made the very word the most hideous in our language, but at that time its vague unknown possibilities made it remote from realistic definition.

My last vision of peace days was taking part in an open-air performance of *The Tempest* given for a local charity at Leintwardine House, Herefordshire, on the afternoons of August 6th and 7th. Kennard played Ferdinand and I Caliban. A week later I went to a recruiting office and was immediately assigned to a 'dockers battalion'. I had hardly reported there, when I was abruptly switched to the Inns of Court Officers Training Corps. I can remember nothing of these months, of how we were trained or what our duties were, but in due time I found myself a second lieutenant posted to a new volunteer battalion, the 13th Royal Fusiliers. I arrived in Shoreham in charge of a platoon of recruits as raw and as unacquainted with matters military as I was. How slowly I came to terms with military procedure can be illustrated by two small incidents.

War seems to stimulate rain, for it certainly rained almost without ceasing during that winter in Shoreham. In billets it was well enough, but under canvas often intolerable. One evening a new draft of youngsters arrived and I was on duty. They had of course all volunteered for service, with all that it implied in willingness and in loss of normal life. No arrangements had been made for them, perhaps indeed they were not expected; but there they were, and no bedding or blankets for them—just a couple of sodden tents with their soaking tent boards. Spare dry blankets etc. were safely locked away in the Quartermaster-Sergeant's Stores. These I was told could not be issued without a chit from the Adjutant. 'Where was the Adjutant?' 'In London!' I decided it was a case of my draft seizing them by force or risking a couple of pneumonia cases. We seized them. The next morning was officially a grim one for me.

The second incident was on a night manoeuvre; and I thought my very cleverness would ensure at least promotion. I was ordered to take a patrol through the 'enemy' outposts and bring back a report on their positions. It happened to be a full moon that night which made secrecy difficult; so I commandeered a hay cart that was moving in the direction we had to take and hid my few men in it—to make the disguise even securer, caps were exchanged with the farmer and his son. In this way I was able to make a good get-away and a fairly accurate report. To my surprise I was given to understand that if I played the fool in this way I had better go elsewhere. As all of us realised, we were simply wasting these early months in play acting—no proper uniforms, no proper rifles, elderly retired officers instructing us in methods long discarded. I remember listening to a lecture on the Camel Corps and to one on nautical knots. It required a lot of imagination and confidence to remember that we were training to face the gigantic German war machine. That the Germans were well prepared and trained was continually hammered home to us in the news, and here I can recall a strange hint of this in pre-war days. My elder half-brother had spent a few terms at Heidelberg and made friends there. On returning to England he told my father that at his farewell dinner some students had assured him to his surprise that when they came to London they would see that no harm came to him, or words to that effect. In the light of future events, these parting words took on a sinister implication.

The months went slowly by in Shoreham or Worthing, but I gather that gradually we reached a standard of some efficiency, for I still have the brief diary of our last few days in England, and of our arrival finally in France.

July 26th—pioneer work, filling in trenches, Perham Down.
  ,,   27th—lecture by Gleichen on nothing in particular.

July 28th—Transport goes via Havre.

„ 29th—equipment inspection—eternal route march, mud everywhere.

„ 30th—Tents struck, camp cleaned up, paraded 4.15 p.m., left Ludgershall amid band playing at 5.15 p.m. sailed from Folkestone.

I know that it is superfluous to attempt today any further account of a man's experience of war in France during 1914–18: so many poets and writers have portrayed its realities, neither over-emphasising nor distorting, and, where my own battalion is concerned, the story has been brilliantly written by Guy Chapman in his book *A Passionate Prodigality*. My excuse is that these four years are so deeply etched on my mind that I cannot make a logical form of my life without depicting them. Luckily I have letters and diaries written at the time which tell what I did and thought and saw; without them the gap now of fifty years would be a canyon too broad to cross. Did I really crawl on my belly in the mud at night towards the German trenches patrolling with Mills bombs in my pockets and a revolver in my hand? This picture is now as unreal as a scene from an old film, but once it was a tense reality. Characteristically my father kept all the letters sent from the front by Kennard and myself, and had them set up in beautiful type. I find most of mine make dull reading. It was not so much the censoring that prevented a vivid account as a natural reluctance to let those at home know how bad conditions often were. As my brother Kennard wrote in a letter to Howard 'One simply *has* to write some sort of "cheer O!" stuff. Really, of course, I tremble at the knees "from morn till dewy eve".' All the same I shall quote a few extracts from letters as well as diaries to fill in some of the detail.

### Extracts from Diary

We sailed for France on Friday July 30th 1915. The transport and the machine gunners had crossed from Southampton to Havre the previous day and were to meet the battalion at a pre-arranged rendezvous several days later.

We moved off in two batches, the commanding officer going with the right half battalion, and the second in command with the left. I was detailed as acting adjutant to the latter, which duty narrowed down to looking after a pile of large green forms which were never demanded or required. It was a beautiful night, calm and warm, with a full moon; the boat was crowded from bow to stern, and was escorted most of the time by a destroyer on either side, which communicated signals of any approaching submarine by means of stern lights. In spite of a perfect crossing many of the men who had never crossed the Channel before were very sick.

We landed at Boulogne around 2 a.m., and had a long wait near the landing stage until all the equipment had been checked ashore. Finally we marched off through the silent town, then up one of the stiffest hills I can remember to the rest camp. Many thousands of troops had used it en passant, and it was in a filthy condition. I found the tents full of lice, so we slept in the open air.

The next afternoon I got leave to go into the town and have a swim. From the beach could be seen the masts of several vessels showing above the sea where they had been torpedoed. I was told that until the British Admiralty took over the defence of the harbour German submarines could creep into it with impunity.

The next few days were spent in travelling east towards the sector of the line we were eventually to occupy. We marched to Pont de Briques and entrained there at 10 p.m. The men were herded into cattle trucks labelled to hold eight horses or forty men, and were packed in so tight that in each truck the overflow sat with their feet dangling in space: the officers were in carriages of indescribable dirt.

The journey was slow and wearisome, with all lights out, and with frequent stops and jolts; its top speed never exceeded fifteen miles per hour. But at last at 2 a.m. we arrived at a little station, Watten, tumbled out, formed up and marched off seven miles in drizzling rain to Nortleulinghem. After seeing my platoon under cover, I turned into a barn and slept. Later I took a turn round the village, typical of the many we were subsequently going to make our temporary home—an old Flemish church, the house perhaps of the curé or monsieur le maire, and a collection of farms, outhouses, barns. In these the men were quartered, lying just as they had flopped down, anyhow and anywhere, exhausted and asleep. All the work of this village as of all the others was carried out by the very old or the very young, and with every inch of ground under cultivation very hard work it must have been.

The next days were spent in arduous marching. We would start say at 3.30 a.m. and be on our way before the sun was high, but fifteen miles on a surface of pavé, with the August sun getting ever hotter was a good test of fitness for a man carrying 60 lbs. on his back. We were the rear company of the brigade, and anyone who has done much marching knows what that implies; however slow the pace in front, those in the rear seem always to be breaking into a run to keep up. We became oblivious of scenery or villages, and only looked up when an estaminet came into view, and then 'the eyes right or left' would have done credit to a battalion of Guards.

The divisional H.Q. was at Caestre, and on August 6th I found myself mounting guard over the G.O.C.'s house. The monotony of this was relieved by an invitation to dine at one of the Staff Messes. I slept on a packing case in a little épicerie, and was away as early as possible next morning.

On our way to our destination in Armentières we broke the journey at Bailleul. Another officer and I shared a room in the doctor's house just off the square. To keep up our spirits the housekeeper told us that our room held most gruesome memories. It seemed that other English officers had been billeted there from time to time, and all without exception had come to a tragic end. One had been gassed, another had lost both legs, a third had gone off his head, and still another had been blown to bits by a shell that he was taking home as a souvenir. Perhaps to her disappointment we slept soundly. My Company Commander who had seen active service elsewhere was a real genius for extracting the best of what little was going. He found a small hotel in the square which served as a most comfortable mess: the Mademoiselle who served us with good food and wine told us that not many months before the Germans had used our mess room as a stable.

The entrance into Armentières was not prepossessing—the endless long straight street with the dirty little houses on either side mostly untenanted, with broken windows and no doors, seemed sunk in complete depression. The centre of Armentières did not show much sign of being battered, though the church in the square had blocks knocked off its tower and several of the houses near by had suffered from shelling. The Germans on the whole had left its thoroughfares intact, probably holding it as a hostage against our good behaviour to Lille. Our officers secured a good house in the Rue Sadi Carnot, while the men were billeted in empty houses close by. Our house had been the home of the Deputy, and had a fine big dining-room divided from the living-room by sliding doors. Although no valuable furniture had been left, it must have been in its days of prosperity very attractive, and the old caretaker, who refused to leave, was very ready to talk of the gay happenings in pre-war days. What made it particularly useful to us was that it had a big bathroom and a not too decrepit piano. We learnt next day why we were stationed in Armentières. We were to supply working parties every day to dig lines of defence just east of the town: these were to move off with their rations at 9 a.m. and report back at 5 p.m. The area for digging was named Gunners Farm and was approached by a road that was under observation by the Germans who were enterprising enough to have observation posts up the factory chimneys in Lille. It was their habit to send over a few salvoes of shells every day into this farm, and we were lucky to get our first experience of shelling with but a few light casualties; but I think there are few more unnerving experiences than leading a slow moving column of men from A to B, knowing that over a stretch between these two points we are observed and present an easy target to the enemy's guns.

One of the rewarding chances in war is coming suddenly on former friends serving in other regiments. Most officers found their way to the Café Marguerite, where there was a piano, and between tea and dinner time there was a continuous medley of sound coming from this meeting-place. Canadians, who were holding Ploegstreet at the time, added to the gaiety, and helped to take my mind off a persistent toothache from which I was suffering. I had made various ineffectual attempts to get it treated. I had applied to two French dentists who had given me some ridiculously ineffective paint to put on my gums. I went to Bailleul on leave to find a dentist there, but in vain, and I was really becoming unfit for duty when I heard of a private in the A.S.C. who had done some extractions, and he yanked it out very neatly with what looked surprisingly like a pair of adjustable motor pliers. I bled freely but felt a new man.

To quote again from my diary:

Aug. 19th 1915 in firing line for the first time, with the 11th Middlesex, to put us wise.

Heartily dislike rest billets—always shelled, and men killed in latrines. Mess in small smelly estaminet, flies a plague—cannot use better place, as l'Abbé insists we shall rape the women.

Sept. 4th— marched to Hannescamps—arrival 2.30 a.m. and took over from the French. No guides, and trenches in a ghastly state—nothing but cesspools and open latrines, dug-outs very verminous. Cleaning up and fatigue parties ad nauseam.

Sept. 30th— sleep all morning—read *Julius Caesar*—wrote to Elgar and Parry—had rat hunt that night—they attacked at 9 p.m. with intense bombardment of clay, then charged! A and I completely demoralised.

Oct. 14th— Wiring all the morning, ride on Doctor's horse 'Beauty' to Pas in afternoon for a hot bath. C.O. appears in our mess for the third time. I fear there is trouble brewing. Pub-crawl (i.e. trench inspection) with K. Read *Times* 'Broadsides' and throw away useless ones. Keep 'Hence, loathed melancholy', four poems of Shelley, Wordsworth's 'Intimations'; Tolstoy's *War and Peace*, letters of Lamb to Coleridge and essays of Bacon.

Nov. 8th— Wicked day to relieve trenches: Lulu Lane (main communication trench) under water: had practically to swim down: men fell into sump pits up to their shoulders: lost our cooker. C.O. sends round an alcoholic pledge to be signed! Refuse.

Nov. 9th— 3.30 a.m. started with 200 men and three other officers, heavily laden, for working party at Bienvillers—gale blowing—driving rain—work in pitch darkness—lose men by machine gun fire—soaked through—troubled by infernal boils, a ghastly night!

Nov. 17th— In the trenches, very cold, do not feel very fit. Try rifle grenading. P. accidentally shoots himself cleaning rifle, a sad loss—letter from Lady Elgar, read Conrad's *Victory*.

Nov. 23rd—Took 30 men on patrol: A. and P. shot: lost 5 rifles: made three attempts to recover them from no-man's land: successful the following night.

Nov. 29th— Kennard leaves England with 134th Brigade R.F.A. Very depressing week; the whole place, with continual rain, an utter mud heap. C.O.'s conference, usual hour of boredom. W. hit by shell—post very irregular.

Dec. 7th— Experience our first prolonged bombardment—shelling for 2 hours—a fearful ordeal, with nothing to do but sit and endure it—casualties including Capt. A.—rumour of Prussian Guards behind Monchy.


The monotonous routine of the front line continued through the winter months, miraculously lightened by a sudden 'leave' to England. It was like exchanging one planet for another, and to make use again of my own piano at home gave me indescribable joy. I found in France, as so many others did, that the appreciation of a moment's beauty had been greatly intensified by the sordid contrast around: one's senses were so much more sharply on the alert for sights and sounds that went unnoticed in peacetime because taken so for granted. But a butterfly alighting on a trench parapet, a thrush's songs at 'stand to', a sudden rainbow, became infinitely precious phenomena, and indeed the sheer joy of being alive was the more relished for there being the continual possibility of sudden death.

Here are some extracts from letters to my father at that time.

*February 6th 1916*
. . . Our present line has three places that I do not like to stop in for any length of time. One is the cross-roads in the little village behind

the trenches; this is a very open spot and is always very lively with falling shells. Another is a small length of road, leading to a communication-trench from the village, which is constantly being swept by the enemy's machine-guns. The third is where a large tree has fallen across our trenches, and commonly called the 'Fallen Tree', which furnishes a fine mark for the enemy's artillery and trench-mortars. On coming out last night I cut off a large lump of this tree as a souvenir, and I will send it home one day by some man going on 'leave'. Well, when we go off to a new line we shall go unprejudiced, which is a very comfortable feeling.

Please keep the photo of Captain Anthony\* for me. Many thanks for attending to the gramophone spring. I'm sure that Corporal Baisting will be awfully pleased that he took this home for me. I am greatly looking forward to hearing all the new gramophone records. Yes, I have safely received the Mother Superior's charm and also the wrist-watch that you got mended at the Army and Navy Stores for one of my fellow officers. He has given me the money for it. Many thanks also for attending to my tunic.

I received, by the same post as your very welcome letter, one from Lady Elgar who has now recovered from her motor accident. Says Sir Edward is very occupied with writing new masterpieces.

Well, I must stop now. With best love,

ARTHUR

*February 13th 1916*

Here we are! just moved into our new billets! We changed last night amidst pouring rain. We are not very far from our old place, but it seems quite a different country, being rolling instead of flat, and high instead of low down. The village, where our reserve billets are, is quite a large place and is comparatively untouched by shells. In fact a Frenchman told me they had not had a shell here for many weeks. A French Territorial Regiment occupied it previously to our coming, and all the civilians here are afraid that it will now get badly knocked about. They say that the British always 'strafe' a lot, and stir up the Germans to retaliate!

I have now the best billet since I have been in France, and have a decent bed with sheets, and a nice large Mess. The inhabitants are typical of all these French villages. They're all over ninety years of age, and they take no interest in anything but food, which they are always cooking. Their rooms in consequence always smell of last week's supper. Still, they are very hospitable, especially as we are the first English troops they have seen. They gave us soup when we

---

\* Captain Anthony had been killed on December 15th.

37

got here, and appeared very much amused by our uniforms, etc. Later on they will begin to distrust us and, as generally happens, we shall part in open hostility.

I haven't yet seen our front line trenches, though I hear they're very muddy. We want to hide from the Germans the fact that English troops are now opposite them; but they apparently knew of it the first night, for the regiment going in was welcomed with high explosives. Still, it is fairly quiet here, and I believe the enemy at present call this 'The Happy Valley'! . . .

*March 20th 1916*

. . . A battalion of Regulars has gone in the trenches after us; and, curiously enough, the Company Commander who took over the line from me was at Bilton with me, and a great friend of mine. So, too, was the Second in Command. I was awfully pleased to meet them again and to hear something of their experiences. These were most varied. Seckham, the O.C. Coy., was wounded at Mons, gassed at Ypres, went to Gallipoli, was wounded there, and now has just come to France again.

We shall move right away from the fighting zone, and will be billeted, I expect, some twenty miles back. It will be a great and welcome change, and will give to all the men a chance to recuperate and get fit again. I have been playing this afternoon on the one piano of this village, belonging to the Curé. The Curé from the next village lives with him, as his own village, which he always refers to as 'my poor, poor home', is always being shelled. He is a dear old man, nearly deaf, and was a Professor of Music at one time. He had a lot of old music, mostly of the Corelli-Bach type, which it was great fun dipping into again. I haven't touched a piano properly for six months, not since I was at Armentières, except during my week's 'leave' at home at Christmas.

Many thanks for all the parcels, all of which have arrived safely. You ask about Captain Goodman. He was shot through the heart by a party of Germans, early one morning just before dawn, whilst he was taking some of his men along to fire upon an enemy party that he had seen. I enclose an obituary notice of him, cut from the *Daily Telegraph*; but we have not, of course, seen 'The very heavy fighting' alluded to in the obituary.

We move out from here tomorrow, and shall march about twelve miles. In my next letter I shall be able to tell you what the place is like to which we are going. Even as I write I see two or three small children going off to school, each with a satchel containing a smoke helmet. It all seems so very strange! . . .

In letters to my father I find myself asking for more gramophone records for my portable instrument. These were to include the second part of the *Meistersinger* Overture (replacing a smash), the slow movement of Debussy's Quartet, Overture and March from *Prince Igor*, Tchaikovsky's *Theme and Variations in G*. I wrote 'It is of the greatest possible advantage to have something worthwhile to listen to, worthwhile to read, and worthwhile to eat, probably too in that order'.

My father and friends answered such requests with the utmost generosity. I was continually thanking for whisky, brandy, port, cigarettes, honey, asparagus, vermijelli for vermin, Harrogate rock candy and Fuller's sweets, the *Times* 'Broadsheets' and Elgar's *Falstaff*, tins of calorite and a pair of Mallock-Armstrong ear-defenders, anti-boil remedies and a special 'trench' pipe, a medal from a Mother Superior and the libretto of Stanford's opera *The Critic*. How all these and similar gifts to brother officers reached the front line was one of the war's miracles.

In early spring we were resting well behind the lines, but even this relaxation had its dangers. These were the times when highly-placed staff officers descended on us like a swarm of angry hornets. The number of forms that had to be filled up to appease military computers increased. For many years I kept one that some wretched runner had risked his life to give me as we attacked on the Somme. It was marked 'urgent' and I expected it to be of immediate import-ance, relating to our critical position. The message ran 'How many men in your Coy. are left-handed?'

Following the preliminary inspections came two ominous ones, for they *must* mean that we were now 'for it'. The first visit was that of Haig. He summoned my friend and fellow officer J. K. Gwinnell and myself to him, shook hands with us and uttered a few congratu-latory words. It was curious to see at close quarters the man whose final orders probably put in motion one's chances of life or death. A few days later Kitchener inspected our battalion. Perhaps it was the recollection of his staring eyes and fiercely pointing finger on thousands of recruiting posters that gave the actual man a suggestion of the sinister. As he walked slowly along the ranks I had the impression that his strange eyes were focusing on two objects at once. Both inspections were happily lightened by comedy.

One of our companies was temporarily commanded by the best bridge and poker player I have ever met. He was a most reliable officer on foot, but his experience of horses was nil, and mounted on one for the first time in front of his company, he was plainly mis-cast. As Haig and his staff approached, my friend's horse, startled by the crashing salute given, plunged suddenly forward and carried his rider away off the parade ground and out of sight. It said much for the company's discipline that the men remained poker-faced. At Kitchener's inspection another company commander's horse showed a different side of its nature. It fell asleep, head drooping to the ground, oblivious of the great man's presence. Luckily the only subject that interested Kitchener was the efficacy of our steel helmets. These two inspections undeniably indicated a move, but though we were drafted to a new sector of the line, and gas cylinders were installed by a special unit, nothing untoward for the moment happened.

As May opened I was sent to the 3rd Army School of Instruction for a 'refresher'. Again I had the feeling of being fattened up for the kill, but the conditions of living were too comfortable to allow much foreboding. Such topical necessities as courses on gas and lachrymatory shells with *practical* experiments, on 'the bayonet as a weapon of offence', on revolver shooting were varied with lectures by a general on 'the personal characteristics of Great Commanders'. He outlined the peculiar genius of Alexander the Great, Wellington, Napoleon, von Moltke etc., not forgetting to slip in mention of some improvements(?) that he himself had made to the art of warfare.


The Somme Battle opened with two days' prolonged shelling of the enemy positions, and in pouring rain we were driven in buses to Busieux and thence marched to the reserve trenches near Albert. Amid the ruins of the town were battery after battery and the famous statue of the Virgin hung pitifully down from the cathedral. On the night of July 6th we moved to the front line trenches from which we were to launch an attack on the site of La Boisselle the following morning. In my diary I wrote 'the scene of confusion looks like Hampstead Heath on a Bank Holiday painted by a madman'.

Troops were everywhere: artillery after their two days' fearsome barrage on the German lines were still firing and the sky was luridly lit up by flashes. I led my heavily laden company slowly across the cratered moon landscape in single file; the two guides soon lost their way, no blame to them. What was the use of a map reference when shelling had transformed the terrain? Somehow we stumbled into our trenches facing the Germans and waited. The enemy guns were so silent that either they had been silenced by our prolonged shelling or they were waiting. As we climbed out of the trench sharp at 8.30 a.m. and advanced in a long extended line, we knew which alternative was the right one. They were waiting. I saw men falling on either flank and then I felt as though I had been struck a heavy blow on the leg by an iron bar. I fell in the mud and crawled to some hole for shelter. Later in the day when the battalion had got astride the

Bapaume Road, stretcher bearers, those brave and welcome adjuncts to any attacking force, found me and took me down to the First Aid Post. A tetanus injection, and then I was in an army ambulance jolting down the road to the reserve posts. Below me in a bunk lay a mortally wounded friend whom I had last seen in Cambridge days.

My wound was a slight one, but after a year's experience I felt exhausted, and I remember only as in a dream the slow return to England. I seem to remember a barge on some river, flowers thrown down on the wounded from a bridge, then crossing by sea, and at last a hospital in London.

That autumn was a tragic one for my father, for news reached him that Kennard had been killed on the 28th of September.

A letter from the gunner who was with him at the time deeply touched my father.

> 'D' Battery, 59th Brigade, R.F.A.,
> British Expeditionary Force,
> France

Frank E. Bliss, Esq.,
21, Holland Park,
London, W.                                   October 31st 1916
Sir,

I was with Lieut. Bliss that day as his signaller. The infantry had advanced, and Mr. Bliss went forward as Forward Observing Officer. We reached the advanced infantry about 2 p.m., but being unable to observe clearly from there Mr. Bliss went forward about thirty yards. The enemy were shelling heavily, and about 3 o'clock a heavy shrapnel burst close overhead and he fell without a sound. A piece had pierced his head, and I started to dress his wound; but his death must have been instantaneous.

I carried him back to the trench; and, being rather shaken, I laid him in a sheltered place out of the way of the advancing infantry, where later a party recovered his body. Thus you will see that my being with Mr. Bliss was part of my duty, for which I have been more than amply rewarded by being awarded the Military Medal. I am only too proud to have shown any respect to a brave officer, who had endeared himself not only to me, but to every man in the battery. . . .

> M. I. VALENTINE
> Gunner

I was thankful that my brother Howard who had suffered delicate health ever since his school days had been rejected for the Army on medical grounds, when he presented himself at the Recruiting Office in Cambridge.

When I left France I had not seen Kennard for nearly a year, though on several occasions we had been in the line only a few miles apart, without, of course, being aware of the fact. But on June 1st he walked into our rest billets, as my company were indulging in bayonet-fighting exercise! I rode out to his mess a few days later, heard his gramophone (much Berlioz), saw his gun-emplacements and had a sumptuous meal. I wrote to my father 'Really, if he always dines as well—soup, lobster mayonnaise, roast beef and chips, asparagus, sweets, savoury, washed down with good white wine and liqueur brandy, the R.F.A., gastronomically speaking, is a greatly superior place to the R. Fus. K. is very contemptuous of his Major. The latter is certainly the sort to drink port (someone else's) in gulps from a tumbler, and is according to K. totally incompetent; but he is affable and easily led, and apparently always goes to K. for advice on technical matters.'

This was the last time I saw Kennard, but before his death my brother Howard and I received some letters from him, and I was eager to preserve them, for his indomitable, independent and sardonic spirit shines through them.

'D' Battery, 231st Brigade, R.F.A.,
British Expeditionary Force,
France
July 31st 1916

(Apologies for so serious a letter at this gay event,* but levity is not fitting in war!)

Dear A.

I very much doubt if this letter will reach you on your birthday, but it may make a good attempt.

Well, and I suppose you are looking forward to returning to the front, aren't you? Isn't the joy of sacrifice and the lust for honour hot within you again? Away with a life of ease and idle pleasure! Why waste money on an opera ticket, when you can present the Empire with a hand grenade? I have no gift to bring you! Whilst you are petted and in luxury, I nobly am spending sixteen hours out of twenty-four in sleep, four out of the remaining eight in food, and the other four in novels, chess, and military discussion (armchair variety). I might add that I spend ten minutes nightly in 'chat'-hunting (I am looking forward to reading father's note on this word!). I have had the misfortune to run upon some of these amiable and social beasts in our O.P. dug-out, which is so patronized by the more windy of the infantry as to be no longer tenable by a clean liver.

* i.e. My birthday.

42

I no longer hear the guns down south. There is also a rumour of 'leave' starting shortly. Can it be that the 'Great Offensive' . . . ? But no! Anyone who fed his scepticism on the daily 'Roll of Honour', combined with a study of the map, would be reassured at once by Mr. W. Beach Thomas' frantic eulogies. Don't you think so, mon Capitaine? But I know you do! 'Stout Britishers all'! And so farewell, and fervent wishes that next year's August 2nd will find the wound (in your brain) healed, never to re-open.

KENNARD

To Howard

*'D' Battery, 231st Brigade, R.F.A.,*
*British Expeditionary Force,*
*France*
*August 22nd 1916*

Dear H.

. . . My latest occupation is the decoration of a large letter-box for the Mess. I have painted on the front, against a dark-red background, a yellow woman fantastically dancing on some red, green and brown cushions, with a dark-green cat at her feet. On one of the sides, against a background of bright orange-yellow, zig-zagged with emerald, all wet and running together like shot silk, a tall, thin, sinewy negro (in a sort of greeny-purplish colour—Wonderful!) with arms taut and outstretched, stands on one foot at the top of some steps. The whole is seen through two thin, round arches of a dark, very luminous green. It is absolutely superb in harmony of colour. I have never done anything finer. ('Easily said!' I fancy I can hear you remark!) The figures are drawn in the William Blake style ( = bad Michelangelo). I enclose a study for the negro. The finished drawing is more vigorous even than this, and the arms better drawn. But nothing could equal the easy precision of the leg he is standing on, could it? (No? Thank you!) If we should move from here I shall send home these drawings, together with a caricature, done on the back of a cartridge-box, of the Major holding a glass of (my) port. This last drawing has become quite popular in the Brigade!

What are the 'Promenade' programmes like? I read in the *Daily Mail* the usual grouse about British composers faring so badly in them. What works of Berlioz are they doing?

The puttees have arrived. A thousand thanks! You might tell father that I think the *Saturday Review* is wasted on me really. I am sorry, but 'tis so. I like reading the other side, and should prefer the poor old *Spectator*, if it be not too much trouble to make the change. . . .

'D' Battery, 59th Brigade, R.F.A.,
British Expeditionary Force,
France
September 4th 1916

Dear A.

Many thanks for your letter and Rootham's. I am having, in a way, an interesting time. We had a little (unsuccessful) battle, yesterday, at dawn till noon. It was a pretty sight at first, before it became light. We reached our objective more or less, but had to retire. They shelled our O.P. and smashed a telephone, direction-finder, and maps of a 'Heavy' officer who was using the trench just by the door, but did no other harm. They also fired gas shells round the battery for two hours and a half last night—and must have wasted hundreds. They had the range wrong, and the wind blew the stuff away from us,—a very feeble exhibition. We are moving again, I don't know where to.

It is rather amusing being in a battery where the O.C. knows something about gunnery. He is very charming and pleasant to work with; a serving soldier, but of course very stupid about anything unconnected with his job. I haven't been able yet to speak with freedom about the British Army, but have rather hurt his feelings on the subject of Conscientious Objectors and the importance of 'Peace-at-any-Price'. He said 'I think Militarism is the best thing for a nation.' I asked him what he meant. Of course it was 'Oh! Look at all the weedy youths one sees.' Delightfully naïve, these hired assassins; but he is honest, which I couldn't have said of the detested Major. He, by the way, refused to let me bring my horses (one of which he wants himself), or my servant with me. I share the biggest, stupidest fool you ever saw with another subaltern, and have no horse at present. The men are largely old Regulars or Special Reserve men, stupid, kindly, well-disciplined and dull, with fierce, bullying, servile servants (the type par excellence of our professional splendid Army). I miss my dear civilian crowd enormously, especially the telephonists. I have not seen a spark of brain yet—only efficiency. . . . If you come across any paper-covered books by decent authors, please send them out. I am hard up for literature.

Events march! I am glad to see the Greek people asserting their rights against the Government. If only all would do the same! But I believe we shall have revolutions yet, somewhere. . . .

KENNARD

# Chapter III

## 1917–1919

AS THE YEARS PASSED I came to realise more and more what a poignant loss to the family Kennard's death had been. Poet, painter, musician, he was the most gifted of us all, and to *me* his rebellious nature would have been a stimulant, his caustic comments a sharp corrective through those years when I was struggling on my own for musical expression.

After being passed fit for duty, I was posted, as an instructor, to an officers' cadet battalion in Prior Park, Bath, the beautifully laid out eighteenth-century house and park designed by Ralph Allen. From our quarters on Combe Down we got a fine panorama of Bath itself. Our staff was made up mainly of regular officers, but to my delight one of the 13th Battalion Royal Fusiliers officers, wounded in France, was also sent to join us.

The instruction consisted of drilling and physical training, map reading, signalling and surveying, work at the rifle range, exercises in trench warfare and lectures of various kinds. There was leisure to explore Bath, and I made full use of a room with a piano that I found near the Abbey. I now associate the hours in this room almost entirely with the music of *Götterdämmerung*. Apart from *Die Meistersinger* I had not yet seen any Wagner operas. *The Ring* existed for me only in a piano transcription. I was deeply immersed in a romantic attachment, and Wagner's music seemed to provide just the right outlet for the emotions: in that little room in Bath I stormed through the conflicts between Brünnhilde and Siegfried with much ardour.

It was at this time that I first met Robert Nichols, with whom I was to have a close but uneasy friendship for many years. His was a complex personality compounded of many warring elements. Sometimes he would be wildly exuberant and excitable, at others he would sink into black depression and self-pity. Always generous and loyal to his friends, he would then alienate them by some mad Quixotic action, embarrassing to both giver and taker. He belonged to that class of friend in whose presence we feel it impossible *not* to quarrel, but whom when absent we stubbornly defend. What kept our friend-

45

ship alive was my respect for his creative gifts. He did not leave behind the rich legacy he should have; his brilliant imagination spilled wastefully over into thousands of letters written on all subjects, and to almost everyone he had ever met: these glitter with ideas, fantasies, plans, quotations, comments on music, painting and literature, advice of all kinds, and self-analysis. The pen moved so fast that they were often almost impossible to decipher, but should by some happy chance these scattered letters be collected, edited and published, they would give permanence to a very gifted poet whose lineaments are, alas, fading into oblivion. At our first meeting in 1917 he entered like some attractive young faun in uniform, elated at the success of his first published poems.

Some friends of the Elgars were also staying in Bath, among them Lalla Vandervelde, the wife of the Belgian Minister of Justice. She suggested that she should visit Prior Park and entertain the cadets with a recital. My commanding officer viewed any diversion with interest, and agreed without in any way realising what was planned for the evening. The recital consisted of exuberant renderings of poems by Claudel and Maeterlinck, and ended with a performance of Elgar's *Carillon*, written to accompany a poem of Emile Cammaerts. In this I gave what help I could at the piano to support the ringing voice of Madame Vandervelde but it was the last frenzied cries of 'à Berlin, à Berlin' that established the evening as a real 'diversion'.

Our Colonel happened to be acquainted with Kipling, and unknown to his junior officers invited him over to Prior Park one day to see what sort of training the New Army was getting; I believe Kipling at this time was busy collecting material for a book on the subject. At the hour of his visit I was on the miniature rifle range with my cadets, and we were desultorily engaged in puncturing holes in small targets supposed to represent the head and shoulders of an enemy at (say) two hundred yards.

I was suddenly summoned by our Colonel to confront a small man distinguished by thick overhanging eyebrows, keen eyes behind magnifying glasses, and a jutting chin. 'And what are you doing here with your men, Captain Bliss?' he quietly asked—I imagined a pencil poised above a note-book. I remained completely tongue-tied. Our present occupation in the miniature rifle range seemed far too remote from any experience to be faced in the front line. No words came from me, and Kipling walked away, beside the displeased Colonel, despairing, I suspect, of our military future.

During my absence in France my father, with the professional help of Eugene Goossens, had seen two early chamber works of mine through Novello's printing works—a string quartet and a piano quartet. The string quartet (1915) was dedicated to Dent, who used

46

to say that *all* young composers embarrassed him by putting his name at the head of their earliest and most immature chamber works. I dedicated the piano quartet, written in the same year, to my friend Lily Henkel and her Quartet. This latter work was given a public performance in Bath while I was there, and the event was considered by my commanding officer sufficiently noteworthy to have the cadet corps officially represented at the concert! So his Second-in-Command stoically came into Bath with me, and sat through what turned out to be the first serious concert he had ever attended—an endearing example of protocol duly observed. Perhaps a more appropriate companion would have been the cadet, R. D. Gibson, who in after years became the respected director of the music publishers, J. & W. Chester.

The months went by and, with new officers on sick leave coming as instructors, it was getting time for me to go. I should like to have been sent to rejoin what was left of my old regiment, but the chances seemed very remote and so, acting on a suggestion of a friend who was in the Grenadier Guards, I decided to join this regiment in London. I say 'I decided' but it was not so easy as all that: first I had to have two acknowledged sponsors and then seek a personal interview at Wellington Barracks. If you were favourably viewed you could then find yourself stationed at Chelsea Barracks. The situation was exactly as if a man who had just taken his degree at Cambridge should by magic be transported back to his preparatory school.

In spite of a year of active service in France and then months spent in instructing others in military procedure, there I was again on the Square, rifle in hand, listening with my fellow subalterns to the commands of a regimental sergeant-major. There were lectures on the history and tradition of the Brigade of Guards, and minute regulations dealing with what *could* and could *not* be done: the taboos were numerous.

I had a little flat at that time just off Sloane Square and sometimes found myself, when not on actual duty, detailed to attend Society dances, where young men were at a premium. The choreography of 1917 was slightly different from that of 1897 but I inwardly thanked the formidable Mrs. Wordsworth of that former period for making me overcome initial awkwardness.

A more dramatic episode that I remember was the shepherding, with several brother officers, of (I do not know quite what word to use), a herd, flock, team of land girls who were to be marched to Buckingham Palace and there be inspected by the Queen. I have to use country similes, because it was like so many sheep dogs that we ran up and down their ranks trying to keep their exuberance in check. In spite of our zeal they surged into the Fore Court of the Palace, armed with agricultural implements, as might fiery young revolutionaries have stormed the Bastille.

When I was a boy I had watched the spectacle of the Changing of the Guard, but never in my strangest nightmares did I conceive being an actor in this ceremony. The ordeal was far less nerve-wracking than expected, and whatever anxiety I might have felt in not having taken the stage as a true professional was smoothed away by the excellence of the dinner provided for the Officers on Guard that evening, in St. James's Palace. For that compensation I had to thank King George IV for his munificence, and the Captain of the Guard for his fine taste in food and wine.

During the months I was stationed in London two events took place which radically affected my life. The first concerned my family. After many years of loneliness my father decided to remarry. His choice fell on a widow with two small children, whose husband had been killed early in the war, and whose family lived close by us in Holland Park.

I remember my father's hesitation (so rare in him) when he told me of his intention, and my surprise, for I had hitherto no inkling of his feelings. I gladly consented to be his 'best man' at the wedding, which took place in June 1918. His wife, Ethel, was to bring him affectionate companionship in the years that remained to him and when later a daughter, his first, was born to him, his happiness was great.

The other event was a personal experience. During my first year in France I had been buoyed up by the conviction that, whatever the danger, I myself could not be killed. The bullet that bore my name had not been cast. The sense of my own vital individuality was too strong to allow the thought that a chance shell could in its haphazard way blot out *my* existence. The coming return to the same battle-fields now made this brash confidence waver. The throw of luck had so far been all on my side, but as odds usually go, the cast should now be against me.

As a family we had never held deep religious convictions; my father had a stern New England consciousness of what was right and what was wrong, and formal outward observance seemed superfluous. At school, at the age of Confirmation, it is true that I felt a momentary spiritual quickening but, with religious services relapsing into routine habit, whatever exaltation there had been soon faded palely away.

But now I felt the urgent need for some reassurance that sudden death did not automatically annihilate the human soul: perhaps Faith could prove stronger than a stubborn disbelief. In search of a solution

48

Myself in Tyrolean
costume, aged seven

(*above left*)
My mother, Agnes
Kennard Bliss, 1893

The Bliss family,
1899.
(*Standing*)
My half-brother
George and my father;
(*sitting*)
my brothers Howard,
Kennard and myself
(aged about eight)

Howard, myself and Kennard
on holiday, 1906

At the time of
the *Colour Symphony*, 1924

In the
Grenadier Guards, 1917

I went to a priest at the Brompton Oratory for instruction, and later was received into the Catholic Church.

The fifth summer of the war passed with frustrating slowness. I seemed to be just marking time with instruction at Tidworth on bombing and revolver shooting, varied by a riding course in Knightsbridge Barracks: but at last, early in September 1918, I was ordered to France to join the 1st Battalion, Grenadier Guards. I found myself taking a draft out and on the way in France passing my old trenches near Monchy au Bois and Adinfer, south of Arras, then down the Bapaume Road to Lagnicourt and our divisional H.Q. Letters home and excerpts from my diary take the story forward.

To my father

*September 9 1918*

I have just heard that I am posted to the first battalion so my address will be:

Lieut. A. E. D. Bliss

1st Battalion Grenadier Guards, B.E.F.

In great haste

ARTHUR

*September 11 1918*

My first adventure in this land of chance is to catch 'tonsilitis', so at 10.00 this morning I go into hospital at the depot. I am angry about this, as I was to join my battalion this evening, and it looks bad to go ill on the eve of going into the line, but I can't help it: it is no use going up feeling really sick as I do at present. I hope it will only be a question of a few days.

*No. 2 General Hospital, Havre*
*September 15*

It appears I have *not* got tonsilitis after all, but a very aggressive wisdom tooth, which has to come out to-morrow in company with two or three other old friends of mine. What a curse is laid on me that whenever I come to France I have toothache! I never suffer so in England.

*No. 2 General Hospital, Havre*
*September 21*

The cutting out of my wisdom tooth was quite an international affair; in attendance, a French dentist, an American anaesthetist and the resident English doctor! I feel much better now it is gone. The American anaesthetist 'put me off' with the words, spoken slowly, ponderously, with pauses: 'First you feel a tingling sensation . . . in your legs . . . in your arms . . . a loud knocking will sound in your ears . . . as of many anvils beaten together . . . listen only to *me* . . . you are now going to the land of dreams . . . think of pleasant subjects . . . and your dreams will be . . . will be . . .' (I'm off!)

I have been reading *Essays and Studies* by members of the English Association. It is published by the Clarendon Press, and appeared first, I think, in 1911. Could you sometime get and keep some of the volumes for me?

> *Guards Division Base Depot*
> *September 24*

I left hospital this morning feeling, I am glad to say, quite fit. I shall probably join my battalion to-morrow. What a mysterious letter that was from Holland! Howard wrote to me about it. Having nothing better to do I tried à la Holmes to discover a code in it but failed, as Watson would have done. In hospital I met an interpreter with the Chinese Labour Corps, who told me that there are thousands of them in France on a three year contract. He said that their ingrained idea of the superiority of the European is fast vanishing!

I do envy you the Russian Ballet!

To my brother, Howard

> *October 4*

I am sitting in a rigged up tent, trying to keep warm with the aid of a brazier. It is not an inspiring view from here—a canal with all its bridges battered in, two miles of flat country behind with the usual accompaniment of ruined trees, dead horses, and cemeteries! Well! I freely admit that I would rather be handling a mashie with you in Raynes Park, or smashing out the *Danse Macabre* in someone else's charming studio. (NB. From my diary I see that the battalion was moving steadily east. The names of villages Harrincourt, Ribécourt, Mercoing, Magnières, all south of Cambrai are mentioned and then Wambaix, Bevillers and Quiévy.)

To my father

> *October 7*

I have to guess the date. I know it must be a Monday for yesterday I attended Mass in a canal lock just in front of our bivouac. All is well with me.

*October 10*

The last two days have been spent on the move. Last night we messed in a billet that had only just been evacuated by the Germans. They had cleared out too quickly to raze the village to the ground, and we had the luxury of a roof over our heads and beds of a sort. The roads are choked with troops of all kinds advancing—cavalry, artillery, engineers, every branch of the services; we pass regiments coming from the line and large batches of prisoners. In the billet in which I am writing my cook found for me a battered German cornet. I don't know whether I can add it to my kit, which is growing enormous. I am sitting at the moment on a ruined piano stool!

*October 15*

We have had rather a rough time lately, fighting a pursuing action, not knowing exactly where the Germans are. The villages we passed through were almost intact, proving a hasty but disciplined retreat. The few old peasants that were left welcomed us, crying hysterically. I feel well.

*No. 8 General Hospital, Rouen*
*October 26*

Since last writing I have been in two night attacks and, during the second, had the ill fortune to swallow a gulp of gas. Hence the above address. It is very slight but means remaining quiet for a week or two, and I shall probably be sent to Trouville for a short recuperation. I am on ordinary diet and there is nothing to be anxious about. My only worry now is my kit, which apparently has been lost. I have nothing but a steel helmet and a pair of pyjamas!

The man in the next bed is an American who caught the gas worse than I did, and is being sent to England. He knows no one there, and I told him to write to you when he gets to a London hospital. He comes from New York and has an overwhelming desire for 'pie' (apple variety).

*No. 72 General Hospital ( M4 ) B.E.F.*
*October 27*

I am now ensconced here and shall probably remain for a week or so: it may depend on when I get my clothes—the addition of a toothbrush brings my list of possessions to three!

We are about a mile out of Trouville, high up overlooking the sea, in huts. I was glad to get out of hospital in Rouen, which was crowded, stretcher cases covering the floors.

To Howard

As you will have learnt from my letter to father this above address
gives no cause for alarm. I imbibed a dose of gas one night and
suddenly collapsed while my Company was relieving the 2nd Scots
Guards. It was a toss up whether I came here or was evacuated to
England, but it was decided I was not bad enough for the latter.
By a coincidence I am being attended by the consulting doctor of
Rugby, who has a son about to go to our old house there.
This place is going to be deadly dull, I can see, and the inhabitants
duller, the music from the 'Bing Boys' crashing out from the pianos
and gramophones, and 'old man' and 'old bean' and 'cheerio' flying
about in true hearty fashion. I am staggering through a treatise on
Caius Julius by Froude—what an opera the subject would make!
The more I read about that garrulous and pompous mediocrity
Cicero, the more I believe X is his reincarnated image. I shall write
and tell him so. I know he will be pleased to be associated in thought
with some one who rose from plebeian status to consul by sheer
garrulity.
December 3
I have been given sick leave for a week or ten days. I have determined to go to Lourdes, and see something of the Pyrenees.


*From my diary*
December 11 1918. Started back to Pau and Base H.Q.


   Christmas Day was spent guarding German prisoners. This was a
distasteful task, especially at that season. The rank and file, very
young, clay coloured of face and uniform, were a pathetic lot; many
spent the day carving little crosses or ornaments out of little bits of
wood which they presented to their captors. The German non-
commissioned officers on the other hand had lost none of their arrogant parade-ground bearing towards their men, though they were
unpleasantly subservient to any British officer whose duty it was
periodically to have the prisoners counted. They bullied their
wretched charges in true Prussian style, and stirred me at any rate
to retaliatory measures.
   Early in 1919 I got my release from the army: one large part of
my life was over and another, in prospect totally different, was to
begin. I was twenty-eight.

# Chapter IV

# Post-War Years,
# 1919 and 1920

WHEN I USED TO PLAY the music from *The Ring* in Bath with such excitement, I comforted myself by the thought that Wagner had been a slow starter, that his early work showed little signs of the formidable power that was to develop later, that there was still time even for me, if I set to work immediately and with concentration. I resolutely planned that these next few years should be crammed with musical experiences.

I started on a full length quintet that I could play with my friends of the Philharmonic String Quartet (Arthur Beckwith, Eugene Goossens, Raymond Jeremy and Cedric Sharpe) who had already given several performances of my early string quartet. A scheme was formed to give the first performance of this work in Paris later that year. The impetus came from the composer Josef Holbrooke who had arranged to play in his own Symphonic Quintet at two recitals of British music there. I shall tell of our misadventures in due course.

In the meantime I had made friends with two painters each of whom was to have an influence on my career. Claude Lovat Fraser was a painter passionately devoted to the theatre. Designs for sets and costumes, in beautiful colours, poured from his brush. Whenever I visited his studio I found him at work, however many visitors were there, and round the walls were hundreds of his imaginative sketches. His wife, Grace, was a brilliant and vital personality, overflowing with exciting ideas and plans for the future, and the possessor of a fine soprano voice. Thanks to their friendship I met Nigel Playfair and Arnold Bennett who had just acquired artistic control of the Lyric Theatre, Hammersmith.

My first commission was to arrange suitable music for their April production of *As You Like It*, with scenery and dresses designed by Lovat. For the performance of the music I was indebted to the wife of another artist. I had often visited Edward Wadsworth and his wife, Fanny, in their house in Church Street, Kensington. I admired his somewhat clinical approach to painting, and the hard excellence of his drawings and tempera paintings (one of my first collected pictures was a woodcut of his, a sketch of blast furnaces at night). Fanny had a string quartet of her own, all women, and it was this ensemble that I used for the music in *As You Like It*. Dressed as pages and playing in Arden, a forest of white birch trees, they performed arrangements of music from late Elizabethan sources and also of songs by Arne.

From Nigel Playfair I got permission to use the Lyric Theatre on Sunday evenings during October and November for six chamber orchestral concerts. British music figured conspicuously in these, and my little season ended with a stage performance of *La Serva Padrona* with Grace Lovat Fraser as Serpina. This was preceded by a lecture from Edward Dent. A press cutting, that I have kept, says of one concert that 'it was notable for a surprisingly fine performance of Ravel's Trio by Lady Ross, M. Defauw and Mr. Howard Bliss'.

The English works in my six programmes included a new string quartet by Armstrong Gibbs, a *Comedy Suite* for clarinet and piano by Herbert Howells, an *Old English Suite* by Granville Bantock, *Songs for Orchestra* by Cyril Rootham and Denis Browne, a group of songs with piano by Vaughan Williams, and John Ireland's Trio No. 2, with the composer playing the piano, and Rhoda Backhouse and Felix Salmond the violin and cello respectively.

Ireland was an excellent soloist in his own music, but it was very difficult to get him to play in public. He seemed to have convinced himself that his music could not possibly interest a post-war audience. I frequently visited him in his studio in Gunter Grove and once there would instinctively ask him what he was writing, and if he would show it to me. Reluctantly he would go to his piano, but before playing he would turn round and mutter 'You won't like this, you know'; then at the end would come the inevitable question '*That* didn't interest you now, did it?' This morbid distrust in his own ability to win attention grew on him and I consider it an achievement to have inveigled him to appear at one of these concerts, in one of his finest chamber music works.

At this time I was writing two short pieces for unusual ensembles—*Madam Noy*, A Witchery Song for soprano, flute, clarinet, bassoon, harp and double-bass, and *Rhapsody* for mezzo-soprano and tenor (wordless), flute, cor anglais and string quartet. Both were to be given performances in 1920 and were to start me on essays in the exploration of sound right up to the time of the *Colour Symphony* in 1922.

I found the words of *Madam Noy* in an anthology of poems given to me by Grace Lovat Fraser, which was called, if I remember rightly *Black and White Magic*. The words of the 'Witchery' song, a variation of the nursery rhyme 'Old Mother Hubbard' were signed E.W.H.M.

I later found that the author's surname was Meyerstein, a scholar, novelist and poet. But I cannot recall any letters passing between us, and I do not believe he ever heard my setting of his words.

*Madam Noy* did not meet with much critical appreciation in spite of its advocacy by the accomplished Anne Thursfield; the comment by the writer in the *Westminster Gazette* of June 25th 1920 is fairly typical:

> It was an eminently modern programme which Miss Anne Thursfield offered at the Wigmore Hall yesterday afternoon, and if it was not possible to find intense enjoyment in everything she did, one could at least admire in almost every instance the art which she displayed in her interpretations—even when the material upon which it was exercised was of the least grateful character. Such, for example, were some of the Arnold Bax songs which she gave with the assistance of the composer at the piano.
>
> In a French group which came later she was more happily suited. . . . Less effective was an elaborate would-be humorous song, *Madam Noy*, by Arthur Bliss, which had not been heard before.
>
> This was a setting of some verses of the nonsense order for voice, flute, clarinet, bassoon, viola, double-bass, and harp, though what there was in such childish lines to induce anyone to expend so much energy in the setting of them it was hard to discover. Nor was there anything in the resulting music to explain matters either, since, apart from its piquant scoring, it seemed no more inspired than the lines which it illustrated.

A tiny copy of *Madam Noy*, about the size of a postage stamp, found its way into the musical library of Queen Mary's Doll's House!

However my second essay in timbre, *Rhapsody*, met with a more cordial reception, the *Musical Standard* of October 23rd in describing Dorothy Helmrich's recital in the Wigmore Hall on October 12th wrote:

> The clou of the evening was Arthur Bliss's *Rhapsody* for two voices, flute, English horn and string quartet. Bliss has as yet produced little, but every work bears marks of a unique personality. His *Rhapsody* is one of the few works precisely corresponding to that title, exquisitely coloured, but without preciousness or anaemic poeticism. Real poetry is there, however, of entrancing spirituality, a spirituality not produced by metaphysical pretensions, but by an intelligence which illuminates the rarest qualities of sensation and emotion, creating a glamour akin to Celtic legend. Bliss's music is a musique féerique, made up of dreams moving

in the realm of emotional imagery of a curiously imaginative mind. But he is no vague visionary: he knows the value of instrumental timbre, and has a keen sense of fluid form. Above all, he is aware of that elusive quantity we term beauty. He is certainly a musician who counts. The *Rhapsody* was repeated in response to applause.

Meanwhile, rehearsals of my piano quintet preceded our long-planned visit to France. Josef Holbrooke, of course, came with us and for most of the journey from London added much to our gaiety. Unfortunately, he had omitted to comply with the current passport regulations: he was also a bad sailor, and the crossing was a rough one. As he tottered off the boat, a very sick man, he was refused admission to France and had the ordeal of recrossing to England. We in the meantime went on to Paris, where Holbrooke wired us that he was in hospital and that the first concert at which he was to appear must be postponed! Our agent in Paris was completely bouleversé: he had with great difficulty, he said, packed the Salle Gaveau with those who *should* be there, and not one of these would think of turning up again at a later date. To add to our confusion a second telegram from Holbrooke warned us that he was not coming at all, and that we had better now take the arrangements into our own hands. When the changed date of our concert at last came and I went on the platform of the Salle Gaveau to play, I thought at first on looking round that the hall was completely empty: then I observed a dozen or so at the back, who at once shifted to the front for a more cheerful effect, led, I was most grateful to see, by Darius Milhaud.

The excitement of being in Paris soon wiped this fiasco from my mind, and I greatly enjoyed being part of the stir that the young hornets, Honegger, Poulenc, Auric as well as Milhaud were causing. Edwin Evans, the music critic, had given me a letter to Maurice Delage, the composer of the *Poèmes Hindous*. He was living at the time in Auteuil, and he told me I could not possibly miss his house as there was a giant sunfish hanging over the outside door. My reception was slightly embarrassing as no sooner had I entered than he led me to the piano, and asked for fifteen or sixteen bars of my own music, not more, he emphasised, so that he could appraise my musical personality. A light touch on my shoulder stopped me, and my personality was not again referred to. However he illustrated his theory by showing me a few bars of manuscript from Stravinsky's *Petrouchka*, triumphantly asserting that the whole man was *there*.

I remembered this incident many years later when I was sitting on a panel with Frank Bridge to award composition prizes. As score after score was passed to him, I saw him immediately turn to the last two pages; he affirmed that the ending would give a very fair inkling of a composer's individuality—no need at once to plough consistently through the whole work!

It was Maurice Delage who brought Ravel to lunch that day in Auteuil, giving me the chance, of which I have already written, to tell him of my early love for his music.

In his letter to me on my seventy-fifth birthday Benjamin Britten mentioned my 'possibly apocryphal Parisian exploits' at this time. Alas! What the exact nature of these was is now too deeply buried by the intervening years to re-lift to the surface of memory. I dare say they were just such as those scintillating, exciting, anarchistic years of the early twenties offered to any young seeker after excitement. Even now the thought of the sign 'Le boeuf sur le toit' lights up momentarily the darkening past like a welcoming neon sign. But I did not stay in Paris long enough to be much affected by its capricious excitements.

Back in London, a second performance of my quintet was given the following spring at a concert at which I also included Stravinsky's *Ragtime*. The hunt to find any good cymbalum player for this kept me busy for a long time, but the contradictory and amusing press accounts of the squib made it worth the trouble.

That same spring of 1920 I joined a party chosen by Adrian Boult to go to Amsterdam and see Nikisch conduct. The other members on this trip were Armstrong Gibbs, Scott Goddard, Leslie Heward, and Boris Ord. We arrived in time to hear a performance of the *St. Matthew Passion* under Mengelberg, and two concerts with the Concertgebouw Orchestra conducted by Nikisch. I wrote a short account of our experiences for the Royal College of Music Magazine, and I have the present editor's permission to quote from this:

Every concert hall develops its own peculiar personality. The Queen's Hall, I feel, radiates a happy holiday humour, is out to enjoy itself, overlooks mistakes, and applauds with indiscriminate relish; the Salle Gaveau, on the other hand, wears an air of brilliant snobbery, anxious not so much for its musical traditions, as that the society it has invited shall not demean themselves by any excess of enthusiasm; lastly the Concertgebouw shows a serious mien, as though within it sat a conclave of prosperous shareholders about to meet their chairman, conscious of his promise of a 10 per cent. dividend, and withal determined to meet this expected prosperity with due moderation and respectability. There are no late-comers—the soloists appear—Mengelberg enters in silence— the baton is raised—the *Passion* commences.

I have met such a personality before, in less happy times, in days gone by when one was but a marionette whose head, legs and arms danced at the bidding of a powerful and all-compelling personality, to wit, the drill sergeant at Chelsea. I smiled to myself as I thought that the eminent flautist could no more phrase a passage as he felt it, than could I have marked time in triplets against my neighbour's twos, that no fiddler could use a down bow in defiance of the rest, any more than I dared turn left consciously instead of right; uniformity of bowing, of phrasing, of dynamic force was absolute, and the result achieved was magnificent. And yet, in spite of one's admiration for a well-nigh perfect rendering, there would intrude this thought—'If only our Drapers, our Brains, and our Jameses were here, just to show this orchestra the effect of several unique musicians infusing the general interpretation with their own individualities.' Mengelberg may be a superb musician, he may be a superb conductor, but he has not got the same gift of awakening enthusiasm in an orchestra that one gentleman has, who came several days later—Arthur Nikisch.

Meeting Nikisch was like being confronted with some giant of the past, of whose titanic exploits one had read but whose personal existence one felt sure must be a myth founded on legendary lore. I am certain I shall feel no greater surprise when faced with Plato, King John or Blondin. A little older, a little greyer, a little sadder maybe, he is still the leader of indomitable fire and energy, the inspirer of enthusiasm and loyalty. The preparation for his concert, which was to contain two symphonies, the *Eroica* and the Schumann D minor, preceded by the *Euryanthe* overture of Weber, was not long. First, two or three hours' rehearsal with the orchestra, then a dress rehearsal, to which the public were admitted on the payment of a small tax; and finally, the concert on the following evening.

I find it difficult to put into words an impression of a Nikisch rehearsal. I suggest that he goes for the broad interpretation of the whole, rather than for the perfection of any detail, that he appeals to the imaginative faculty rather than to one's faith in historic tradition, and that he has a way of purposely over-emphasising points of dynamic interest and changes of tempo at his early rehearsals, which fall naturally into their proper proportion to each other and to the whole by the time the concert performance is reached. His shrewd knowledge of men, founded on his many years' experience of orchestras throughout the world, was surely never shown so vividly as in the manner in which he chose to end his first rehearsal with this orchestra—the first for twenty years or more. If you look at the miniature score of the *Eroica*, page 176, you will see a pause, and it was on that pause, held long with a mighty crescendo on the violins, that the rehearsal came to an end.

You could see the band, like so many Oliver Twists, asking for more, if only for an additional three bars or so.

Nikisch had a special gift shared by few other conductors that I have seen—the apparent ability to generate at will some electric current which galvanised both players and audience alike. Beecham had the same power. Each might be proceeding with no more than professional musicianship through a score, when suddenly a musical passage would excite them either by its beauty or its rhythmic vitality and the heat was on.

In the autumn of 1920 I wrote a third work for chamber orchestra and voice, *Rout*, which gained some popularity at the time. I wanted to evoke the sound of a carnival overheard at a distance. A soprano was given a medley of made-up words to sing and so add to the impression of a crowd's jollity.

*Rout* was originally designed for a musical party given at the Piccadilly home of Baroness d'Erlanger, and it owed its initial success to the dramatic singing of Grace Lovat Fraser.

To read what was written about one's music so many years ago is not unlike poring over obituary notices; it gives one a macabre feeling. I stopped taking any collection of press notices after the *Colour Symphony*, but I like to gloat a little over these early ones. This is what *The Times* said about *Rout* on December 17th 1920.

### A Musical 'Rout'

At a chamber concert given at 139 Piccadilly (by permission of the Baroness d'Erlanger) on Wednesday night, a new work called *Rout*, by Mr. Arthur Bliss was given a first performance. One hardly knows whether to describe it as chamber music or programme music, street music, or 'Jazz'. It has elements from them all. The cast begins like chamber music, and ends like orchestral music; mezzo-soprano voice, flute, clarinet, string quartet, double-bass, harp, side drum, and glockenspiel. The composer said that *Rout* was used in the Old English sense, or one of the Old English senses. His was not Chaucer's sense—

*The sterne wynde so loude kan to route*
*That no wight other noise myght here,*

nor the 18th century sense of 'a fashionable evening assembly,' but in the sense of a popular jollification, a Hampstead heathenish bank holiday rout. So the programme accounts for the street music and the 'Jazz' emerging from a number of rakish tunes for the voice, the clarinet, the flute, and the strings tumbling over one

59

another in wild confusion, while the double-bass cuts capers, the harp thrums accents, and the orchestral 'kitchen' behaves according to its kind. It is exceedingly clever, and proved quite captivating to an audience who belonged to the other kind of rout, the 'fashionable evening assembly'; they demanded and got its repetition. One has some misgivings about it however. Having heard several of these whimsical excursions one begins to wonder where they are leading. Are they forming an individual style with which Mr. Bliss will be able to say something when he has really got something to say, or is he becoming a fashionable joker? His abilities are much too good for the latter.

And here is a delicious cutting from *Eve* on December 30th 1920, I leave the sex of the writer for the reader to determine:

### *Eve said Unto Adam*

Talking of newness, and the need for it, there's a boom (let the poet say what he will) in romantic and unusual dressing just now. I went to Baroness d'Erlanger's chamber concert in that most amazing house of hers, and saw much that was good in the dress line. Grace Crawford, the singer, who was singing in Arthur Bliss's new *Rout*, wore a tight sheath dress made of thirteenth century Japanese Daimyo brocade—orange with great golden birds and clouds all over it—and wore with it heelless gold buskins laced over flesh coloured stockings. The *Rout* was so liked that after they'd encored it they had to give it all over again at the end of the evening; a brilliant and wonderful thing. Madame d'Erlanger was very lovely in jade and black, her girl in black velvet and white ermine. Viola Tree was in scarlet net, Karsavina in black with a huge wreath of green and cherry flowers. Everyone in the world of art was there—Viola Meynell, Francis Meynell, John Drinkwater, and Ezra Pound of the writing world; Vladimir Rosing and Hilda Saxe of music; Paul Nash, Albert Rutherston, Edward Wadsworth of the poets (sic). There was a stage made at the end of the long drawing room, where the arches and the golden altar-piece made a background.

Later, at the invitation of Diaghilev, I scored the work for a larger body of players and in this guise it was given by Ansermet as a musical Interlude in the programmes of the Russian Ballet.

I followed this with another chamber work to enliven a musical evening in a big house, a quintet which I named *Conversations*. The five movements all had titles (1) 'The Committee Meeting'

60

(2) 'In the Wood' (3) 'In the Ball Room' (4) 'Soliloquy' (5) 'In the Tube at Oxford Circus'.

Five noted soloists gave it a good send off, and I give their names for they recall pleasant memories of laughter and gaiety at rehearsals, Woodhouse (violin), Raymond Jeremy (viola), Cedric Sharpe (cello), Gordon Walker (flute), Leon Goossens (oboe). For 'In the Ballroom' I used a bass flute, and for the 'Soliloquy' a cor anglais. 'In the Committee Meeting', with its ineffectual but stubborn chairman vainly trying to get his motion carried amid the frequent interruptions of his colleagues, can still raise a smile.

The public chamber orchestral concert given by Edward Clark in the Aeolian Hall which included *Conversations* met with some hostile hissing, and the *Daily Mail* of April 4th 1921 was particularly severe:

### Blare Music
#### Bellowing trombone & Tango Rhythms

Mr. Edward Clark and a small picked orchestra yesterday at the Aeolian Hall, New Bond Street, W., played some of the new—the newest—music, English and French. That is to say, we had bellowings on the trombone, dissipated cries from a cornet, tango rhythms, an outdoing of the brutalising circus 'orchestration', a soprano ejaculating in Dadaistic-French 'Marin cou le pompon moustaches mandoline, Linoléum en trompe-l'œil, Merci, Cinéma nouvelle muse,' etc.

Mr. Arthur Bliss with five new instrumental *Conversations* was the Englishman. From France came bouquets from Mlle Germaine Tailleferre and M. Poulenc and Milhaud, three of the much-talked of 'Six' who interpret the new spirit of the age. It is an irreverent age. Was music once a holy art? Did the masters once contrive sublime syntheses of Love, Life and Death?

We are much too knowing nowadays for any such hollow romance. Nothing today sounds more absurd than a grand symphonic apotheosis. 'Analyse, analyse!' says the scientific spirit which has been duped by synthesis once too often. Beethoven described in music Mankind in its millions embracing in Universal Brotherhood (improbable), and Wagner, the Retribution of World-Guilt by Renunciatory Love. Mr. Arthur Bliss composes 'A Conversation in the Tube at Oxford Circus'. It is really the triumph of Nietzsche, with his motto, 'Let instinct live', over his pretentious old enemy.

A very fair idea of my musical preferences can be deduced from a paper that I read at this time to the Society of Woman Musicians.*

* See Appendix A.

I confess to blushing on re-reading what I then said forty-seven years ago, an embarrassment shared, I am sure, with many who nonchalantly lay down aesthetic laws in their youth, and who in after life discover their hollow arrogance. But those were my convictions at the time of speaking, and I have reprinted them because I find that a similar creed is prevalent today, namely that sound for its own sake is a satisfactory solution for music.

Time, of course, has moved quickly on, and today's 'sound' composers can make use of electronic devices, prepared pianos, unlimited percussion and a freakish use of ordinary orchestral instruments. To a young composer who may not be endowed with much emotional content all this provides an easy but fascinating approach. What saves mere sound is of course architectural form, but even sound plus shape gives only the skeleton, and some emotional substance drawn from the composer's experiences is needed to clothe it—at least to hold *my* attention. As regards my enthusiasms in 1929 I soon became an apostate and sought new allegiances.

# Chapter V

# 1921—1923

IN ORDER TO GAIN experience as a conductor I was at this time conducting the Portsmouth Philharmonic Society, taking over the post from Adrian Boult, who was too busy elsewhere to continue. The Society had a large and excellent chorus and an orchestra of local professionals and amateurs reinforced by members of the resident military band. I greatly enjoyed our weekly rehearsals and they kindly endured my youthful inexperience. I remember performances of Berlioz' *Faust* and Bach's B Minor Mass as being particularly rewarding occasions for me.

Early in 1921 a new opportunity to write music for the theatre came my way, a production by Viola Tree and Louis Calvert of *The Tempest* at the Aldwych Theatre. This was an extraordinary amalgam of all styles—all styles of acting, all styles of scenic design and especially all styles of music. I was called in to compose special music for Scenes 1 & 2, Scene 3, Act III, and Scene 1, Act IV. I used a sound-combination of tenor and bass voices, piano, trumpet, trombone, gongs and five drummers. My other collaborators were Arne, Sullivan with additions by Raymond Roze, and Frederic Norton of *Chu Chin Chow* fame.

My original plan was to hide my drummers in the auditorium placed at strategic points, where the audience could feel itself, as it were, immersed in the storm. But the management took fright, and on the opening night some of the drums were with the singers and players in the pit, while two long-suffering timpanists hauled their drums up into the 'flies'.

At this time the utterances of Ernest Newman were to be awaited with considerable trepidation. He rarely, so he said, went to the legitimate theatre himself, so what kind of lightning would flash from his pen after his known visit to the Aldwych! He let me off lightly in the *Manchester Guardian* of February 10th 1921.

There is nothing very much to be said about the music itself to the new *Tempest* at the Aldwych, but that curious production is the sort of thing that sets musicians thinking. In a show that is itself a higgledy-piggledy of styles and formulae, both in the acting and in the décor, it is perhaps not surprising to find the music a hotch-potch of periods and ideals. Arne's 'Where the bee sucks' is inevitable, of course: but Sullivan and Raymond Roze might have been given a rest, while one searches the back corners of one's brain in vain for an explanation of the association of Shakespeare and Mr. Frederic Norton in Act III. The only music that matters is that of Mr. Arthur Bliss, who, with a fearsome array of kettle-drums, has given us a storm in the opening scene that is not only terrifying in an imaginative way, instead of the merely noisy way of the old stage thunder, but has the additional and great merit of reducing the scenery and the actors to their native insignificance. For the scene in the fourth act, in which Prospero and Ariel and their satellites tease the shipwrecked lords with a visionary table of delicacies, Mr. Bliss has written some music that I should like to hear again under more satisfactory conditions than those of the theatre. It has a strange remoteness and mystery: here one felt, as nowhere else, unfortunately, during the whole play after the storm scene, that Shakespeare's vision of an island enchanted had been realised. It is the most imaginative piece of theatre music that I have ever heard. Mr. Bliss is a young musician of a curiously lively, questing mind. He has experimented a good deal in unusual instrumental combinations, and always we feel that there is a reason, rooted in the thought itself, for the music being laid out just as it is. He has done some striking works on a small scale for strings and wind and voices. He is particularly fond of vocal works in which the singer merely vocalises instead of singing words. There is certainly a future for this method of treating the voice simply as one instrument among others; it allows it a welcome freedom and entry and exit and colour change. Altogether Mr. Bliss strikes one as a composer from whom something may be expected.

Later Edward Clark gave a concert performance of my *Tempest* music at one of his enterprising evenings in Queen's Hall. As the *Westminster Gazette* of the time said, perhaps quite truly, 'never before, it may unhesitatingly be asserted, has such an unholy row been heard in a London concert room' but he gave me a little pat by adding 'and yet there is no denying the cleverness of it all. The composer displays method in his madness, there is "purpose and significance" in his scoring, and in its preposterous way the thing is quite effective.'

It was very difficult in those years for a young British composer

With Trudy in *Beggar on Horseback* at the
Lobero Theatre, Santa Barbara, 1924

My father, Francis Edward Bliss, *circa* 1928

to get the chance of hearing his music in public if it called for the use of a full orchestra. One of the few opportunities to learn by experience was offered by the Patrons' Fund scheme of public rehearsals at the Royal College. To take advantage of this I wrote *Two Studies* for full orchestra, one grave, one gay, and sent them in for consideration. They were accepted for these rehearsal-performances, but before getting the parts copied, I felt the need for someone much more expert than I to glance through my score. By great good fortune I got the assent of Holst. I had heard movements from his gigantic suite *The Planets*, and to have a lesson from a man who could make an orchestra sound so magnificently vivid as he could was a wonderful opportunity. I took my *Studies* along to his room in Brook Green.

One is far too apt to take for granted the exceptional artist who can be seen living daily in our midst. There he is, just like us, getting on a bus, or sitting and eating in a tea-shop! If we miss an opportunity to meet and talk with him—well, there will surely be other chances. And then he dies, and there *is* no second chance. I now feel this deeply about Holst. I was with him only a few times, but each is indelibly engraved on my memory by some short pithy statement that he made. He had the utter honesty of opinion that riveted attention: there was no possibility of misunderstanding what he thought or what he felt. He has passed this rare integrity on to his gifted daughter Imogen.

On this first occasion at Brook Green he pounced on a tune that I had rather weakly given to the cellos: 'But this is a trombone tune,' Holst said, 'it *can't* be anything else!' How right he was, when I heard it! In my second and rather lengthy 'Study' he looked at the first and second page and then suddenly turning to me said, 'But *when* is it going to begin?'—devastating criticism but accurate. It hadn't really begun. I knew that instinctively.

When in 1923 I went to America with my father and his family, Holst was on board the same boat. One evening we were looking over the stern at the vanishing wake of the waves, and Holst said 'How heroic the men with Columbus must have been!' He paused here and I thought he was thinking of the tiny boats, compared with ours, that made the dangerous crossing: but then he added 'for in their minds the earth was flat, and the night horizon that they saw perhaps the final edge'. Later, in 1930, I was sitting next to him at a first run-through of Vaughan Williams' *Job* in Norwich. The composer was taking the rehearsal. Suddenly Holst, and when he was listening to music he listened with a frightening intensity, said to himself 'That doesn't come off. I must go and tell him.' He stepped on to the platform, looked at the score with Vaughan Williams, discussed and suggested, and then came back to his place, while the

65

composer spoke to the players. The section was then tried over again, but with what a difference of sound!—clarity instead of thick obscurity. Holst always probed like a fine surgeon to the root of the difficulty. I wish I had grasped the chances to know his unique personality better. I was able to repay a little of his kindness by giving three performances of his one-act opera *Savitri* at the Lyric Theatre, Hammersmith in late June 1921. As *The Times* wrote 'it is a perfect little masterpiece of its kind, and we can think of nothing else which belongs to the same kind'. The three singers in these performances were Dorothy Silk, Clive Carey and Steuart Wilson. Before the opera I gave three of Holst's *Hymns from the Rig Veda*, sung by women's voices with harp accompaniment. This opera was the last work for the theatre that Lovat Fraser designed, using richly coloured dresses against a sombre background of dark trees and fading night sky. His early death at thirty-two put a tragic finish to a career of inspiring creative work. Holst himself was pleased with the performance and with the audience's warm appreciation, and he gave me, as a memento, a signed copy of the full score of his *Hymn of Jesus.*

My two *Studies for Orchestra* were duly performed in the over-resonant Concert Hall at the Royal College of Music together with an orchestral piece by Leslie Heward. I remember we sat up all the previous night correcting the countless mistakes in the parts, naturally cursing the copyist.

At the same time I was busy with the preparation of my new work, a Concerto for pianoforte and tenor voice with string and percussion accompaniment, which was given for the first time in the Wigmore Hall with Myra Hess and Steuart Wilson as soloists. In order to use the tenor voice as a fine sound, and not at the same time as a definite expression of some poem's mood, I resorted to a third experiment. The voice should not vocalise as in my *Rhapsody*, nor sing nonsense syllables as in *Rout*, but instead rely on English words chosen for their sound and rhythm, but of so abstract a character as not to interpose a logical meaning. Although the work was encored at its first performance, I knew that this experimental idea had failed. As one paper wrote: 'I read that the concerto was to be regarded as pure abstract sound. Pure abstract sound! It may exist in the mind of God, but not in the Wigmore Hall on a Saturday afternoon.' I therefore put this score aside, and rearranged the musical content for Ethel Bartlett and Rae Robertson to play as a double piano concerto with normal orchestral accompaniment. The original score was lost during the Second World War when a bomb crashed into the warehouse where, with a lot of other manuscripts, it was stored.

Through the Lovat Frasers I had met Tamara Karsavina, whom I had so long admired in Diaghilev's ballets. I am lucky to have

66

seen her introduce *The Firebird* to London: she made the role one of incomparable beauty and drama. She was now planning to give a summer season at the Coliseum, supported by M. Novikoff and an English corps de ballet. She had invited Holst and Arnold Bax to provide special orchestrations for her, and she asked me to make an instrumental transcription of Sinding's *Fire Dance*. I am sorry that all remembrance of this dance has completely passed, with the music, from my mind.

I have remarked before on the difficulty that a British composer encountered in those days in getting orchestral works performed. An exception must be made in the case of the Queen's Hall Promenade Concerts. Henry Wood was indefatigable in his wish for new music of a reasonably professional standard, and I was one of the many composers who owe to this fatherly figure their first chance with a fine orchestra. For his autumn season of 1921 I had finished a ten-minute work which I entitled *Mêlée Fantasque*: this I dedicated 'to the memory of Claud Lovat Fraser'. I tried to depict in it the brilliant colour and movement of the theatre that he loved and to weave into the texture an elegiac lament for his loss.

I have never taken kindly to the race of conductors, and all my life have avoided rather than sought the attention of those who are called 'international figures', but to work in any capacity with Henry Wood was to work with a man free of conceit or megalomania, one wholly devoted to music, and generous to those younger and less secure than himself.

The rehearsal schedule of the Promenades in 1921 was like some nightmare jisgaw puzzle. How Henry Wood managed to complete his long and exhausting programmes in the short hours of preparation allotted remains a miracle to me: yet skimping the better-known works he would allow the young composer the fullest measure of time he could. There was one endearing feature he showed at performance; as I nervously waited to go on the platform he would hold me back: 'Just a moment till I get to my seat' he would say, and then bounding up to the dress circle he would sit overlooking the first violins and watch your performance. It gave me a warm feeling of support. It was Henry Wood who, two years later, sent me a telegram to Gloucester when I was rehearsing the first performance of my *Colour Symphony* telling me he wanted to include the work in one of his forthcoming symphony concerts: and this *before* the performance had taken place, a performance that bitterly disappointed me. When I think of the arrogant attitude of some other 'famous' conductors in their dealings with me I gladly pay tribute to this warm-hearted and dedicated man.

Another friend whom I recall with gratitude is the publisher Felix

Goodwin. Enthusiastic and ambitious for British music, he began to issue beautifully produced scores. In my case he brought out *Rout* with a vivid colour design by Lovat Fraser, *Conversations* in a limited edition with a pen-and-ink drawing by Wadsworth, *Mêlée Fantasque* with a strong design by William Roberts, and the *Colour Symphony* with a pencil sketch by Wyndham Lewis.

The last-named artist wanted to do some drawings of me and I hunted him out in his lair in Adam and Eve Mews in Kensington. Lewis liked to surround himself with an aura of secrecy and mystery, but though absolutely reticent about himself, he was far less so about his brother artists. He greatly enjoyed blasting and bombardiering. He made several three-quarter portraits of me, treating my rather long Nordic head in an El Greco manner.

At that time we planned a revue sketch to be offered to Cochr n called 'The Street comes into the Room'. The stage was to show a typical office with secretaries and typists: a large window back stage was to show a glimpse of a busy thoroughfare. Every noise outside was to materialise and pass through the office in concrete form, shaped in a flat profile. Fire engines, motor-cars, buses, barrows, newspaper boys etc. were to float, apparently invisible to the office staff, between desks and over typewriters. It was to be an abstract ballet for which I was to supply the appropriate sounds. Eventually the collaboration came to nothing, which was as well for it would have meant a lot of work expended on an ephemeral stunt.

I conducted my *Mêlée Fantasque* in the Queen's Hall on October 13th. Programme notes written by someone other than the composer are often nothing but shameless advertisements heightened by glaring colours, and the Promenade 'analysis' of my *Mêlée Fantasque* was certainly no exception. It gave the *Observer* of October 16th 1921 every right to accuse me of inconsistency:

> According to the long description in the Queen's Hall programme on Thursday night, the *Mêlée Fantasque* of Bliss is one of these new attempts to do away with 'expression'. There is the usual talk about the objectionable 'subjectivity of the nineteenth century', about 'the success of an effect depending simply on its being capable of giving pleasure', and about the aim now being to 'convert such effects into distinctive artistic values that shall constitute something akin to the absolute objective art that largely depended on sheer physical enjoyment'. For myself, I am afraid I consider 'absolute objective' music as elusive a conception as 'simple impersonal truth', and very likely a good deal of my honest, innocent enjoyment of Mr. Bliss's work during the last twelve months has been of the wrong sort—enjoyment of the passages

in which he most markedly fails to attain his object. Analysing my memories, I believe one cause of my pleasure in many of his creations has been that abounding youthful vitality of his, which often compels him to sweep on one side his theories, and write down what he feels, in all its native heat. If Bliss is really aiming at this cold suppression of his humanity, he has again betrayed his theoretical self in a work which, as the programme tells us, contains passages where 'the solo violin gives out, tranquillo e molto cantabile, a beautiful melody accompanied by a warm background harmony in the tutti strings' where the drums 'unchain a more impassioned restatement of some of the preceding material', where 'a glow of deep emotion seems to be thrown over all these strands of melody', where 'the work ends very poetically in the hushed mood of the Introduction'—and so forth! Technically, my present criticism of the piece is that it is too broken, and contains passages which appear to be mere interpolations included to show us some orchestral possibility.


My inner life at this time was far from being of that orderly disciplined kind which best conduces to creative work; it was indeed very much the reverse. I was entangled in a feverish love affair with a young girl accidentally met at an evening party in London. She was a wonderful dancer, and her beauty exhaled an animal magnetism which immediately enticed the male. At all times she needed men, and knew how to get them. The attraction being almost entirely physical was all the more exciting and unsettling.

During those many months our love affair on both sides was of the 'odi et amo' order and the relationship became so tense that her guardians sent her off to Switzerland. I was still irresistibly drawn to her, and made a dash across Europe to see her—only to find another man in possession.

Like some character in an Aldous Huxley novel I had made the ineffectual gesture of taking her some settings of love poems. I remember that back in my hotel room that night after the confrontation in her flat I savagely tore my manuscripts to pieces. Sheer sensual frustration?—perhaps. Wounded vanity?—certainly, allied to rage with myself for being so enslaved.

# Chapter VI

# 1921—1923 (continued)

WHEN I STARTED to compose again after the end of the war I became friendly with the singer Anne Thursfield, whose stylish and intelligent interpretations I much admired. So, for one of her recitals, I wrote three songs to poems by Walter de la Mare. His exquisite verse was much sought after by composers; I am sure he must have grown tired of giving permission to all and sundry to use, and sometimes to misuse it. However, he generously gave me leave to try, and in addition invited me to come and see him in his home near the Crystal Palace. There are certain memories when meeting a man of genius for the first time that never leave one. I have one such of de la Mare that is fixed in my mind. I had tea with him and his family, and then he took me for a stroll in his garden. It was a fine autumn day in September. He was speaking to me when he suddenly stopped and riveted his attention on an object close to the path. This was a perfectly constructed spider's web, glistening with dew, in the centre of which hung a large garden spider, waiting motionless. De la Mare stood still, gazing at it minute after minute, absolutely forgetful of my presence. It was as though the poet had suddenly realised an image of poignant importance to him; it permitted no interference to shatter his inward vision. I remember nothing more of the visit but the picture of his rapt and loving attention to this minute marvel of nature. I am glad that I still possess on my shelves his collected poems in two volumes and the novel *Memoirs of a Midget* signed by him with his personal good wishes.

In January 1922 Adrian Boult conducted a concert of British music in Prague, and I went with him. His programme consisted of Butterworth's *Two Folk Song Idylls*, my *Mêlée Fantasque* and Elgar's Second Symphony. With us also came the English Singers led by Steuart Wilson: they had an overwhelming success with their madrigal singing, the audience insisting on their reappearing after the Symphony and giving a final group, ending with Vaughan Williams' setting of *As I Walked Out One Morning*. This had to be repeated three times! Prague certainly showed us great kindness, putting on a special performance of *The Bartered Bride* at the National Theatre on the afternoon before our concert.

Our same group went later that spring to Vienna for concerts. I see from a report sent to the *Musical News and Herald* by Egon Wellesz that I conducted my *Rhapsody* and *Tempest* music, the latter according to Dr. Wellesz 'exciting some philistines to a very high degree'. Alas! What may have seemed scandalous forty-five years ago can sound inordinately mild today. Will our grandsons think the 'advanced music' of 1967 as pitifully harmless in 2007? Again in Vienna it was the English Singers who carried off the chief honours, members of the audience following them to the station and demanding more encores right on the platform.

Hitherto, I had only tried short flights in music, but now there came the opportunity to attempt something much more ambitious. It was an added stimulus that this should come about through the instigation of Elgar. In December 1920 he had asked several musicians to have lunch with him at the Royal Societies Club. I had no idea who else might have been invited or the reason for this kindness. When I arrived I found Adrian Boult, Anthony Bernard, Eugene Goossens, John Ireland, and W. H. Reed, who was the Leader of the London Symphony Orchestra at that time. The luncheon went a bit awkwardly with Elgar at his most nervous; then, when the coffee came, he suddenly told us the reason of our being gathered there. He wanted Howells, who was not present, Goossens and myself each to write a new work for the Gloucester Festival of 1922: no limitations on the form of the new works were imposed. Howells complied with *Sine Nomine*, written for soprano and tenor soloists, mixed chorus and orchestra; Goossens with a work called *Silence* for chorus and orchestra, and I wrote a symphony later to be called the *Colour Symphony*.

I have always found it easier to write 'dramatic' music than 'pure' music. I like the stimulus of words, or a theatrical setting, a colourful occasion or the collaboration of a great player. There is only a little of the spider about me, spinning his own web from his inner being. I am more of a magpie type. I need what Henry James termed a 'trouvaille' or a 'donnée'. So for weeks I sat before a blank sheet of manuscript paper trying to make up my mind what shape, what character this new big work should have. And then one day, looking over a friend's library, I picked up a book on heraldry and started reading about the symbolic meanings associated with the primary colours. At once I saw the possibility of so characterising the four movements of a symphony, that each should express a colour as I personally perceived it. There was to be no attempt at a semi-scientific basis whatever, if there *is* such a thing. I was fully aware that colours

71

arouse quite different emotions in different people, and that I was speaking only for myself in composing this symphony. For that reason I did not at first give it any name except 'Symphony in B'. Later I was won over by the argument put forward by Percy Scholes that if I *had* found initial inspiration in the idea of colour, it was timid not to proclaim it. Hence its title *Colour Symphony* with the subtitles to the movements of Purple, Red, Blue, Green.

A rewarding interlude during this time was preparing and conducting the first performance of Vaughan Williams' one act chamber opera *The Shepherds of the Delectable Mountains*. This took place in July 1922 at the Royal College of Music, and the production was in the hands of Proctor-Gregg. Hugh Allen wanted the scene of this pastoral episode from Bunyan's *The Pilgrim's Progress* to reflect the majesty of the rolling South Downs. The young baritone who sang the part of the third shepherd is now the Director of the College, Keith Falkner.

August 1922, the score of my symphony completed, found me in Salzburg with a group of English musicians for a series of international chamber concerts, which for the first time formed an adjunct to the Mozart and Reinhardt Festival. The first was of polyglot character. Recent songs by Richard Strauss, the patron of these concerts, sung by Elizabeth Schumann, a chamber work for wind trio and piano by Milhaud, played by Louis Fleury and his colleagues of the French 'Société Moderne d'Instruments à Vent'. I then conducted *Rout* with Dorothy Moulton singing the soprano part supported by the French wind players and German string players (Hindemith honouring me as violist). An Austrian played the percussion and an English critic, Dunton Green, managed the harp part on a piano! This was followed by *Passacaglia* for piano played by the composer, Felix Petyrek, and the concert ended with Bartók playing his first violin sonata with an Irish violinist who had settled in Vienna, Mary Dickenson-Anner. It was only at the third concert that uncouth incidents occurred. The cause of these was a performance of the *Five Movements for String Quartet* by Webern; never could music of this nature have been so badly placed in a programme. These tiny musical crystals immediately followed a dadaistic work by a Czecho-Slovak composer, designed to set audiences laughing good humouredly. As soon however as the Webern work started, laughter broke out again: there was something unpleasant and hostile in it, and with two opposing factions shouting at each other, the music simply wilted away. I had a chance a day or two later to hear these sketches played under dignified conditions in a private home, and a miniature score in my possession with an appreciative message from the composer fixes the occasion in my mind.

It was the first time I had met Schoenberg, Berg or Webern. I greatly regretted that my ignorance of German kept me from talking to Webern, though I should have had to admit to him as I did years later to James Joyce that I had not found the clue to real appreciation. James Joyce answered that it was quite possible that he himself did not know where he might be led, but that the journey was so exciting that he did not worry about the goal. I rather doubt whether Webern would have expressed himself so: he struck me as a man who knew with absolute clarity what path he was on.

I have hinted that the first performance of my *Colour Symphony* in Gloucester Cathedral on September 7th 1922 was a disappointment to me. It was a difficult work to play and a very intricate one to conduct. Rehearsals were inevitably very restricted, and with wrong notes in new parts to be found and corrected, there was virtually no time for the players to learn the work. A final blow fell at the actual performance, when it was discovered there was not room on the platform erected in the Cathedral for the chorus, who were also taking part in the programme, and my huge orchestra. So, just before I went on, a posse of my players seated on the sides were removed. I certainly saw the tuba ejected and one or two other players on whom I relied. It was not a happy occasion for anyone. Some forty years later I had the satisfaction of conducting the Symphony, again with the London Symphony Orchestra, in the same Cathedral at a similar festival, and in a brilliant performance obliterating from my mind any unhappy memories of the past.

In spite of my forebodings due to the miserable first performance of my Symphony, the papers were unexpectedly cordial. I give *The Times* review of September 8th, 1922 and I am glad to have kept others, for to compare them with the sentiments of these writers' sons (grandsons?) in the papers of today is to receive a lesson in historical perspective, the then and the now.

Bliss's Symphony marks a new stage in his career, an important one, because the first thing which must impress everyone is its earnestness. Some time ago it seemed an open question whether Bliss, with all his talents and facility, would develop as a serious composer, or be content to play with the resources of modern instrumental tone-colour and do little things for the astonishment of those who feed on astonishment. The Concerto seemed to me, at any rate, to show that he was out for the bigger thing; this Symphony leaves no doubt about it. Whether the title, *A Colour Symphony*, and the description of the four movements as purple, red, blue, and green, is a happy way of bringing his hearers into touch with him is an open question. For my own part, I found

73

myself referring to the programme to find out whether I ought to be seeing red or looking blue at certain moments, and some of it certainly made many of the audience feel green.

But though he has chosen, or been persuaded, to tell something of his scheme of moods by the analogy of colour, the thing does not rest on any finicking illustrative idea. It is a symphony in its strong, melodic outlines and its processes of contracted episodes. Its form is severely logical, granting its premises, and the last movement, of an elaborately-developed fugal type, is as strict as such things can be expected to be. Clear diatonic melodies spring forward at times, and have definite characters of their own. The harmonies— or should we call them the conflicts?—of parts have the feeling of inevitability; they are certainly no affectation.

One feels that a razor-edge mind is at work, a young mind because it despises weakness and sentiment, and it is there, probably, that Bliss still has some growing-up to do. The music never seemed to appeal in the sense of wanting sympathy or giving it. Where it struck me as beautiful, as in the latter part of the first movement and the middle theme of the third, it was a cold beauty, and I felt all the time that what I liked best might be something on which the composer set comparatively little store. Probably the work was not altogether performed to the satisfaction of Bliss, who directed it (such first productions rarely are), but it is worth while to add that the orchestration all came out with extraordinary clearness. There was no difficulty in following the detail in even the most complex passages.

I did a lot of preliminary work on this Symphony in the home of Vaughan Williams in Cheyne Walk which he and his wife Adeline shared with his brother-in-law, R. O. Morris, and Jane Morris. There was a wonderful atmosphere of quiet sustained work in that house. Vaughan Williams lived on the top floor, then below came R. O. Morris' study, whilst I had the room on the ground floor. Morris, who was a quiet worker, contributing critical articles to magazines and compiling his scholarly work, *Contrapuntal Technique in the XVIth Century*, acted as a sound-proof barrier between Vaughan Williams and myself. At times, though, I heard slow moving chords that seeped into my room from above; I think at that time Vaughan Williams was making one of his periodic revisions of his *London Symphony*—I loved working there in so sympathetic and creative an atmosphere. I got to know R. O. Morris very well, or as well as he allowed anyone to penetrate his reserve. He loved claret, and he loved cats: with one of the latter curled up purring on his lap, and a glass of claret at hand, he would challenge me to chess, his elegant fingers moving the pieces with sure logic to my final defeat. Years later I dedicated my ballet *Checkmate* to him in memory of those happy evenings. Like Holst he was absolutely downright in his opinions. It was 'yes' or 'no' without any diplomatic hedging or vague hesitations. His kinship with the cat tribe was very understandable: he had the same proud disdain, the same self-sufficiency, and the same dislike of change in the way of living that had become habitual with him. A concert of his works was once given in the Wigmore Hall where I had the support of the Fachiri sisters in performing his fastidious and finely constructed concertos. I know he resented this public intrusion, but his many friends and pupils were happy in thus showing their affection for him.

I conducted my Symphony in Queen's Hall on March 10th 1923, and there for the first time met Prokofiev, who was playing his D flat Piano Concerto at the same concert. His hands were markedly large and powerful and as I watched him at rehearsal it was as though he was gripping great chords and flinging them from the keyboard.

# Chapter VII

# America 1923–1924

SHORTLY AFTERWARDS preparations went forward for the Bliss family to leave for America. In his seventies my father suddenly felt the urge to return to his own country, so in June that year he, his wife, her two children, my father's new daughter, Enid, and Enid's nurse, and I, sailed for New York; my brother Howard was to follow a year later.

Once in New York, my father tried to find the site of the office in which he had worked as a boy, but it was a hopeless task in that completely rebuilt city. But he did find his old University, Brown, in Providence, looking much the same, and was invited by the present young occupant into the rooms he had once used himself.

The Bliss family then moved on to Canada, and crossed the Rockies, stopping off at Banff and Lake Louise. A few days were spent in Vancouver, then the journey continued down the Pacific coast to San Francisco. Here I first met the composer, Albert Elkus, who was to prove such a good friend to me at the outbreak of the Second World War, when he was Chairman of the Music Department at the University of Berkeley, and I was visiting Professor there. The Pacific coast seemed unbelievably beautiful to me, and Santa Barbara its greatest gem. It was there that our long trek ended, my father buying a house in Montecito. He was to live there until he died in 1930.

Santa Barbara appeared primarily a playground for the wealthy in the years before the Wall Street crash, but it also prided itself on maintaining an interest in the arts. This was fostered, as in many other American cities, by a Community Arts Association. I was soon actively engaged in this, accepting a request to write incidental music for a current play on King Solomon at the local theatre. I placed my modest little band in the wings, and contrived to simulate the sounds of the building of the Temple by a rhythmic tapping on steel bars of different pitches.

I spent that winter of 1923 in New York, in a small bachelor apartment just off Times Square. It was a sort of poor man's Albany, and has long disappeared; but its position gave me then the feeling

76

of being at the very heart of New York's electric vitality. If I am not mistaken, I could hear through my bedroom walls the presses of a great daily paper churning out the next day's news.

There is something about the cold champagne air of New York in the autumn and winter that marks the place out from all other great cities. Whenever I pass through it during those months of the year I experience the same exhilaration; 'Life will now start anew!' New York seems to scream, 'nothing is unattainable'. I could never do serious work there, far less live for any length of time—the pulse throbs too excitedly—but for an electric shock to the imagination it is unique.

It was not only the air and aspect of the city that distracted me from getting down to any work; it was also the meeting and getting to know a new exciting type of inhabitant. For the first time I encountered the 'American rich girl'. She not only had seemingly inexhaustible wealth which enabled her to live like a princess, but appeared free of obvious impedimenta such as responsibilities, family, or work of any kind. Should she feel so disposed, she could dash off to Europe, or make a tour of Mexico, charter a yacht for a sunshine cruise, or go to Switzerland for ski-ing.

There was a little band of such young women with whom for a short time I became acquainted; they were clearly self-sufficient to themselves, hardly needing attendant men. If you added ten years to the ages of the 'Frieze of Girls' at Balbec described by Proust, endowed them with great wealth and an intelligent interest in the arts, especially in whatever was new, you would get a pretty fair idea of the glamour they exerted. The frieze would not stand out against a seascape, but be silhouetted by the jewelled lights of New York's Aladdin's Cave. Great riches emit a heady intoxicating perfume, but the aroma can quickly enfeeble, and indeed stifle artistic ambition.

I escaped for a visit to the MacDowell colony for artists. Here were numerous isolated cabins for musicians and writers. A midday meal would be silently deposited on your doorstep so as not to disturb your thoughts, and in the evening everyone met together for supper. It sounds an ideal atmosphere in which to work but I found it difficult to do so. I became self-conscious, and felt the responsibility to provide like a hired labourer my daily quota of work, a heavy one. I was grateful for this kind interlude, but with some relief returned to the exciting arena of New York.

The League of Composers had just been formed to give concerts of modern music. This enterprise owed much to the organising ability of Mrs. Claire Reis, who has since written a history of the movement. During that winter two very active members were Varèse and Salzedo, and at their invitation I managed to write a short work for voice and chamber ensemble for one of their concerts, *The Woman of Yueh* to poems of Li-Po.

I also visited Boston to hear Monteux give a performance of my *Colour Symphony* with the Boston Symphony Orchestra. It was the first time I had heard a great American orchestra and I was astounded; I had never imagined such virtuosity to be possible. At his first rehearsal I learnt one useful practical lesson. Monteux had had to spend a considerable time over one particular passage in my score, and in the interval he pointed out how much easier I could have made it for the players if I had adopted a simpler notation. Ever since then I have avoided the temptation to make my music *look* intricate, and so, perhaps, more interesting to an armchair score reader: the orchestral player must be the first consideration.

I have another vivid recollection of that concert. Casals had just been rehearsing Dvořák's Concerto with Monteux, and was sitting in the stalls listening to the latter at work on Debussy's *La Mer*. When the orchestra came to the short passage for divisi cellos in the first movement, Casals asked whether he might rehearse them alone for a few minutes during the interval. When the interval came there was Casals leading the cellos through the passage, making suggestions as to bowing, while other string players sat around eagerly listening. Happy the orchestra where conditions make such an experience possible! Time, leisure and an assured future: these are the best foundations on which to build a great orchestra.

Leisure! I remember that in 1939, when I conducted the same orchestra in Boston in *Checkmate*, there was a small party after the concert given by some of the principal players, and during it I sat down with the horn player and cellist, and just for sheer enjoyment played through the Brahms Horn Trio with them. Chamber music *after* an orchestral concert! In London?

I also went to Philadelphia to see and hear Stokowski. I use the word 'see', for to watch was to add to the drama of the concert. The whole evening was like a great theatrical production on the part of both players and conductor. I heard a performance of Tchaikovsky's Fifth Symphony that made my very hair rise. No two conductors could be further apart in their approach to music than Stokowski and Monteux. Both were great artists in sound. Stokowski revelled in its dramatic power; he was always experimenting with new ways to achieve a maximum effect. He was also a strong disciplinarian. My first impression, as I sat in the Academy of Music, was of a super Rolls-Royce being driven by a man who had himself made every gadget; yes, but *driven*.

Monteux did not drive. He allowed his players freedom to take part with him in the interpretation. He too knew exactly how to produce the texture of sound he wanted. He teased thread from thread, skein by skein, realising a stereophonic clarity from the most complex score. His magic lay in his sensitive ear and wonderfully intelligent eyes, not in the dramatic gestures of hands. This power of making a score both transparently clear and glowingly luminous seems the special gift of French conductors: today Pierre Boulez also has the secret.

When I returned to Santa Barbara I found to my delight that Howard had arrived from England, and with a good violinist, Roderick White, we formed a chamber ensemble to give concerts for the Community Arts Association. I had often played at home in London with Howard, thus getting to know much of the cellist's repertoire, and had also come to rely on him for understanding and criticism of my own music. All through my life there has been hardly any first performance of mine that he has not attended, and when my works began to be broadcast I was always sure to receive a postcard or letter commenting wisely, and sometimes sharply, on what he had heard. I owe him much.

Apart from playing I undertook other musical tasks in Santa Barbara, lecturing, conducting, and writing occasional music; the growth in interest for music there was accelerated at this time by an unexpected visitor.

Morley Fletcher, the artist, was taking a class in painting in the town, and through him an invitation was sent to Donald Francis Tovey to come and give recitals and lectures. I found his immense learning and authoritative manner rather overwhelming. I had never met anyone with so encyclopaedic a knowledge or with such a retentive memory. At a musical evening in a friend's house Tovey would go to the piano, gaze around and say 'I would like to play some Beethoven— but what? Any suggestions?' No request seemed to give him much trouble, even when asked for comparative rarities like some of the *Bagatelles*. This phenomenal memory for music went hand in hand with a compensating vagueness in practical matters. An endearing picture comes to my mind of Tovey on the beach with me, preparing to bathe. As we undressed Tovey was discoursing—he never chattered, seldom talked—on Brahms. I was ready first and moved towards the sea. Tovey followed, one boot on and one boot off, and quite oblivious, still the expositor, waded in.

Another figure in Santa Barbara whom I found very stimulating was Henry Eichheim. He and his wife Ethel had a beautiful house not far from where we were living. For many years Henry had been a violinist in the Boston Symphony Orchestra; then he married and

79

was able to carry out a long-cherished dream, that of exploring the East and its musical traditions. He returned with a big collection of instruments from Java, Bali, Japan and elsewhere. There were groups of wooden xylophones, whose intervals were spaced wider and wider as one ran up the scales; miniature cymbals which, when clashed, rose in pitch: magnificent gongs with a reverberation of half a minute. These were suspended around his studio, and one had time to touch the nipple of each in turn with a soft-headed mallet, so that they sounded together producing a gloriously bronze sonorous chord. Ethel was an excellent pianist, and like Henry specialised in French music: German music was out. Every detail of their house was exquisite, and it became a welcome focus for visiting artists who came to Santa Barbara.

I drove down several times to Hollywood—the old road along the sea's edge was lovely—but I did not have any technical contact with the film world until much later in my life. However, conducting in the Hollywood Bowl was an experience that I am glad I did not miss: everything combined to make music more magical—the velvet starry sky, the soft air, the vast bowl of the auditorium in which one could sit so far distant that the shell in which the orchestra played looked like a toy, and the conductor but the size of a match-stick. The first music I heard there was the First *Peer Gynt* Suite. I have never wanted to hear it since, for lying at ease on the slope remote from the players and looking up into the dome of stars, its first notes were wafted to me with a beauty of sound that cannot be repeated. When conducting there, I felt far from any audience, and their applause sounded like the crepitations of dry leaves blown about by the wind.

An even more dramatic setting for music was the theatre in the Bohemian Grove, north of San Francisco. Every year the Bohemian Club camped there for a week, and during this period an opera was produced, the giant redwoods forming the wings of the stage. The libretto was generally written by one of the members, and on the occasion when I was a guest I remember that an important actor in the cast was the full moon which, when invoked in song, appeared promptly and brilliantly centre stage.

Amateur efforts were much encouraged in Santa Barbara, and I was urged to get up a performance of *Elijah*. A good sized chorus was gathered together, and rehearsed hard, and a sprinkling of good local players formed the nucleus of the orchestra. For the wind and brass I had to draw on players from the Los Angeles Symphony Orchestra. To my delight, amongst them were some former players from Henry Wood's Queen's Hall Orchestra.

They motored up to Santa Barbara the day before the concert

and we held a full dress rehearsal that afternoon. My old friends from London and I had dinner together that evening. The contingent from Los Angeles had been picked by Alfred Brain, one of the famous family of horn players. These were the years of prohibition, not so rigorously observed in California, and Brain was an unofficial source through which some drink could be obtained. His supply made the evening a merry one, but in the early hours of the following morning I felt very ill indeed—I had no doubt that I had been poisoned. The doctor came early, diagnosed wood alcohol as the cause, gave me a pill (strychnine?) and told me to lie quiet. On hearing that I had to conduct the concert that afternoon, he gave me a second dose to take in the artist's room just before I went on the platform.

In a still feeble condition I was driving down to the theatre when I suddenly remembered the others of last night's party. Were *they* too in a similar plight? Should I find empty seats in the orchestra, or, at the best, very sick looking players? As I reached the rostrum I glanced around. Straight in front of me was the beaming face of Alfred Brain; and all his colleagues too looked in the best of health. I could only think that long practice had completely inoculated their insides against any dire effects. Shakily, but comforted I started *Elijah*.

I sometimes varied my music-making by attempting musical journalism for the local paper. I remember getting into trouble through an article on Geraldine Farrar, who brought a potted version of *Carmen* to Santa Barbara, and who stormed into the newspaper office the next day to demand vengeance on me. To offset this, I had the privilege of reviewing a recital given by Myra Hess who gave the most beautiful performance of Chopin's B♭ minor Sonata that I had ever heard.

One day a young and determined American composer came to see me. His name was Roy Harris, and he was living in Los Angeles at that time. He arranged to come up by foot and by friend's car the ninety miles to Santa Barbara to show me his orchestral scores. I do not know whether I helped him very much, but I liked his independent and vigorous outlook, and when in later years I heard Koussevitsky give his Third Symphony in Boston, I felt that in this fine score I was hearing real American music for the first time, free from European influence.

There is a tendency to depreciate a national idiom in favour of some international style, whereby it is often difficult to tell whether the composer is a native of Manchester or Osaka, Stuttgart or Minneapolis. Personally, I get bored with this musical Esperanto. I prefer infinite variety in all aspects of life, whether in cooking, language, architecture or music. I hope the distinctive and refreshing flavour of regional genius will always have a welcome.

81

# Chapter VIII

# Marriage and Return
# to London
# 1924–1925

ALL THIS TIME AN EVENT was slowly approaching that was to determine the course of the rest of my life—my marriage. A fine new theatre,
in the Spanish style, had been built in Santa Barbara to house theatrical
and musical enterprises. It was beautiful to look at, both inside and out.
To inaugurate this it was decided to put on a two weeks' run of a play
that would utilise local talent. The choice fell on *Beggar on Horseback* by
Kaufman and Connelly, which had been running successfully in New
York. The plot, in outline, dealt with the plight of a young and struggling composer. Should he marry the daughter of a rich tycoon, thereby
obtaining security at the price of surrendering his artistic conscience,
or should he marry the poor girl who is warmly sympathetic to and
keenly understanding of his musical ambitions? The cast was all
amateur, but a professional producer was brought from Hollywood
to cajole and force it to performance level. As the chief role had
to be filled by someone who was not only obviously musical but able
to prove it by playing the piano on the stage, I was offered the part.
Acting opposite me as the 'poor girl' was a twenty-year-old girl,
just home from Radcliffe College for her summer vacation. Her parents
lived in Carpinteria, close to Santa Barbara, and her name was Trudy
Hoffmann. At our first meeting her charm was immediate and winning,
and I began to look forward eagerly to rehearsing our scenes together.
I had been in love many times in my life, and had been made unhappy
and disturbed by each experience. The emotional crises always came
when I had to make the final decision as to whether marriage would
bring fulfilment to life, or an eventual frustration.

Perhaps there is a hard core in the composition of every artist
that makes him wary of a lasting tie, of deliberately fixing in a groove
the free mechanism which is his true inner self, his creative talent.
This cautious, perhaps cowardly, egotism must make the artist an
unsatisfactory object to a woman. He is magnetically drawn to her,
and then sheers off, warned by a tough sense of self-preservation that,
however adorable, she is not the inevitable choice.

I remembered the teller of fortunes in Chelsea whom I used to consult in my Cambridge days when burdened with a romantic problem, and how she insisted that I should not marry till I was over thirty, and then it would be for life. If that old Scottish woman was right, the time was now approaching. I should like to think that, as in classical myths, this climacteric was being marked by a special portent, for that rare phenomenon, a total eclipse of the sun, was due at this very time. Many of us in Santa Barbara motored over to Gaviota to see the eclipse at its best. As the moon's disc gradually crept across the sun every bird ceased singing, and at the moment of complete coverage, when the daylight was sickly grey, a sudden cold shiver of wind swept over the grasses. Twenty-five years slipped away and I was back in my first children's school, absorbed in that newly given prize book, *King Solomon's Mines*.

Intensive rehearsals for *Beggar on Horseback* began and I fell into the habit of driving Trudy back in the evenings to her home in Carpinteria, through the miles of scented lemon groves bordered by the phosphorescent Pacific Ocean. The mise-en-scène could not have been more beautiful. In between rehearsals we shared picnics on the shore, or in the foothills, or made expeditions to the Casitas Pass and the Ojai Valley.

On one of these trips an incident occurred which I still remember with a tremor of anxiety. We had motored up the Casitas Pass, and then scrambled into a fenced enclosure which looked the ideal place for a picnic; it had a wide view all round except on one side where a wood crept up towards us. Spreading our things around us we began to eat our lunch. The only sound came from a deep-toned cow-bell away down somewhere in the wood. It is a curious thing that Trudy, who is in every other respect quite fearless, has a fear of cows; even today to walk across a field where these docile animals are grazing causes her a flutter. So, naturally, when the cow-bell on the Casitas Pass sounded nearer and nearer, and finally the leader and several other animals appeared, I threw missiles at them. This was a mistake—they were not cows, but bulls, and they charged us. We ran like mad, and put the fenced enclosure between them and us in record time! Abandoning the lunch did not matter, but unfortunately the keys of my car were left behind with the food, and these had to be got back.

We discussed a wily Odyssean plan. Trudy was to draw off the bulls by threatening shouts and grimaces to a different sector of the enclosure, while I was to creep like a silent tracker to our picnic site and smartly recover the key, and anything else I could. This man-oeuvre was executed with perfect timing, but I realised that there was nothing of a matador's spirit in me.

83

The play opened its run in the Lobero Theatre, and it was soon evident to our audience that where I was concerned the drama on the stage was being re-enacted in real life off the stage. Perhaps I should say at this point that in *Beggar on Horseback* the composer does not marry the rich girl. I knew that I had at last met the girl who not only allowed me to be truly myself, but who could make me a more worthwhile man and better artist. I had a challenge to meet here, for I was by no means the only one captivated by her looks and charm.

When the run of the play ended I was invited to join her family for one of their periodic camping trips in Southern California. Trudy's father was a noted botanist and ornithologist, and he could make any expedition a real exploration. Her mother and sister were experienced campers, and with an artist friend to join us, the six of us set out for the Mojave Desert and the Yosemite. I believe that today metalled highways make such expeditions luxurious, but in the early 'twenties there was plenty of rough going. There were wonderful things for the newcomer to see—the hot colour of the desert and the sandstorms, the gigantic Joshua trees, the cool greenish skies at dawn and sunset, the delicacy of peach and apricot blossom in spring and great drifts of Californian poppies after the rains. We camped in Owen's Valley and then climbed into the Sierras on horseback. With my senses sharpened by love I thought I had never seen such grand and dramatic landscapes.

In September Trudy returned to Radcliffe, and I pursued my purpose, first sending her a beautiful Persian kitten and then following, myself, to Boston where she had relations. By Christmas we were engaged, and in the spring Trudy returned to her family in California. My feeling of happiness was heightened by my father's obvious affection for Trudy. On June 1st 1925 amid a host of relations and friends we were married at the Old Spanish Mission Church in Santa Barbara. From now onwards I shall drop as far as possible the intrusive 'I' and substitute the more sympathetic 'We'.

I always thought of my two years in Santa Barbara as a temporary interval in my life, and well knew that my future inevitably lay in England. So, my wife and I decided to leave at once for London and start our married life together there. Trudy had never seen England, and I know that those first years there must have tried her courage a good deal: the contrast between her past life and her present one was great. Instead of the beauty of California there was the grim aspect of Redcliffe Square, in which we found a studio-flat: instead of the comfort of her family and the companionship of college friends she had to face the unknown groups with whom I had been brought up. Whatever nostalgia she must have frequently felt she bravely minimised, and our life was varied and happy. To feel even closer to my musical life Trudy at this time went regularly to the Royal College

84

of Music, where she studied theory with R. O. Morris and took singing lessons.

I soon realised that I also had to make a fresh start. I had written little music during the intervening two years, just a few piano pieces and songs, and, on a larger scale, a string quartet which, sent in for a prize, had mysteriously vanished en route.

Musical memories can be quickly overlaid, and I found that to retain any footing in the changing musical scene I would have to work hard. But before starting on intensive work, I wanted to show Trudy a little of England, so we set out to motor slowly through the West country. My brother, Howard, had for some time been a friend of Thomas Hardy, collecting with zeal what letters and manuscripts of his were available. Thanks to him an invitation came to us, as we went through Dorset, to take tea with Mr. and Mrs. Hardy at Max Gate.

When I was a student, I had set to music one of his poems 'The dark-eyed gentleman' from *Time's Laughingstocks*, and I remembered how Stanford had angrily told me to take what he considered a most unpleasant poem away from his desk. It was difficult to equate this gentle little old man with the writer of the tragic novels and of the often ironical and pessimistic poems. True, his wrinkled apple-cheeked face told the tale of much experience, and his blue eyes were brilliantly penetrating; but his modest, absolutely natural manner towards his two unknown young guests was a surprise and an enchantment. He talked about the old instruments that he had heard as a young man in church services or at village dances, and which he has described in several of his novels. Hardy must himself have had some practical experience of music, for my brother once possessed his cello. As he stood in the evening light at his gate and said good-bye to us, my wife and I felt moved at having met the writer of the Wessex Novels face to face.

At tea Mrs. Hardy had said 'If you are going in their direction you must meet our friends the Granville-Barkers. I will ring them up and tell them.' So next day we found ourselves invited there for lunch. No greater contrast in environment could be imagined. We arrived too early, and were told by the majestic butler that Mrs. Granville-Barker always worked at her writing, in bed, right on until lunch time, and had not yet dressed. Would we like to take a stroll through the gardens? This we did until our watches told us it was precisely one o'clock. The inside of the house was exquisite, and so seemed Mrs. Granville-Barker as she entered the dining-room with a brightly coloured cockatoo perched on her wrist. She was a gracious hostess but I longed to get Granville-Barker himself to talk; after the easy natural atmosphere of Max Gate, we found the social formality rather stifling.

I have never been able to think very clearly, much less work with success, in very wealthy surroundings. I have sat in magnificent music-rooms in America, kindly placed at my disposal, without being able to think of a single note. I just blankly wandered around, staring at this *objet d'art* and at that; taking this book and that down from the shelves, returning once more to the concert grand—but in vain.

On my only visit to the Vatican I imagined how glorious it would be to work in one of the splendid long galleries, the Galleria dei Candelabri for instance, with a grand piano at either end. I would strike out a theme on Piano A and then slowly pace the 260 feet to distant Piano B. By the time I had reached there, my theme would have sprouted. I would play the growing shoot on Piano B, then slowly return to Piano A. In this way, treading many a mile, the musical conception would flower into finality. The dream was from every possible angle nightmarish, for I can only work well in a small remote room, where every object and even every muddle is friendly, and the cosy ambience invites concentration and effort.

True, I should like some great rooms near by, with high ceilings and plenty of floor space, such as perhaps Goethe found in Weimar when he left his small study to greet his friends in the reception rooms; but surrounded with too much luxury, I feel inhibited, the expensive bric-à-brac stares at me too demandingly. In that home of the Granville-Barkers I sat for a few minutes at a beautifully inlaid harpsichord: I just could not summon any music to my aid.

There was to be a meeting with another notable literary figure that winter. The idea sprang from a conversation at the Café Royal, after a concert, with Scott Goddard and a friend of his; as unfortunately I cannot recall the friend's name I shall call him X. X was telling us of his admiration for the writings of George Moore, and how he would occasionally catch a glimpse of the author at his window in Ebury Street, opposite to where he himself lived. We asked him why he did not pluck up courage, call on George Moore, and tell him of his appreciation: everyone likes a bit of hero-worship. X replied that he did not have the nerve, so to stiffen his resolve we others suggested that a joint letter should go to George Moore from us all, requesting the chance to see and thank him. This four-handed effort, written on the table of the Café Royal, naturally came out pretty stilted and contrived, and to give it some grace, we rashly added 'and to present you with some token of our appreciation'.

The letter was duly posted and in a few days came the reply addressed to my wife. Starting with 'Dear Lady and Gentlemen,' George Moore went on to say that at his age he gladly welcomed any surprise, so would we call on him at nine o'clock one evening, and he mentioned a day a week hence. Now came the question of the 'small token'. X was empowered to enquire of George Moore's housekeeper what was his favourite food or drink. The reply was negative: 'Mr. Moore was dyspeptic.' Books were obviously excluded, and pictures were too expensive. It was finally decided to buy a Venetian vase and, as an overture to the evening visit, to despatch a bouquet of deep-red roses to his house. We agreed that the ceremony of presentation should be a formal one, so white ties and tails were the order of the evening. To put ourselves into the right mood we first had a good dinner at Rules and then, precisely at nine, assembled on George Moore's doorstep in Ebury Street, my wife clutching the Venetian vase, and the whole four of us somewhat hilarious. We were ushered upstairs and received by our host, in a tweed jacket and carpet slippers, standing on his Aubusson carpet. He offered us a choice of port or hot cocoa, arranged us in a circle around him, and then proceeded to entertain us. With effortless ease and in a voice slightly tinged with brogue he talked of Paris and Manet, of Ireland and literature, of Wagner and music. His melliferous words flowed on, and an hour glided by. He then rose, thanked us, and said good-bye, giving me on leaving a fine copy of his *Perronik the Fool*, assuring me it would make a perfect libretto. Alas! Wagner had already written *Parsifal*.

A little later we invited George Moore to have dinner with us in our little studio-flat in Redcliffe Square. We had asked a few carefully picked friends to come in afterwards and meet him. On the advice of my brother we warned each one of our friends to keep off the hazardous subject of Thomas Hardy: he and his writings were absolutely taboo.

One day on one of our Californian camping trips, my wife's mother was driving the car. Our route lay across the Mojave desert, flat sand in front, to right and left. Only one object stood conspicuously out in the middle distance, and that was an old motor tyre lying abandoned, with a sharpish spike sticking out of it. My wife's mother, fully aware of this dangerous object in our path, naturally wished to avoid it—no difficult job, as she had the whole desert for a diversion. But as though magnetised by some malignant spell she drove straight to it, over it, and then *we* also had a punctured tyre.

In just the same way our evening with George Moore had a fatal termination. All had gone brilliantly until just at the end (was it the chance mention of Dorset?) our talk neared the danger point, fluttered wildly around it and then swooped directly on the name 'Thomas Hardy'. George Moore burst out 'dreadful, dreadful *gritty* writing! How can anyone with a love of beautiful English ever etc. etc.' The evening was marred, but even this fatal error did not prevent George Moore from inviting my wife to the Tate Gallery where, in a crowded room, he suddenly asked her in a loud voice 'Do you admit many lovers?' These moments with Moore were embarrassing just because one could not believe in his role of the experienced roué.

# Chapter IX

# 1926–1932

THE WINTER OF 1925 was a busy one for us both, and included a visit to Winterthur where I served on the jury to select the new works for the 1926 Festival of the International Society for Contemporary Music.

Our generous host was Werner Reinhardt, and among my colleagues on the jury were Dent, Honegger, Scherchen and Szymanowski. I found helping to choose the new works, simply by examining the scores, immensely difficult. Appreciation and criticism of new music being a personal bias—there is no such thing as an objective judgement—I chose the works that I best liked the look of, and put aside those that I did not like. I suppose the other jurists did the same, so, as all our sympathies were disparate, the final recommended choice was probably a gambler's throw.

There was another consideration which made itself felt round the table. Among the scores submitted were some very puzzling-looking ones. What *would* they sound like? We were all curious to put this to the test. Alongside these were many scores of established composers whose ideas could be easily comprehended. Was our choice to be based solely on the merit of the music, or on its curiosity appeal? I leave the conundrum to be clarified by musical history.

On our way back to England my wife and I stopped for a few days in Paris, where we heard a performance of *Meistersinger*, sung of course in French. I have never heard *Pelléas* sung in German, but the disguise must be equally laughable.

Trudy was at this time pregnant and on July 18 1926 she gave birth to a daughter whom we christened Barbara after the town where we had first met each other. Trudy's mother came from California for the event, and I certainly needed her affectionate companionship and support, my mood being one of anxiety and fear, then mounting to thankfulness, relief and pride. Trudy pointed out to me that the little girl had much of my look, and indeed she was soon to show evidence of her Bliss ancestry, just as our second daughter, Karen, was to be, in appearance and in character, an obvious Hoffmann. Trudy and I

89

took our daughter, during the golden September of that year, to Swanage where thirty or so years ago my brother and I used to spend part of our holidays.

I had been working hard through these months of 1926. With the sound of the Philadelphia and Boston Symphony orchestras still in my ears, I felt eager to write works for each of their conductors. I dedicated my *Introduction and Allegro* to Stokowski, who played it in Philadelphia the following year, but I actually gave the first London performance myself at a Queen's Hall Promenade Concert in September 1926. I followed it with my *Hymn to Apollo*, which Monteux introduced in Amsterdam two months later. Trudy and I went for this to Amsterdam; then on to The Hague by train with Madame Monteux and Pierre to hear his second concert there. Monteux had warned me that the conservative audience in the Concertgebouw did not respond quickly to new music, and that he had come to rate silence as tolerance and a sprinkling of applause as real appreciation. *He* certainly was most warmly welcomed, and on his suggestion I took the scattered claps that greeted my *Hymn to Apollo* as definitely reassuring.

Many years later I made revisions of both these works. During my career I have continually found that my second thoughts are usually better than my first, and the third sometimes better still. I am not one of those who can carve the final form out of the material at the first attempt. If I were a painter, for example, I could not be happy with Corot's creed; 'Soumettons nous à l'impression première'. I have to let my works be buried for a time, then exhume them for re-examination. I can then see how a tightening here, a loosening there, a thinning of the score at a third place will contribute to the perfection of form or sound. Through my life I have suffered the disadvantage that conductors have only known the original score, and, perhaps through criticism of the flaws, failed to renew their interest with my final and revised editions.

Rewriting an earlier work may bring the danger of spoiling what bloom it may have had, but in my case facility, quickness, and the urge to move on (ingredients in my character I have had cause to mistrust before) must be countered by the arduous task of revision.

In 1927 Trudy and I with our one-year-old daughter took a trip to California, by sea and then across the continent of America by train. My father was now eighty years of age, and we wanted him to see and greet his first granddaughter. We were accompanied by the nurse who had looked after me when a child. She had entered my father's household as a young girl, and had stayed on in Holland Park long after we three brothers had grown up, indeed until the day when my father left to live in America. Now she was again attached to the Bliss family; after she reached the age when she could no longer continue to act as nurse in our house, we kept in close touch with her until she died at an advanced age, a devoted and cherished friend to three generations.

While I was in America I had met the famous patroness of chamber music, Mrs. Elizabeth Sprague Coolidge. Among the rich women I have known who have supported music, she was unique in actually knowing a great deal about it, in being able to play it, and in recognizing what an artist stands for, and so treating him as a friendly colleague. I once came across the wrong type of millionaire patroness in America, who having engaged an eminent string quartet to play in her palatial music-room, sent them to the housekeeper's room for supper while the guests regaled themselves elsewhere. Since they were my friends I naturally joined the quartet in their humble quarters, and then to our delight the door opened and in came Mrs. Coolidge, who happened to be one of the guests of the evening. Spluttering with indignation she sat down with us, and I have reason to believe the rival patroness later learnt a salutary lesson in behaviour.

Mrs. Coolidge's festivals in Europe were noted ones, and when she asked me to write a special work for Leon Goossens to play at her festival in Venice in the autumn of 1927, I set to work most happily and composed my Oboe Quintet. It is always a joy to write with a superlative artist in mind, and besides the sound of the oboe with strings is exquisite.

I had not been in Venice since boyhood, a stiletto being the sole reminder, and for Trudy it was her first visit to Northern Italy. We first went to Como, then Padua, and long before the train neared Venice, Trudy's head was out of the window in expectation. The whole festival was a happy occasion for us: Leon and I used to take a gondola across the lagoons to the Lido to rehearse with the Venetian String Quartet, and the performance in the Conservatorio Benedetto Marcello was all that I could have desired.

Trudy and I had been invited by Francesco Malipiero and his English wife to visit them in their house at Asolo. I had already written with enthusiasm about his *Sette Canzoni*, and we were received with charming hospitality. Malipiero had a repugnance to destroying any living creature however insignificant; even spiders indoors were to be left undisturbed in their webs; in the kitchen were two small owls perching on short poles. When Malipiero approached them and hummed softly they would slowly shift from leg to leg as if performing some ritual saraband. From Asolo we drove with Mrs. Coolidge through the Dolomites to Vienna. She had the misfortune to suffer from approaching deafness, but motoring seemed to relieve this; she and her guests would accordingly motor hundreds of miles on end without a stop.

The programmes of the Venice Festival were repeated in Vienna, and I was much gratified by a few words that Alban Berg spoke to me in praise of my Oboe Quintet. We motored thence to Berlin, and while there, my wife and I wanted to repay Mrs. Coolidge's kindness by some return; we knew that one of her greatest pleasures was going to see a film: these were the days of silent films and she could easily follow the action on the screen. She chose her cinema, and we reserved seats for her and her rather large entourage. When we arrived in force we found that there had been a misunderstanding and that not enough seats were available for our party. Anger is a great incentive to hidden memories. I knew very little German, but suddenly my wife, who up to the age of four had spoken nothing else, let fly with a torrent of indignation which immediately produced the manager, then chairs in the aisle, and a decisive victory over incompetence. I remember feeling absolutely astounded that a small child should have known those imperious words at all!

Our next place of call was Amsterdam and on the way a small scene took place which recalled the end of Act II of *Die Meistersinger*. Suffering from a sore throat Mrs. Coolidge drew up one evening outside an 'apotheke', in a small town. The shop was closed, but on sounding the knocker, a shutter flew open above, and a head in a night-cap leant out. Mrs. Coolidge knew no German, and had to resort to miming; putting her finger down her throat she loudly gargled. The repetition of this two or three times brought a few passers-by to us, partly to see what this majestic figure was doing, and partly to help if they could. Other windows sprang open, and, as I have said, the scene was not unlike what Wagner pictured except that here everyone was doing their best to suggest and advise. Success crowned the miming: the chemist descended, produced a gargle: Mrs. Coolidge thanked all those around, and on we went to Amsterdam.


About this time I met Harold Brooke, a director of Novello's and the conductor of a small choir in the City of London. He suggested my writing a choral work for one of his concerts, the music to be published by Novello's. In this chance way I became associated with that great publishing firm, initiating a close alliance which has now been maintained for forty years. As is usual with me, I had to wait until some lucky incident set my creative talent in motion.

In the spring of 1928 two American friends of ours from Santa Barbara invited us to join them in a visit to Sicily. Trudy and I met them in Naples, and from there we motored down through the wild scenery of Calabria, crossed to Messina, and saw the beauties of Palermo, Agrigento and Syracuse. It was at this latter place, when one morning I had set out to explore the site of the classical fountain of Arethusa, a copy of the *Idylls* of Theocritus in my pocket, that I found the theme for my choral work. The southern light, the goat herds, the sound of a pipe, all evoked the image of some classical, pastoral scene. I began to collect a short anthology of poems which should depict a Sicilian day from dawn to evening. In later years I wrote a short programme note for this thirty-minute work which I give here as an accurate description of what I intended to convey. I used modest resources—a small choir, a solo mezzo-soprano, a flute, timpani and strings.

This *Pastoral* opens with Ben Jonson's summons to shepherds to celebrate their spring 'holyday' in honour of Pan. A rhythm of drums then ushers in the Hymn to the god, set to the words of John Fletcher, at the end of which the singers call four times on Pan to appear. The sound of his flute is heard on the hills. A stately Saraband is danced in his honour, and the chorus recall the story of Pan and Echo, in which Pan vainly invokes her love, and Echo mockingly sends back a distortion of his appeals.

The sun rises in the heavens, and water-nymphs invite the shepherds to seek rest and solace with them. This poem by Robert Nichols entitled 'The Naiads' Music' might be an evocation of some picture by Poussin.

In this short choral work I have tried as far as possible to vary the vocal texture in each section. Starting with a four-part chorus, I have next used the voices antiphonally, then women's voices alone, and now a single mezzo-soprano sings 'The Pigeon Song', the words again by Robert Nichols. In this poem a young girl whispers her story of love to her tame pigeon and then sends it as messenger to her lover in the fields.

Verses from Theocritus form the text of the next section. Men's voices accompanied by the shrill whistling of the piccolo sing a lusty prayer to Demeter to bless the fruit and grain.

Dusk falls, and the singers recalling the classical love stories, Venus and Adonis, Leda and Jupiter, Diana and Endymion, ask each other why they too should not follow the gods' example.

This was the first occasion on which I employed the device of the anthology for constructing a musical work. I found it very attractive to choose verse from quite different epochs, each poem having the same general subject as its theme. However widely separated the centuries music has the mysterious power of linking them together.

I was to adopt a similar principle in my choral symphony *Morning Heroes*, in the cantata *The Beatitudes*, and in the cantata *Mary of Magdala*.

I dedicated the *Pastoral* to Elgar. There was a good reason for this, quite apart from my long years of admiration for his music. Since the performance of my *Colour Symphony* in 1922 an estrangement had grown up between us which is evident in the first letter of his.

*Tiddington House,*
*Near Stratford-on-Avon*
*November 8th 1928*

My dear Bliss,

Your letter gave me great pleasure and satisfaction and I am obliged to you for writing it.

I do not refer to the concert now but to what you say about our friendship: this I valued and shall value again if you will allow me to do so.

Frankly, I was greatly disappointed with the way you progressed from years ago. There was so much 'press' of a type I dislike and newspaper nonsense. I can easily believe you were responsible for little or none of this but it rankled a great deal because I had great hopes for you: I had affection. It will seem vulgar to you if I add that commercially you have (I believe or was led to believe) no concern with the success of your works—an unfortunate side of art which we penniless people have always with us, and try to ignore. I hoped you were going to give us something very great in quite modern music, the progress of which is very dear to me; and then you seemed to become a mere 'paragraphist'. I am probably wrong and trust I was.

Now I have written at greater length than you will like but my reason (not excuse!) must be that you are one of the very few artists in whom I took an interest, to use the word again, affectionate interest.

Believe me, my dear Bliss,
Yours most sincerely
EDWARD ELGAR

The concert to which he refers at the outset must have been one in the Queen's Hall at which he had been conducting, and I must have then reopened a correspondence. I am glad I did so, and that his two remaining letters written in so friendly a spirit are still in my possession.

*Tiddington House,*
*Stratford-on-Avon*
*February 1st 1929*

My dear Bliss,

I accept, with grateful feelings, the honour of the dedication of your new choral work: may it flourish exceedingly.

With kind regards
I am
Yours most sincerely
EDWARD ELGAR

*Stratford-on-Avon*
*May 9th 1929*

Dear Bliss

Under conditions far from good I listened to the performance of the *Pastoral* you so kindly dedicated to me: the transmission or reception (I know nothing of the workings of the BBC with aerial sprites) was not good. But I could judge that your work is on a *large* and *fine* scale, and I like it *exceedingly*. The Pan sections suited me best but that is only a first hearing notion. Some of it naturally puzzled me, but I am none the less sympathetic: thank you!

Yours very sincerely
EDWARD ELGAR

At the same time in 1928 I had embarked on a work of a different character. My wife and I had been attending some of the concerts held in Mrs. Samuel Courtauld's house in Portman Square. I remember one particular evening when I first heard Schnabel play. It was a programme of Schubert. Remembering my early present at the age of twelve of the sonatas, I was well aware of the awkwardness and difficulty of much of Schubert's piano figuration. Schnabel's performances were those of a complete master; I have never forgotten them, though I have since heard many great players play the sonatas with quite other conceptions. Schnabel was a formidable arguer with a Johnsonian manner, brooking no interruptions, as I found to my cost. I thought his comparison of Schubert to Rembrandt an odd one, but perhaps it gave some clue to his very personal interpretations.

Mrs. Courtauld and Malcolm Sargent were planning a series of enterprising public concerts, and for one of them I wrote a *Serenade* for Baritone and Orchestra.

The idea of the *Serenade* came to me one day in 1929, as I sat in a

95

gallery looking at a picture (was it a Fragonard?), in which a pleasure-loving group frolicked in one of those romantic gardens, with temples, grottos and all, so favoured in the eighteenth century. I thought—why not revive the tradition of the vocal serenata, in which the lover himself sings his songs of courtship? In these four movements, therefore, I first introduce the serenader himself as a somewhat swash-buckling and cocksure fellow, and then let him sing a setting of Spenser's Sonnet *Fair is my Love*. In the third movement, his lady is depicted, and in the fourth, a second song is addressed to her, and she is praised in the words of Sir J. Wotton's *Tune on my pipe the praises of my love*. The work is dedicated to my wife.

The *Serenade* is scored for a comparatively small orchestra, and was first performed at one of the Courtauld-Sargent Concerts in the year of its composition, with Roy Henderson as the baritone and with Sargent conducting.


By this time, 1929, my wife and I had moved from Redcliffe Square and found a house in Hampstead. After the studio-flat, East Heath Lodge overflowed with character. It had a fine position, abutting right on the heath, with a splendid view—from our roof we could look straight across to the Crystal Palace. It must have been built by some lover of Italy, for there were fasces emblems on pillars in the porch and on the balcony, and the mantelpiece in the living-room carried the arms of the Borgia. This living-room on the first floor provided a beautiful studio to work in, and it was here that I started on my most extensive work since the *Colour Symphony*, a choral symphony to be called *Morning Heroes*, destined for the Norwich Festival of 1930.

Although the war had been over for more than ten years, I was still troubled by frequent nightmares; they all took the same form. I was still there in the trenches with a few men; we knew the armistice had been signed, but we had been forgotten; so had a section of the Germans opposite. It was as though we were both doomed to fight on till extinction. I used to wake with horror.

I was now at last decisively to exorcise this fear. If sublimation, the externalising of an obsession, can be thought of as a cure, then in my case I have proved its efficacy.

*Morning Heroes* is a symphony on war, and in Appendix B I have written the short description of the work that I sent to Vancouver for the use of the chorus there when I went to conduct a performance in 1967.

Again I used the form of an anthology, choosing poets as different in age and style as Homer, Walt Whitman, Li Po, George Chapman,

Trudy and
Barbara, 1931

*Lenare*

Trudy and
Karen, 1934

View of Pen Pits (architect P. J. B. Harland) from the orchard, 1935

Music room in the woods at Pen Pits, where the opera *The Olympians*
and the ballets *Miracle in the Gorbals* and *Adam Zero* were written, 1944-9

*The Architect and Building News*

Wilfred Owen and Robert Nichols. The first of the many orators who have since declaimed the passage from the Iliad and the Wilfred Owen poem was Basil Maine, and his was perhaps the most moving performance of all who have taken this role.

The problem of mixing spoken words and music—so as to make the amalgam satisfying to a musical listener—has to be solved anew on each occasion when the need for this alliance seems to arise. It can be argued that its use really begs the question, and that in any case the result is some kind of hybrid or 'sport', but I maintain that in *Morning Heroes* I was perfectly justified in nominating an orator to declaim the chosen texts. These depicted two intensely dramatic incidents, the first in prose, the second in verse. In both it was necessary that the words should be clearly projected, and that the varying pace at which an experienced actor might wish to speak them should be of prime consideration.

An additional problem for me was that in the Homeric scene there were two protagonists, Hector and Andromache. No doubt I might have set this as an operatic duet, but I rejected the idea as tending to soften the impact of their final farewell. Instead I maintained behind the speeches a soft orchestral texture which should heighten the emotion, but in no way restrict the orator's free declamation.

When I came to select the Wilfred Owen poem 'Spring Offensive', I found its content so poignant and its appeal so immediate, that I knew only a hint of distant gunfire was necessary to introduce and 'punctuate' it, pointing in as economical a way as possible the stark change of mood from the preceding fiery Choral Scherzo. I am always aware, when conducting this Symphony, that in these two movements, where narration joins with music, the emotional temperature of an audience rises.

The journeys to Norwich with my wife to rehearse the festival chorus as each movement was written and printed, returning in the evening through the lovely summer landscape of Norfolk, have left ineffaceable memories.

At this time I had come to know Bernard van Dieren, the most enigmatic personality I have ever met. In paying a tribute to his memory after his death I wrote that he partook of the nature of a Leonardo da Vinci, so multifarious were his inventive interests. He not only played a musical instrument, but he could make one, he not only wrote books such as his monograph on Epstein, but he was a beautiful binder of books; he was a linguist, a chemist, and a composer of many songs and much chamber music. Continuous illness, borne with much courage, kept him mostly confined to his house, but friends went regularly to see him in St. John's Wood as to some rare Delphic oracle. When I came to write my clarinet quintet in

1931 I dedicated it to Bernard van Dieren in gratitude for the many stimulating hours I had spent with him and his wife, Frida, content (and this I know is a rare thing with me) simply to listen.

Trudy arranged a small musical party in our Hampstead house to mark the first performance of the quintet, and Frederick Thurston with the Kutcher Quartet gave the work a most auspicious start. I do not think van Dieren was well enough to come and hear his work, but I have kept with care his appreciative and characteristic letter.

> *68 Clifton Hill,*
> *St. John's Wood N.W.8.*
> *September 30th 1932*

My dear Arthur,

I am getting on very well, but even writing a letter is a very great effort. I therefore make use of a siren that types and I hope you will not think it a less personal communication if I do so on this occasion.

I feel very pleased and honoured by the promised dedication. If the clarinet quintet is going to be at all like the oboe quintet it will be *anything but a trifling tribute.*

My love to Trudy and also from Frida.

> Yours ever
> BERNARD

Frida was herself as remarkable a personality as Bernard, and the two with their young son formed a trio of indomitable determination in face of continued difficulties. Frida told my wife a story that indicates her son's character very well. She had been to see Shaw's *Saint Joan* which had greatly interested her, and she was anxious to obtain a published copy of it. Her schoolboy son, knowing this and realising that times were hard, borrowed the play from a library, and in his spare time copied out the whole of the text in clear and model handwriting and then presented it to his mother.

Bernard, because of illness, seldom left his home, but on one occasion being anxious to see Charles Laughton in Edgar Wallace's gangster play *The Ringer* he came out with me to the theatre. The only seats we could get were in a stage box, and leaning well forward Bernard keenly followed the story based on Al Capone's life. In one scene, either before or after a killing, Laughton, mixing sentiment with ferocity, the characteristic antithesis in a gangster, went to the organ in his spacious living-room, and started to play Gounod's *Ave Maria*. At this moment Bernard could not contain himself, felt himself an active participator in the scene and began shouting Italian at the astonished actor. This absorption in the instant was typical of the intensity with which he lived.

98

# Chapter X

## 1933–1934

IT WAS THROUGH van Dieren that I made the acquaintance of Jacob Epstein. I had long wanted to possess, if possible, one of his bronzes, and a day came when I received an invitation from him to see over his studio.

Mr. and Mrs. Epstein were then living in Guildford Street near the Foundling Hospital. When we three sat down to tea, I became aware that there was a fourth person present. An inert form lay on a sofa, a long slender dark girl. Was she ill, or just asleep, or in a trance? She did not stir, nor did my host or hostess make the slightest reference to her; I began to imagine that I must have mediumistic powers, and be seeing something unobservable by others. I resolutely kept my gaze averted. Finally, Epstein took me into his studio, and I at once fell in love with a bust of a girl, whose strong head and massive brow made her resemble Beethoven. As a matter of fact Epstein told me that she was a well-known Café Royal model, named Betty May, and had written a book of reminiscences called, I think, *Tiger Woman*. Well, I carried away the head of 'the Tiger Woman' and then, taking leave of the Epsteins but not of the motionless figure on the couch, which still remained there as laid out for burial, I staggered into a bus with my bronze, sat down and held it on my lap. It drew all eyes, and I remember thinking that its powerfully modelled features made all the passengers look, by comparison, like sheep.

Epstein refrained from going to the private views of his own new works, but instead would invite friends and acquaintances in later to his house. On one such occasion when he was living in Kensington I took the tube back from his exhibition in the West End, and found myself sitting opposite a very striking looking girl whom I knew I had met before. I am bad at recalling names, but that did not prevent me from crossing over, sitting beside her, and speaking to her. To my embarrassment she turned an affronted shoulder with such a theatrical gesture that all others in the carriage were immediately alerted. It was obvious they thought I had been well

99

snubbed for my crude attempt at a pick-up. Very abashed, I got out at the same station as she did and, as she seemed to be going in exactly the same direction, discreetly followed behind. To my surprise she mounted the steps of Epstein's house, and so did I. Once inside I immediately realised *where* I had met her before; it was at the show from which I had come. Naked from the waist up she had towered in bronze over the visiting crowds. That she was now clothed made no difference to the confirmed impression I had formed, that I knew her. Explanations followed, and my self-confidence returned.

I made another friend at this time with whom I was to work closely in after years, J. B. Priestley. He was then living with his family close to us, in Well Walk. I had had for a long time on my shelves his early book of essays *The English Comic Characters*, and much enjoyed its gusto; and gusto is an appropriate word to use of Priestley as I first knew him. He went at everything with keen zest, whether returning a service at tennis, playing the piano, cueing a billiard ball into a pocket, or marshalling arguments to point his opinions. He quickly sized up the strengths and weaknesses of others, was an excellent mimic, and most enlivening company. I shall have a good deal more to say of him when the time comes for me to describe our co-operation on the opera *The Olympians*.

My father had died in Santa Barbara in March 1930, and in the following year my wife and I paid a visit to America, I to see my stepmother, and Trudy to see her father and mother. This was the last time that she had the delight of accompanying her father on a camping trip, for in the next summer he met his death, falling from a rock face when searching for rare plants. They had been very close in life, and the loss was a great grief to my wife. A consolation was the arrival of our second daughter who had been born in February of that year, and named Eleanor Karen. Her gorgeous red hair was probably inherited from my mother's side of the family, some of my cousins having a similar shade. As on the birth of Barbara, Howard celebrated the new arrival by presenting her with a magnificent painting by Matthew Smith. Trudy and I also owe to him pictures by Ivon Hitchens, from his collection of modern paintings, which have adorned our walls for many years.

I should like here to mention an encounter in Paris with James Joyce, arising out of the publication of *The Joyce Book*, a tribute to the author from a number of artists. In his foreword Herbert Hughes jogs my memory. 'This book', he writes, 'has evolved out of conversations that took place in Paris in the autumn of 1929. The talkers were Arthur Bliss and myself. We were attending a festival of contemporary music arranged by Elizabeth Sprague Coolidge, and James Joyce had accompanied us to the Palais Royal where works of Bliss and Roussel and others were performed. The subjective association of chamber music—that is, of intimate music—with the poetry of Joyce was to us like the association of wind and wave, of light and heat; and the idea of this collaboration, urged maybe by the emotional incidence of the festival, seemed to occur to us at the same moment. Let us, who are his friends, we said, make a volume of songs out of *Pomes Penyeach* and dedicate the volume to Joyce. We thought of selecting four or five. Our conversations were continued at Fouquet's and the idea expanded. It was decided that such a book of music would be incomplete, for *Pomes Penyeach* is a baker's dozen and the settings should be presented as such. There should, too, be a portrait, and poets, and writers of prose (also his friends) should join the musicians.'

The handsome volume contained a pencil portrait by Augustus John, a poem by James Stephens, an essay by Padraic Colum, an appreciation by Arthur Symons, and settings of *Pomes Penyeach* by thirteen different composers. I chose the three-verse poem 'Simples' with the opening lines 'O bella bionda! sei come l'onda!' Joyce wanted a particular Italian refrain used for these words, and this probably accounts for the warm phrases in his letter to me:

> *42 rue Galilei,*
> *Paris VIII*
> *March 3rd 1933*

Dear Bliss,

I write to thank you for your contribution to the O.U.P. I like your song better than any other in the book. It's rich and ample and melodious, delightfully balanced in its movements. You have done my little song great honour. Please accept my warm thanks.

> Sincerely yours
> JAMES JOYCE

I have a certain suspicion that with his Irish charm Joyce wrote a similar letter to each of the other contributors—perhaps he liked them all the best!

Musically speaking, 1933 was marked for me by my friendship with Lionel Tertis, and the completion of a large-scale Sonata for him. Tertis, like two former collaborators of mine, Leon Goossens and Frederick Thurston, was not only a master player, but the inspirer of a whole school of playing. It is no exaggeration to say that through his influence the viola, that Cinderella of instruments, was crowned a princess.

As my Sonata grew, I realised that it was really becoming a concerto for the instrument, and if today I had the energy and patience I would translate the piano accompaniment into an orchestral tissue, taking care that the mellow dark sombre tone of the solo instrument was not obscured by too thick a surround. But even if the length of this sonata was a deterrent it could not have had a more brilliant introduction to audiences.

Tertis and Solomon gave a private performance in our Hampstead house to a few musical friends and then a public one in November 1933 at a BBC Chamber concert. Shortly afterwards, in place of Solomon, Rubinstein accompanied Tertis. I remember Rubinstein only had the score a day or so before the concert, but despite that he gave an electrifyingly assured performance. It is a wonderful moment for a composer when he hears his music given a deeper significance than he himself thought it could bear, and then, with two superlative players there is the certainty that for each and every section the right tempo will be found. I have come to the conclusion that I do not so much mind wrong notes or a disregard of dynamics provided the basic tempo is right. I have heard performances of this Sonata that have taken fully three minutes too long. Perhaps it is fatal to affix metronome marks to one's score, for the metronome may be inaccurate, and I feel mine must be. If my music is to make any impression it must move on, and not be static; that is the very essence of my own character.

A right pulse is for me the first essential factor in pleasurable listening. I digress a little to emphasise my joy in the pulsing flow that great players like Tertis, Solomon and Rubinstein can give to any page of music. I think my Viola Sonata should have Tertis' name coupled with mine as joint composers, for many times in the course of its composition I would be called to the telephone by Tertis with his viola at the other end. I would hear his voice 'On page 17, line 3, do you like *this*'—I would then hear the tones of the viola—'or *this*?' He would then repeat the passage. 'But, Lionel, I don't hear much difference.' 'But you *must*,' he would answer; 'the first time I took two down bows, etc. etc.' Well, as I have written in a previous section, I had a master class in viola playing quite free, and I am grateful.

About this time Trudy and I began to long for some spot in the country where we could take our two daughters for the spring and summer. Trudy set about touring the places offered by estate agents, a wearisome task; either the house was too small or too large, too near a main road, or else shut in with no view. At last we decided to build our own house to our own requirements, and seeing a thirty-acre wood for sale in Somerset we bought it. The land was a tangle of undergrowth and, indeed, almost impenetrable in places, but it stood high and when cleared would have a fine view right to Salisbury Plain. The village was named Pen Selwood (the 'head' of the old forest of Selwood) and the site we had bought was named Pen Pits, and rightly so, for over practically all of it stretched circular pits some 20 to 30 feet across, out of which grew oaks and beeches. In some places the rims of the craters touched, giving the ground all the appearance of having been shelled by howitzers. Archaeologists differed as to the origin of these pits, but all agreed that they were very ancient, and might have been excavated by seekers after special flint stones. Later history maintains the possibility that Alfred used the site as a camp during his struggle against the Danes. It had a dramatic look, and I remember, when the house was built and Paul and Margaret Nash came to stay with us, how the painter delighted in making sketches of these moon-like craters with their attendant trees.

A close friend of ours, Peter Harland, was an architect, and we entrusted him with the design of the house. First of all a drive had to be cut from the road, avoiding the deep pits, then the site of the house levelled and cleared; the ground from the height where the building began sloped sharply to a neglected orchard; walls had to be built to buttress a flat lawn. There was a small, disused gardener's cottage on the property, which was put into repair so that we could stay in it and watch the progress of the building.

A good indication of the beauty of the finished house is given by the tempera painting which Edward Wadsworth did of it soon after its completion, sketched from a bank across the orchard, and showing the front of the house with porch and sun-deck. Peter Harland at first wanted the house to have, from an aerial view, the shape of a grand piano, but expense ruled out this imaginative idea. The house had light, air, and space, and we loved it. As an extra benefit the architect provided me with a separate music-room in the woods some fifty yards or so distant. Here I could be absolutely alone; it was a magical little retreat. From my windows I saw nothing but trees, and the only sounds were those made by the wind passing through them. Pheasants would make their rough nests within a few yards, and quite likely a fox, unconscious of my presence, would lollop by; badgers had their setts within view.

The one disadvantage of the room lay in its dampness, which badly affected my piano. One morning as I was playing I suddenly heard within a few yards what sounded like a gunshot. I leapt to my feet in alarm and ran to the window; nobody was to be seen, and with beating heart I went back to my piano. I then found that one of the bass strings had snapped, and it was this startling sound, in my over-reverberant wooden hut, that had led me to believe I had been shot at.

There was indeed enchantment about the place, and Robert Helpmann once said that it would make the ideal setting for a film of *A Midsummer Night's Dream*, especially in late May and early June when the ground was coloured blue by the massive rivers of bluebells. We kept on the house until the nineteen fifties, when my work made London the inevitable centre.

In 1934, while the house was being built, I gave three lectures on music at the Royal Institution, and at one of these H. G. Wells was present. I do not know why he honoured the occasion, as admittedly music meant little to him; perhaps he came to see how another speaker endured the ordeal of this special audience, for later when I knew him he confessed that from sheer nervousness he himself had dried up after twenty-five minutes, and had had abruptly to leave the lecture hall. Something that I said on this occasion must have caught Wells' attention, for he invited me to lunch, and there and then spoke of his projected film based on his book *The Shape of Things to Come*, and asked me whether I would like to collaborate with him by writing the musical score.

How understanding his attitude was towards the music can be seen in one of his early letters to me:

> *47 Chiltern Court,*
> *Clarence Gate,*
> *N.W.1.*
> *October 16th 1934*

Dear Bliss,

I am at issue with Korda and one or two others of the group on the question of where you come in. They say—it is the Hollywood tradition—'We make the film right up to the cutting then, *when* we have cut, the musician comes in and *puts in his music.*'

I say Balls! (I have the enthusiastic support of Grierson, who makes Post Office Films, in *that*). I say 'A film is a composition and the musical composer is an integral part of the design. I want Bliss to be in touch throughout.'

I don't think Korda has much of an ear, but I want the audience at the end not to sever what it sees from what it hears. I want to end on a complete sensuous and emotional synthesis.

Consequently I am sending you Treatment (Second Version). It is very different from the first and in particular the crescendo up to the firing of the Space Gun, which is newly conceived. I think we ought to have a Prelude going on to the end of Reel I, but I won't invade your province.

Will you read this new Treatment and then have a talk with me sometime next week. Then when we two have got together a bit, we will bring in Biro the scene artist, and then Menzies and my son who are busy on the scenes. I have already a definite scheme for drawings and models.

So far from regarding the music as trimming to be put in afterwards I am eager to get any suggestions I can from you as to the main design.

Yours ever

H.G.

Consequently a good deal of the music was written and pre-recorded before the film really got under way; many later modifications had, of course, to be made, but the dramatic *stimmung* of each section remained unaltered.

Those were the days of size in film production, huge sets, huge orchestras, hundreds of supers: the bigger the ensemble, the more important the film. At Denham whole towns sprang up, to be battered down by bombs and guns, and then rebuilt in a different setting. One section of the film was actually shot to my musical score: there was no dialogue in it; the sequence dealt exclusively with the machines of the future. The scene showed the earth being mined, roads made, houses erected, apparently without the aid of manual labour. This was one of the parts of the film in which Wells took a particular interest, watching the 'rushes' as they were shown, and caustically commenting. He had expressed a wish to hear my music before the 'shooting', so I invited him to come to my house in Hampstead, and there played the music through to him as best I could on the piano. I think at the end his comment was, without doubt, the strangest I have ever heard from any critical listener. 'Bliss,' he said 'I am sure that all that is very fine music, but I'm afraid you have missed the whole point. You see, the machines of the future will be *noiseless!*' Assuring him that I would try to write music that expressed inaudibility I went my own way, and luckily Wells forgot his objections.

As the huge film began to take shape, I realised that Wells was becoming disillusioned. At the outset, I knew he wanted his story of the probable future to be an educative lesson to mankind, to emphasise the horror and uselessness of war, the inevitable destruction of civilised life, the rise of gangster dictatorship and oppression. He felt that only the direction of far-sighted planners with the use of scientific inventions in the cause of peace could lift the world into a new era of prosperity and enlightened leisure. He knew that the mass medium of the film was the most powerful means of conveying his message, but it did not quite turn out like that. In spite of

105

imaginative direction, fine acting, and an expert staff of technicians, the financial necessity of having to appeal to a vast audience meant a concession here and a concession there, a watering down in one place, a deletion in another, so that, instead of having the impact of a vital parable, it became just an exciting entertainment. Everything that Wells prophesied back in 1935 has come to pass, even the dream of shooting young volunteers into outer space moonwards, but though the film has gone round the world, it has not influenced world events, as Wells so sincerely hoped it would.

One of the enjoyments for me of going down to the sets in Denham was watching the skill of the cameramen, the recording engineers, the cutters and, especially, the musical direction. This was in the hands of a young Scotsman, Muir Mathieson, who was to gain a great reputation as a conductor for musical film scores, and in his determined way to influence directors to commission special music from our own composers, Vaughan Williams, Walton, Alwyn, Arnold and many others. It is a fatiguing and anxious job fitting music to a film, and I used greatly to admire Muir at work, baton in one hand, stop-watch in the other, one eye on the film and the other on his players. He was so type-cast for this particularly exacting work, that his great abilities as a conductor of public concerts have been overlooked, and that is the musical world's loss.

I have written several scores for films since then, and I am sure the discipline involved is good for a composer's technique. It certainly teaches him the value of the blue pencil, of having to delete whole bars, sew up the passage neatly to an exact timing, and express his thoughts in an aphoristic form. It is salutary to see how often compression improves the music. Not always, of course: there are certain works whose nature demands leisure and space, but quite a number (and one can tell this from an audience's sudden relaxation) outstay their welcome; ending absolutely punctually is one of the marks of the great masters.

# Chapter XI

## 1935–1937

IN SPITE OF INTEREST in the new medium of the films I got weary of only writing music that illustrated other people's ideas, and as an antidote I started to compose a substantial piece of 'pure' music. I chose the string orchestra for this, not only because I loved the sound of it, but also because after the brilliant colours I had used for the film music the quieter palette of this section of the orchestra appealed to me. I wrote these movements fairly quickly, and enjoyed the labour.

Morning is my only successful time for working, especially so after a good night's sleep; afternoons are intended for a rest from mental concentration, but the interval between tea and dinner can be usefully employed in thinking about next morning's work. Planned meticulously like this, the schedule hardly conjures up the popular idea of the wayward inspired creator, forgetful of time or place, wild-eyed and dishevelled in appearance—I am sure there are many of these to be found, but I am not one of them. I am a bit lazy by nature, and if I do not keep to some kind of regular time-table nothing gets done.

When I started on this autobiography, I said to myself 'This is going to be too much of a task, probing about in my past and getting it all down in proper sequence. I shall give up after a few thousand words' and then a friend wrote 'Try a few hundred words every day, and you will be surprised how your story grows'. I took his advice, for *that* is exactly how a musical score gets written—a few pages every day.

I am a firm believer in letting the subconscious mind do most of the hard work. When composing I often find that in the early evening session my invention flags, then stops. I cannot see the path ahead, I have apparently come to a dead end. It is no use trying to force a way through: alcohol only engenders the false belief that you have suddenly found the hidden road; the clear daylight next day disabuses you. The only solution for me is the deep sleep at night: next day I play through the music right up to the point of stoppage, and most times my fingers without faltering carry me on to the logical solution; in my sleep my alter ego has found this for me.

For me, visits to the studios of painters act as a greater incentive to work than any amount of talk with my fellow musicians. In looking at the struggle for realised form in a sculptor's or painter's work I find something that instructs me in my own art.

At this time in the middle 'thirties my wife and I used to meet Ben Nicholson and Barbara Hepworth at their studios near by. Ben Nicholson was gay and physically very agile; playing table tennis with him was like trying to master a piece of quicksilver. How I wish now that on each visit I had brought back some memento from his studio! Among our treasured possessions, though, is an alabaster carving by Barbara Hepworth, a woman with a child in her arms, which still after all these years retains its vital magic.

Mark Gertler too had a studio in Hampstead, and used to come to East Heath Lodge to work on an oil painting of me as I sat playing the piano. His ambitions as an artist were so lofty that while moved by his ideals I was fearful of what might befall him if he failed to reach the heights he sought. He did not attempt a realistic portrait of me; in the finished painting my head shows as a pale oval rising above the piano; what fascinated him was the beautiful scroll on the raised stand of my mother's Blüthner, a very scarce and early one as piano tuners invariably point out to me; beautifully drawn in black, it gave great substance and decoration to the sketch. I regret that I do not possess this work as a permanent reminder both of the artist and of those years.

I have often been told that I am a 'romantic' composer as though that carried in these days some deprecatory significance. I have not the remotest idea of what is implied by that definition, since the very wish to create is a romantic urge, and music the romantic art *par excellence*. So *Music for Strings*, in spite of its neutral title, is a romantic work, and it received its first performance in a romantic setting, the summer Salzburg Festival of 1935, when Adrian Boult conducted the Vienna Philharmonic Orchestra in a concert of British music.

It was good to see Dr. Arnold Rosé, the leader of the famous Rosé Quartet, at the first desk, exercising his authority, standing up to correct the bowing throughout the whole violin section and muttering at times 'Schwer, Schwer—aber gut!'

Well it *is* a difficult work, written for virtuoso players, but after thirty years, technical proficiency has so grown that student orchestras of today now tackle *Music for Strings* without a qualm.

Afterwards I wrote to Trudy:

Well! the day has come and gone! I woke up early this morning,
walked in the Mirabell Park, called on Adrian, and went over to the
Mozarteum at 9.30 for the final rehearsal. It went well, with the
players obviously enjoying the work. The concert took place at
11 a.m.—a good audience, including Toscanini, Weingartner and
Bruno Walter. Adrian was at the top of his form, and steered the
difficult music through spendidly;—applause, which I acknowledged
three times from the balcony. I wish you had been there, next time
I shall take you, money or no. After the concert I rushed off up the
funicular to the restaurant at the top, where I joined Adrian and some
young friends of his. I was to have gone this evening to a grand ball
at the Residenz, but had no dress clothes! No matter—instead, I
went to a reception at the Princess Starhemberg—Viennese diplomats,
archbishops, and other exalted what-nots—a scene from Lothair;
afterwards to a Goethe debauch—Faust, lasting from 7.30 to
midnight. It was superb; I was as moved as Eckermann!

Tomorrow Adrian and I set off for Innsbruck for a week or ten
days' tramp from hut to hut. I have got two chic little coats for you
and a mass of silver buttons. Love to my hübschen liebchen!

In the autumn of 1935 the *Listener* asked me to write a series of
articles for the BBC on 'Musical Britain', giving me free scope to
go where I liked and write what I liked. This musical *Pilgrim's
Progress* took me from the beginning of October up to Christmas,
and I learnt so much about the humbler activities that get no light
shone on them that I reprint a few excerpts from these twelve articles
to recall experiences that I do not wish to forget.

I have started this week on a musical exploration of England—
exploration defines my purpose exactly, for it is to discover the
lesser-known activities in English musical life that I have set
forth, and not primarily to visit those that are already famous. . . .
I aim if possible at penetrating that immense activity that underlies
the more spectacular high points. I shall be, geologically speaking,
excavating at a lower stratum of musical deposit. . . . I started
from Bath, just because its Municipal Orchestra was the oldest
in the country, having begun its concerts in the Pump Room as
long ago as 1705 under the patronage of Beau Nash. There was
actually a 'band of musick' some thirty years before that date,
which played in what is now the Orange Grove under a large tree . . . .
I then went on to Bristol and thence to Cardiff and the Three Valleys.
I heard children's choruses and children's orchestras but I think

the most moving experience was going out to Mountain Ash to hear an adult chorus rehearse.

Of the hundred that were at rehearsal ninety-odd were out of work, colliers and their families, whose employment for the past eight weeks averaged but three days. Mountain Ash, where once a year in May is held the biggest Festival in Wales—the Three Valleys Festival—is in the heart of a densely populated colliery district. Long rows of houses run through the valley, follow the contour of hills, forming a great tightly packed wedge of stone—there are no detached cottages here. Massed dwelling-places cluster round mines and steel works that are so many skeletons, dead and decayed. What once were prosperous communities are now poverty-stricken centres, where the men have the appearance of drifting ghosts and the atmosphere is thick but unreal, as though life had passed on elsewhere. In these distressed areas the University Council of Music in Wales has redoubled its efforts. It braces the choruses, it forms listening clubs and singing meetings, it keeps stringed orchestras going, it organises yearly and terminal classes in music. This is done at the definite wish of the men, not forced on them. In an atmosphere of such deadening inactivity, a weekly chorus practice assumes a very different psychological aspect. On *that* night, at any rate men and women feel themselves employed.

I then toured Shropshire, saw something of the Competition Festivals and School Music Festivals, and in that county as in the Five Towns, which I next visited, came into contact with some of the many choral societies that proliferate through the whole of England. This is a traditional aspect of our musical life that foreigners find hard to visualise:

Most of these choruses consist of men and women who have been at work all day prior to gathering together and being gingered up by a conductor in the evening. According to the district they may be school teachers or shop assistants or miners, mill hands, farmers, engineers, iron workers; they may belong to every sort of trade in fact. These expert choruses, professional in achievement, are all amateurs in point of standing. Music is just the added relish to a hard day's work.

After the Potteries I went through Lancashire. A heavy grey wet blanket rested on Manchester when I arrived there. It was impossible to distinguish details, everything was sootily blurred. As a centre of music it was too famous to need further mentioning, so I chose four other Lancashire towns for investigations—Rochdale, Burnley, Blackburn and Bolton.

It was at Burnley that an incident occurred that might have come from a television comedy. It was my usual plan on arriving at an unfamiliar town to go straight to the Town Hall and look at the posters of any forthcoming musical event and find out, if possible from the Town Clerk, who were the chief musical personalities there.

In Burnley I found it was a young man well known not only for his musical abilities but for having just got married. I was given his address and set off to walk to his home. On my way, to make sure, I asked a postman for the address. 'Oh yes', he said 'I know him, he has just got married!' Coming to his house, I rapped on the door, and was greeted by, obviously, his young bride. She was anxious at her husband's late return: he had been at a football match. I explained what I had come for (to talk to him about his musical problems in Burnley) while she kept glancing up and down the road in search of him. She was cooking his supper—and would I come in and wait? I asked her if I could help her, and go on talking to her as she cooked. As she was grilling sausages I felt I could be of use, and she gave me an apron while she spoke of all the plans that her husband had.

We were getting on in a very friendly way, when there was a smart rap on the door, and a fierce middle-aged man entered the kitchen. He glared at me, turned to his daughter (of course he *would* be the father) and shouted at her 'What's that man doing in your kitchen?' Saucepan in hand, apron-draped, I really felt at a loss to explain, and when I replied 'I come from the BBC', I thought he was going to hit me for my obvious lie. Luckily at the moment rapid steps were heard and the young husband appeared. Peace was restored, in spite of an occasional disgusted grunt from the father. This was over thirty years ago, and I hope time has dealt gently with that young and charming couple.

Near Bolton, at Westhoughton, I came across one of the famous brass bands of this country, the Wingates Temperance Band. I am sure that any musician when he first hears the virtuosity of these amateur band players is as astounded as I was. I note that Toscanini and Casals also expressed their wonder. Hearing the sound that these twenty-four players can produce, it did not take much to persuade me in the following year to write the Test Piece *Kenilworth* for the annual Crystal Palace Festival.

My days in Newcastle brought me a new experience, the proof of how one man can affect the musical growth of a community:

Newcastle possesses one of the oldest schools in the country, the Royal Grammar School with some 800 pupils in it. The school has a set of good orchestral instruments, and a comprehensive

111

library of miniature scores and gramophone records, and lithographs its own orchestral parts. Out of the 800 boys in the school, ranging from the age of 8 to 19, there are 230 learning music in some form or another. Of these 60 are wind players. There are three orchestras, graded according to technical proficiency, which combine to give an annual concert. There is a conducting class whose members can try their skill on the orchestra. The school can muster a string quartet, a piano trio, and a string trio, and the sixth form are at present analysing the Seventh Symphony of Sibelius with miniature scores and gramophone records.

The Director of Music is Mr. A. F. Milner. He has been lucky in having a Headmaster who believes that music can serve a wide educational and social purpose and encourages every effort towards its realisation. He took up the cello himself so that he could tell from experience the difficulties besetting a young musician.

The year 1935 in Glasgow whither I next went was famous for the production of *The Trojans*, the two parts being given on successive nights, conducted by Erik Chisholm. All the members in this vast undertaking were amateurs, only available for work in the evenings or at the week-end; this applied to principals, chorus, painters, designers, costume makers, and the majority of the orchestra.

A letter to my wife indicates my mood at the moment:

*North British Station Hotel,*
*Glasgow*
*October 23rd 1935*

The cheerful sounds of your party over the telephone were sweet music to my ears. Glasgow in this weather is the dirtiest, noisiest, dourest and most depressing city I have ever been in—'une ville sauvage et barbare', as Mademoiselle would say. I begin to go south to-morrow. O Joy! this northern spot depresses; no one smiles and, visiting the Art Gallery (the only spot of beauty), I was seized on by a fanatical evangelist, who quoted Malachi at me, accompanied me in the tram to my hotel addressing me all the way as beloved brother in Christ *and* fellow sinner, in huge hearty tones. I was absolutely defenceless under the scowl of my fellow passengers. I had a nice time in Leeds; my host was most affable, but had one surprising peculiarity—a mania for writing me notes. When I was in the lavatory, a card would shoot under the door; on it was written 'You will find necessary paper in footstool'! Similar cards slithered under my bedroom door e.g. '*No* tips—we pay our servants extra'! I

112

*Checkmate*, 1937:
the death of
the Red Knight.
Black Queen:
June Brae;
Red Knight:
Harold Turner

*Enthoven Collection,
Victoria and
Albert Museum*

Discussion on
the ballet
*Checkmate*, 1937,
between
Ninette de Valois,
myself and
McKnight Kauffer,
the designer

*British Broadcasting
Corporation*

Trudy, Barbara
and Karen in
East Heath Lodge, 1937

Barbara and Karen, 1937

found myself going round the house with my eyes on the cracks of all doors.

My next survey was in Cornwall; there were many surprises to be found. I certainly did not expect to discover, for instance, opera in St. Anthony-in-Roseland, or good male voice choruses in the fishing villages of Marazion, Mousehole and Newlyn.

I finished my twenty-five hundred miles' trip seeing Ipswich and Norwich.

1937 was an exciting year for me, planning as I was my first ballet. I had often thought, in the years before the First World War, when I first saw the splendour of the Diaghilev ballets, how glorious it would be to have one's own music created anew in the dance; and now the chance had come to write a work to be given at a gala performance by the Sadler's Wells Ballet (as it was then called) in their first season in Paris the following year.

I knew exactly what subject I wanted for my dramatic ballet—the game of chess. This had always fascinated me though I knew I could never be anything but an average player. Where had chess originated? In the *Encyclopaedia Britannica* its invention has been ascribed to the Greeks, Romans, Babylonians, Scythians, Egyptians, Jews, Persians, Chinese, Hindus, Arabians, Araucanians, Castilians, Irish and Welsh. I preferred the theory that it was invented by some astute minister for a Persian Shah who had such a lust for war that he kept decimating his armies in pursuit of his passion. Here was a substitute, a warlike game in which he could manoeuvre his warriors without shedding a drop of blood. In essence the game is ruthless, with no quarter asked or given.

I had as collaborators Ninette de Valois for the choreography and McKnight Kauffer for the costumes and décor. Ninette de Valois, who had danced in the Diaghilev Ballet, was that rare fusion, both artist and organiser. It was due to *her* force of character and inexorably high standards that the English ballet became, under its later title of the Royal Ballet, a group of dancers of international repute, with their own repertoire. She has a vibrant personality, touchy, a bit imperious but warm hearted, and I came to like and admire her very much.

McKnight Kauffer at this date was chiefly known for his striking poster decorations but there is no doubt that his early death robbed the theatre of an outstanding designer. Neither knew anything about the game of chess, and so I held sessions in my Hampstead home, during which I moved the pieces about on a big chess board and demonstrated their characteristic moves, the Knight's jump, the Bishop's diagonals, the Queen's mobility, the King's tottering shuffle, etc.

I wrote my own scenario, and in this I had the expert advice of W. Bridges Adams. My wife and I had first met him in the years following our marriage, when we saw his lively production of *The Merry Wives of Windsor* in the old theatre at Stratford. After giving up his directorship of the Shakespeare Company there, he joined the Drama Department of the British Council, and we often met him and his wife at the country house of mutual friends, the Makowers, Ernest Makower being at that time Chairman of the Music Advisory Board of the Council.

Bridges Adams was familiarly known in his family circle as 'Tiger' and it was a very apt description. Prowling round a room with his long arms swinging, he would declaim speeches from Shakespeare with dramatic commentaries, his voice rising to a roar as he demolished this or that producer for his vanity or impertinence. There was little about the history of the theatre that he did not know, and from his fund of experience he gave me one specially useful tip. It was this: if you are going to play about with an exact intellectual conception like chess, woo your audience with a bit of realism first, and then they will accept your romantic departures from the expected. So, early in the ballet the pieces appear one after another on the gigantic board, and at one precise moment line up in the exact position for starting the game. I like my colours to be brilliant, and with the opposing sets of pieces clothed in red and gold, and black and silver, I certainly got my wish.

There were long discussions about the nature of the two players in the game. At first I wanted them shown as huge shadows over the board, but it was eventually decided to have them in the flesh as actors to open the drama. They could be costumed to depict Night and Day, or Alpha and Omega, or Black and White, or any other obvious contrast. Finally, we chose Love and Death, and here again my first idea was that, though Death wins the game, Love should be seen setting up another row of pieces, demonstrating that Death's win is no final one.

It was a joy to me to see this my first ballet take shape, with the wonderful cast assembled, among them Frederick Ashton as Death, Harold Turner and William Chappell as the Red Knights, Michael Somes as a Black Knight, Robert Helpmann as the old Red King, and Margot Fonteyn leading the Black Pawns. In the first performances the main role, the Black Queen, was danced by June Brae.

The opening was fixed for June 15th in the Théâtre des Champs-Élysées. The almost inevitable last difficulties attending any new production were present in full force. There was considerable confusion in the front of the house over precedence, protocol, who should sit where, and whose bouquet should be largest, but it was nothing to the chaos behind the curtain, due to a sudden strike of scene shifters in the Parisian theatres. This is where the experience and panache of Bridges Adams, acting for the British Council, shone brightly. Ordering food and wine to be brought backstage, he addressed the scene shifters in fluent Stratford-atte-Bowe French, enlarging on the glories of the French dramatic tradition, and on this unique entente between them and a famous British Company. Mellowed by wine, and astonished at his oration, the scene shifters leapt to their feet, the stage was set just in time, and the curtain went punctually up on the first ballet of the evening, *Les Patineurs*, conducted by Constant Lambert.

One nice touch in the expenditure submitted by the French authorities for the evening was the item for pipeclaying the accoutrement of the Garde Républicaine, whose members lined the staircase of the theatre.

Trudy left to visit her family in America a day or so after the première, and I spent a few days longer in Paris, often with Constant Lambert, who had given *Checkmate* such a good send-off. He was very keen on spending one evening at a special Night Club in Montmartre —'Brick Tops' I think it was called—where, he said, a wonderful coloured jazz group were playing. We toiled up thither, rather late, and I sat there with him for hours, listening to what was to me a most monotonous and depressive sound. As we came out into the street in the early morning a rickety fiacre was standing there, both horse and driver equally ancient. The driver was white-bearded and was holding a flute to his lips, on which he was blowing long sad notes. Before taking the cab Constant asked him why he was playing the flute at that hour. 'Pour la Mort' was the response. With a chill in our hearts we stole away. This was not the only macabre incident I have witnessed in Constant's company. He seemed to be a focal point for strange happenings, even to conjure them up. On this occasion I should not have been surprised to find, on glancing back, that driver, horse and flute had all melted into the pale light of dawn.

*Checkmate* has danced itself round a good part of the world since its first performance in Paris, and the Black Queen has become associated in my mind with Beryl Grey, whose beauty and dramatic power have contributed greatly to the success of the ballet. *Checkmate* brought me my only meeting with Toscanini; he had seen the ballet and been sufficiently interested in the music to invite me to come to his hotel suite in London and visit him. I had previously attended the rehearsals of the cycle of Beethoven Symphonies that he had given in the Queen's Hall, and had noted the deep impression that his personality made on the players. There was attentive silence as he entered the hall and went to the rostrum; once there, he immediately began what was virtually a concert performance. There was no sitting or lolling on his part; he stood erect, and his vivid beat was like sword play in the air; the mood of the players was such that they would have felt shame at not responding wholeheartedly to this man, so obviously dedicated to music. I was much impressed, and was overjoyed to have a chance of talking to him.

I shall not forget his first words to me, as they were an example of how courteously to put a humbler musician at his ease. Leading me by the arm to a sofa, and settling me down by him, he said 'Tell me, Mr. Bliss,—do *you*, as an English musician, think that I, as an Italian, take the slow movements of Beethoven rather fast?' At once I found myself talking eagerly and naturally, while Madame Toscanini bustled around, supervising our tea. I have at times in my life suffered from the arrogant manner assumed by some famous conductors, so I like to recall this hour with Toscanini as a signal proof of my contention that a great man is usually also a modest one.

*Checkmate* brought me many years later one more novel experience. In 1962 I was invited to make the opening move in the 38th Annual Hastings and St. Leonards International Chess Congress. I had been asked to do this on former occasions, but had been prevented by engagements. This time I was free and consented to do the little ceremony. I could not have chosen a worse year or season. The Congress opened on December 27th 1962, in the midst of one of the severest winters we had endured for many years. Roads were impassable, villages cut off, trains diverted, so heavy were the snow drifts. Not for the first time did I curse my complacence in accepting long-distant engagements.

I was routed in the train all round Sussex, and when I arrived in Hastings, I might have been in Siberia. No vehicles were in sight, and the only other passengers waiting were two woe-begone individuals in thick coats and fur caps who spoke no English whatsoever; they turned out to be in fact Russian Grand Masters who were to compete in the afternoon's contest. I managed to telephone and get a car to a hotel where they thawed out in the warm hospitality that was awaiting them—and me.

Later that afternoon in the 'Sun Lounge' on the promenade, with sleet beating against the windows, and a stormy sea raging outside, I made the ceremonial opening move on behalf of the Russian champion, tentatively advancing my King's Pawn. With a benevolent smile he replaced it, and began his own intrepid gambit against his British challenger.

116

# Chapter XII

## 1937–1939

In the spring of 1937 I was in Baden-Baden for a concert, at which my *Music for Strings* was played. In a letter to Trudy I wrote: 'There was a reception on the morning of the concert given by the Mayor, the Minister and others at the Kurhaus. We all sat at little tables sipping coffee followed by kirsch, while several officials orated. Not having the faintest idea of the appropriate costume, I wore an evening collar and shirt, a blue suit, and patent leather shoes; this musical comedy effect passed well enough. In the evening came the Concert, with my work second. I darted on to the stage, shook hands and bowed, and then bowed again from the stalls in the known Bliss manner. In the interval, Mayor and Minister confided to me that they liked my contribution best—in suave diplomatic tradition they then passed on to my French and Swiss confrères, and told them the same. The next morning I took a rest from further rehearsals, and went for a walk in the pine woods—authentic fairy-tale smell! I followed rundweg after rundweg, finding myself getting higher and higher, and I may say, hotter and hotter, as it has been drizzling here— damp heat—ever since I came. At the summit (2,800 ft?) there was a little hut with a platform for climbers to admire the view: an earlier tourist was in possession, an elderly bald German who was playing a slow waltz on a mouth organ!'

I had the novel experience of meeting a gambling addict here, a refined, elderly English woman, who might, in appearance, have stepped out of a Jane Austen novel. She had come to the concert, and had buttonholed me afterwards in the artists' room, asking me to come to the Kurhaus for some tea. I knew no one in Baden-Baden, and was momentarily caught. When we were sitting at a table I said 'It isn't tea I want, but a stiff whisky'. To my surprise the old dear said 'Well, that is my choice too!' I now began to take an interest, seeing her put down two undiluted doubles without a tremor and, quite curious, asked her what she was doing in Baden-Baden. She replied that she was only there because she could not get away, and then out came the story of her bad luck at the tables, and out came,

117

too, sheets of papers with calculations, demonstrating that the number she put her wager on *must* by the immutable laws of chance turn up within a day or two. And then the request! She had observed me, she said; I was English, and carried with me an aura of good fortune. Would I stand behind her chair that night at the tables, and bring her good luck? Alas for her, I preferred to do something a little more exciting, but we *did* have another round of whisky before parting.

In the autumn of 1938 I found myself in Brussels as one of the jury for the Ysaye International Competition for Pianists. Most of the jury were pianists of great experience, Rubinstein and Gieseking among them; I think only Bernard Heinze from Australia and myself were not public performers. National pride seems to play an inevitable part in these circuses, which have proliferated all over the world in the last thirty years. Each nation, except perhaps our own, is convinced that its own style of playing and interpretation is superior, so it requires a very firm and unbiased chairman to keep the peace and see that justice is done. Unfortunately on this occasion we had an old pupil of Liszt as Chairman, who was both vain and weak. His habit of exclaiming aloud 'zu schnell' or 'zu langsam' while nervous young players were competing annoyed me to such an extent that I threatened to withdraw, giving the press my cogent reasons, unless he kept quiet during the auditions. At the end of the contest he rashly volunteered to play the Schumann Concerto himself at a public concert, thereby giving us the feeblest exhibition of piano playing of the week. The rightful winners, in some haphazard fashion, generally emerge from these competitions, and on this occasion the remarkable young Russian Emil Gilels sailed away with the first prize. When I visited Moscow in the spring of 1958 to serve on the jury for the Tchaikovsky Prize for Pianists, he was our excellent Chairman, and I was happy to recall to him my part in his prize-award so many years before.

In Brussels the second prize went, after endless wrangling, to one of our own pianists, Moura Lympany. To begin with, our Chairman was much attracted by her appearance, and then secondly she brought off a real coup. The finalists were secluded for two or three days and had to learn during that short period a concerto specially written by the Belgian composer, Absil. This was a difficult piece both for the fingers and for the memory, and each finalist played the work with the score on the piano, except Moura Lympany. To the admiration of the jury she played it with confident accuracy without any music to aid her.

I described the visit in letters to Trudy:

*c/o M. le Comte Cornet de Ways-Ruart,*
*16 rue Belliard,*
*Bruxelles*
*May 17th 1938*

I arrived punctually at 4.5 p.m. after a calm trip except for some really sizeable bumps as we passed over the mouth of the Thames, which made me wonder whether air travel was all it should be. I was met at the airport, and taken swiftly into Brussels, and landed in a huge house, or rather 'hôtel' in the French sense of the word, with big closed gates, a drive-in, stables at the back, a luxurious residence, but needing upkeep. My host was, and still is, in bed with fever: my hostess was in the country—so, unpacking in my elegant bedroom (to wash you have to walk half a mile) I sallied forth and drank a couple of bocks in La Grande Place, which I see my book describes as the finest mediaeval Square in Europe. It is certainly satisfying, and would make a good setting for the Three Musketeers. Returning to the hôtel, I met the Countess, who is an American, and very, very charming. We had a tête-à-tête dinner, and then she departed upstairs, entrusting me with two colossal keys with which to let myself in and out.

same address—*Bruxelles*
*May 18th 1938*

We have now started in real earnest—a first session 9 a.m.–1 p.m. a dash back here for lunch, then second session 3 p.m.–7.30 p.m. (!), a hasty dinner, and *if* you feel like it, a concert later.

I have heard twenty-two pianists play the same piece by Bach, the same piece by Scarlatti, and expect to hear them sixty-three times more. Never again!

The Countess continues most hospitable, but the Count remains invisible. At meals a butler and footman silently watch me, and I handle ancient gold plate; I sleep between coronetted sheets! I gaily told you that I was going off to see an exhibition of Rubens last Sunday. Not a bit of it; it was the day for Boy Scouts; 1,400 marched round and round the Square where the gallery is, and every approach was closed.

The King came to our first session, so you see my innate snobbery is being appeased!

I am learning a lot by listening to these young players—the standard is high—and my Piano Concerto is going to benefit by the experience.

119

Hearing hour after hour so much brilliant piano playing made me wish to write an extended work for the instrument myself. I must have put intense concentration into the wish, for almost immediately afterwards the opportunity arose. In the summer of 1939 a World's Fair was to be held in New York; there was to be a week's participation by Great Britain in which the arts were to be represented, and an invitation came to me to write a piano concerto especially for Solomon to play on this occasion.

As was only natural, Solomon, before definitely accepting, wanted to see what views I held about piano technique and whether he was sympathetic to the general atmosphere of the work. Thus began a close and stimulating collaboration. He was meticulous in making technical suggestions, and, when the whole concerto was ready for engraving, his editing was of the greatest benefit to me. It was arranged that the New York Philharmonic Symphony Orchestra should give the performance in Carnegie Hall and that Adrian Boult should conduct.

The journey to New York was obviously one in which my whole family should share, so early in June we set sail for America in the *Carmania*, Adrian Boult with us, and also Leon Goossens who was to play solos during the British Week.

There are some artists, and they are usually the finest, who suffer intensely from nervous strain just before a concert. It is nothing to do with their confident ability in their own genius, for why should, for instance, Casals and Britten be subject to these moments? The cause is, I believe, the desire on the part of the performer to be at the peak of his interpretative powers—nothing less will satisfy him. This nervous excitement always leaves him as soon as he is immersed in the music, but the foreknowledge of this does not appear to ameliorate the moments before.

In Carnegie Hall Solomon was pacing up and down and saying 'I do not feel I *can* go on and play'. I literally had, in friendly fashion, to push him on to the platform. I have been ruthless to my soloist in this concerto, for the uprush of quick octaves at the opening is one of the hardest passages in the whole work, but as soon as I heard Solomon's clear articulation in these I knew all was well. Nerves had subsided at the first sound of the music, and his hands and heart were under perfect control.

Many pianists have played this work since, but the old 78 r.p.m. records made by Solomon, with Adrian Boult accompanying, still keep their authoritative interpretation. One of the finest exponents of the concerto was Noel Mewton-Wood, whose brilliant career ended so soon and so tragically. One performance that he gave with me, and which I shall never forget, took place in Ankara on the occasion of the opening of the New Opera House in the spring of 1948. As Noel was starting the virtuoso cadenza at the end of the first movement, the biggest black tom cat that I ever saw stalked on to the platform and settled himself down by the pedals of the piano. Noel was too concentrated on his playing to be aware of his companion, but he must have heard the ripple of laughter among the first rows of the audience. The players in the Turkish orchestra, the Presidential Philharmonic, were, however, not so closely concentrating on their music, and the tutti that ended the piano cadenza came upon them, alas, unprepared. After an attendant had removed the cat we then settled down without distraction to the remaining two movements. This concerto is really a man's work, but two women pianists have played it magnificently, Gina Bachauer, the Greek pianist, and Shulamith Shafir, herself a pupil of Solomon.

My old friend Albert Elkus was in Carnegie Hall for the first performance on June 10th, 1939; he was then chairman of the music department at the University of Berkeley, and he urged me to come there in January 1940 for a term or two as visiting professor. This new departure sounded attractive, and I promised to think his offer over seriously, when my family and I had returned to England— we had booked our passage back from Montreal later that autumn. I little thought at the time what a life-saving line Albert Elkus was flinging me.

After the concert my wife and the two daughters went to Stockbridge to stay with an uncle and aunt, while I accompanied Adrian Boult to Ravinia Park near Chicago, where in the open-air concerts he was to play some of my music. Adrian always had a love for trains, and when I used to be his companion on European travels the Continental Bradshaw was, I am sure, his favourite reading. As a train, say, in Germany whizzed past ours he would say 'Yes, the 11.40 to Stuttgart—5 minutes late!' These calculations being well out of my own reach greatly impressed me. His youthful enthusiasm still held good on this visit to Ravinia. A then famous train, 'the 400', ran from Chicago to Minneapolis, and used to pass close to the open-air theatre at about the morning rehearsal's interval. Orchestral players were in the habit of waiting for the silver bullet head of the train to appear and then checking their watches, and sure enough there would be Adrian, the keenest of all the train spotters.

I joined my family in Stockbridge, and the plan was for us to go to Moosehead Lake in Maine for a camping holiday before joining the ship in Montreal or Quebec. During all these weeks there had been ugly rumours of the dynamite that might eventually explode in Europe, but it was not until we were in the remote peace of Moosehead Lake that these speculations became very threatening indeed.

It was impossible to get any definite news where we were, and we determined to return to Trudy's uncle's house in Stockbridge and await events. It was there that we heard the fatal news that war had broken out. A week of desperate indecision followed. What should I try to do, with my wife still holding her American passport, and with my two daughters aged thirteen and seven? At first we attempted to get passage on a later ship from Canada, and then the news of the sinking of a non-combatant ship made it seem madness to risk their lives. Adrian was already back in England, and I cabled him to find out whether I myself could be of any practical use if I returned. His advice was to wait, and in this interim of doubt, I accepted the invitation proffered me from the University of California. In the meanwhile we settled in Belmont, near Boston, where my wife had been born, and I worked every day in the Widener Library to prepare some forty lectures on British music from Dunstable to the present day.

As soon as I began studying the history of English music, I realised what yawning gaps there were in my knowledge. I had to work hard, copying scores and writing notes at morning and afternoon sessions in the library, with a snack in between at a drug-store near by. But by December I had amassed sufficient material to give a fairly comprehensive survey, and I started from the premise, which turned out to be correct, that my students would anyhow know very much less than I did! And during all these weeks I was haunted by the thought of what our absent friends in England were enduring and wondering what was the right thing for me to do.

On one particularly dismal day we all went into the Boston Museum of Fine Arts and suddenly at the end of a long room I saw a picture so glowing with the kind of life of which we had been deprived, so strongly constructive, so full of rich humanity, that I felt ashamed of my cold depression and defeatism. It was Renoir's *Bal à Bougival*. Under the shade of trees two main figures are dancing, a man in a brilliantly dark-blue coat, jersey and trousers, and wearing a lemon coloured straw hat, and a girl in pinkish muslin, with a red hat and ribbons; the same red touches her cuffs and the edge of her dress, below which a frou-frou petticoat is visible. The man's hand is round her waist, and his face bends down to her; he is whispering something at which she turns her head shyly away. Behind them on the left are three figures, two men and a girl, seated at a table on which are glasses of bock; one man is formally attired with a silk hat, the other is in more casual costume, with a soft hat, and with a cigarette in hand; the girl looks up at them, one hand under her chin, the other hand resting lightly on the edge of the table. She is listening, open-mouthed, to her more Bohemian companion. On the right of the picture, just glimpsed, are several more men in silk hats, and a woman between them, again with red in her bonnet, who appears to be watching the dancers. The eye is caught at the bottom of the picture by a small posy of violets, perhaps dropped in dancing, and a smoked cigarette on the ground, with a spent match or two. The luscious green of the trees betokens an evening in high summer. The whole picture breathes an air of untroubled contentment and happiness.

In that one picture art showed its power to triumph over the miseries and brutalities that war brings in its train. Indeed all art worthy of the title should add to the excitement of life. I remember a short story by Marcel Aymé in which the pictures of some indigent painter immediately gave the onlooker the physical feeling of having had a good dinner. When placed in the window of a Paris dealer passers-by gaze at them and miraculously hunger no more. That is a good symbol for the mysterious power of art. How rewarding it would be at the conclusion of a fine Symphony to have the sensation of having had a satisfying and exquisitely chosen banquet!

# Chapter XIII

# 1940–1941

WE SPENT CHRISTMAS with some of Trudy's relatives outside Chicago and then started the year 1940 in a rented house in Warring Street, Berkeley, close to the huge University. My heart felt much lighter when I met my colleagues and started on my work. A number of these fellow musicians have remained intimate friends of ours to this day, and their sabbatical leaves to England are always looked forward to as a time set apart for joint adventures.

Apart from Albert and Elizabeth Elkus, there were Charles and Piquette Cushing. He had studied composition with Nadia Boulanger and was a close friend of Darius Milhaud, who was at this time Professor of Music at Mills College. On their visits to Europe the Cushings would occupy the Milhaud's apartment in the Place Clichy, and we have since had uproarious evenings with them there.

Then there were David and Ruth Boyden; his book on the history of the violin, which he was to publish later, is masterly; also Edward Lawton, a skilled choral trainer, and his wife Helena. In the composition class was the dynamic figure of Ernest Bloch.

Outside the Department our closest friends were Bertrand and Mildred Bronson. A classic work on my shelves is the former's authoritative edition of the *Traditional Tunes of the Child Ballads*. His attainments range from studies on Chaucer and Samuel Johnson to singing Elizabethan airs while accompanying himself on his lute.

Such a group provided a warm protective covering to my feeling of exile and frustration. My class at the University was much larger than I epxected, and I knew that the only way to hold their attention throughout a long course, was to make them illustrate the musical examples themselves. So, I formed a large madrigal group and an excellent string quartet, and encouraged solo wind and brass players. I resorted to a real 'gimmick' on occasions. For instance, when I was analysing the Purcell Fantazias I invited any student who could beg, borrow or steal a stringed instrument to bring it to the next lecture, whether they had ever played one before or not. Some twenty turned up with violins, violas, or cellos. With the bows in their hands and their fingers firmly on the strings to sound middle C they took part in Purcell's Five Part Fantazia on one note, my skilled quartet performing round them. After this participation I felt sure none of them would forget the experience of Purcell's music. Among the many modern British scores that I analysed on records, Vaughan Williams' 4th Symphony and Alan Rawsthorne's *Variations for Two Violins* seemed to interest them the most. While the record was being played I devised a means of demonstrating on the blackboard by diagrams and figures what was going to happen next in the course of a work. As we could not provide scores for all the class I found that this visual aid was an advantage to understanding.

On one of my visits to Los Angeles to conduct I called on Stravinsky and on Schoenberg, both of whom were living in Southern California, the latter giving courses at the University. Stravinsky, as on previous short meetings, was kind, wise in advice and invigorating in manner. If my memory serves me right he was then composing his Symphony in C, and had fully sketched out the first two movements, and perhaps the third also. We certainly played some of the music on the piano for four hands, and he seemed in doubt as to the form the final movement would take. I remember saying with some boldness that I hoped it would end with the same classical serenity with which his ballet *Apollo Musagetes* brings down the curtain.

It was a strange coincidence of fate to bring two such world influences in music as Stravinsky and Schoenberg so close together in one neighbourhood. When I went to have lunch with Schoenberg I found, besides Mrs. Schoenberg, her brother Kolisch also present. Before I had had time to assemble my thoughts I was swept into a game of table tennis in their porch with these three; Schoenberg delighted in the exercise, and also had theories about angle shots and other niceties of the game. These theories were not demonstrated practically, for the game was haphazard and delightfully hilarious.

During lunch Schoenberg spoke of his difficulties in teaching the large classes that came to him, in spite of help from chosen senior pupils who could move around and explain further what he himself was illustrating on the blackboard. After lunch Kolisch brought out recordings of Schoenberg's Fourth Quartet, and we listened to this, score in hand. When it had finished, Schoenberg, who had remained absolutely still and with no change of expression in his face, said quietly and cryptically, 'It will take some years from now before I can recover the mood in which I wrote *that*'; he then asked for the recording of his first string quartet. It had hardly begun before he rose, and walked about, obviously deeply affected. Was he recalling Vienna and his early years there, his struggle and difficulties, and contrasting that memory with his present exile? I do not know, but the sight of him with tears in his eyes touched a similar chord in me, and I also felt moved.

In the summer vacation we were lent a house at Santa Barbara by relations of my wife: it was eerily strange to be staying there once more under such different and sadder circumstances, and my mood at that time is expressed in my settings of seven American poems, by Edna St. Vincent Millay and Elinor Wylie, each one of which carries the burden of a vanished joy or beauty.

As the autumn of 1940 drew to a close I began to be assailed with bitter doubts and anxieties; there was a desperate clash of loyalties, destroying any feeling of sustained happiness. What *should* be the future of my family and myself? There could be no question of *their* returning to England, but what action was right for me? My roots were deeply planted there, and whatever growth I had attained I owed to that country's traditions of thought and design of living. As I walked, morning after morning to my lecture room past posters bearing the words 'London Aflame' or 'The City Burning', I was overcome with a sense of impotence and frustration: my work at Berkeley seemed so relatively unimportant. What our intimate friends in England were experiencing was only too clear from the letters that came through. The following excerpt from one of Howard's letters coming into the peaceful backwater of Berkeley will give some idea of the turmoil set up in our minds.

*31 Collingham Road,*
*London S.W.5*
*September 15th 1940*

As you know, the storm has broken. The church in front of this house escaped by yards when an 'oil' bomb fell in its garden. Just behind this house, a bomb (high explosive) came down into the gardens on the same night—near enough to make me think all was over and this house struck. It was a few minutes only after the alarm warning was given—at Hitler's usual 9.0 o'clock sort of time in the evening. I was making an effort to get some sleep before he started his racket, and was lying down on my little mattress two landings below, in my pyjamas—when the scream of descending bombs suddenly began. I seized my tin helmet and put it on and lay on one elbow wondering whether to get up or not. Louder and louder the scream—until it seemed to get right into the house—then thud, thump, whack! The house just rocked, and I heard through the wall at my head the sound of falling masonry and crumbling brickwork—or so it seemed. I felt sure the top of the house was coming down on me. I got up and quickly slipped on some clothes (one feels somehow more protected than just in pyjamas!) and decided that for the first time I must give way and go right down to the basement until things were quieter. After half an hour our locality seemed safer and I came up to my landing again.

In the morning I went on to my roof. Just at my corner and exactly (as I afterwards paced it) twenty-six yards behind this house was a crater 10 ft deep and 17 ft across where the high explosive had fallen. Earth and stones were everywhere: two trees were uprooted and struck down; on my roof were fallen chimney pots which I tossed, without effort, into the crater below in the garden.

Every alternate night I do patrolling of the streets round here— from dusk to dawn—to keep an ear out for falling bombs which don't explode. It makes me very tired because the alternate nights when I *should* sleep I get very little—because of the nightly racket. To tell the truth, I find being out in the street, and perhaps taking cover in a door-way, *far* less of a nervous strain than sitting up in one's bed wondering whether there is enough above one to give any protection, and I hate the idea of being buried under debris as some poor people have been.

Keeping this up paralyses one's ability to think or concentrate on anything—not the thought of bombs, but the lack of sleep. Ay least that is its effect on *me*—but I am a child for the amount of sleep I like to have!

HOWARD

At such times our small family circle became infinitely dear, and the thought of leaving them an anguish. There is no more painful cancer to the soul than indecision, and for weeks I hovered between one line of action and another. My wife remained always wonderfully understanding, never trying to influence me one way or another: *she* knew with the clearest intuition what was involved, and what might be the consequence in future happiness of the final decision. I had written to Adrian Boult at the BBC and to Bridges Adams at the British Council offering my services when they were needed, but the letters of the latter, those dated September 18th and November 2nd, perplexed me even more. He was one of the inner circle of our friends, wise and unprejudiced, with sterling integrity both as a man and an artist. Was he right? His letters are so full of his per-sonality, and so redolent of the days when they were written that I quote a few extracts from the many I received in Warring Street during the autumn and winter of 1940.

*Badingham Old Rectory,*
*Suffolk*
*May 15th 1940*

Butter, if you please! I can't imagine any kinder or more practical help. But you mustn't do it again: believe me, we are so far quite

127

unaware, as far as the inner man goes, of the existence of rationing. We have also 60 ducks to date, and as to rabbits—they do not believe in long engagements.

Quite apart from that the essentials of life show no sign of diminishing. We want news of you all however: one satisfactory aspect is that you are being *English* in California.

I haven't written because of an odd feeling that all one's friendships are in cold storage for the duration: a kind of general bolting of watertight doors, many other people have felt the same. Quite unreasonable and wrong; but I find myself putting a plasticine gas mask on my bust of Shakespeare in the same spirit. *Some* day the bust will be heated on a hot plate until the gas mask drops off— and may you both be here to see!

Meanwhile life proceeds for us by an unchanging ritual, which has always a stabilising influence. On Tuesday to the British Council by the early train, staying at the Savile Club: earnest young civil servants all day, wise old men at night. On Friday, down here— breeding hutches and fowl houses all day, and my wise Peggy at night. The news, I am sorry to say, takes precedence of our normal fireside amenities, that is a pity as it is breeding a race too alive to the moment to live for eternity. Your *Checkmate* clicked in Holland in spite of some bad work by the Haarlem Orchestra. I don't know whether you have heard about this yet. After many rebuffs, jibbing at further inertia, I persuaded a doubtful Lloyd to let me send the Sadler's Wells Ballet to The Hague, Haarlem, Amsterdam, Brussels, and Antwerp. They got as far as Haarlem, where they played to a rapturous and astonished house (it was in the danger zone) half an hour before the Germans marched in. They showed our flag and, much more important, the banner of all artists all over the world, to such effect that the Dutch cheered them to the roof when they had breath to spare from gasping at their pluck. I had based them, thank God, on The Hague throughout, with their own coach and scenery lorry. They got back, the drone of their own engine drowning all other sounds, to The Hague at about 3.0 a.m. and at 4.0 a.m. were awakened by the doings—they stood for an hour on the roof in their dressing gowns, watching dog fights and street battles, too excited to take care. Then a long journey under fire by night, a peaceful day in a deer park (this was full marks to the Legation) and at last an embarkation to the hold of a freighter where they lay on straw for 10 hours or so—no life belts, two life boats and 700 passengers— and so to Harwich and eventually Liverpool Street, where I met them at 2.30 a.m.

The first to emerge was Constant Lambert, with an immense bandage round his head. 'My God,' I thought, 'they've been shot up.'

'You're hurt,' I said. 'Yes,' replied Lambert 'cigarette ash in my eye!' The whole outfit, in fact, were unscathed. But I don't mean to go through it again. Seventy pretty legs I kept thinking! I was on to the Legation eleven times, sometimes with strange noises sounding, but always the neutral world-weary diplomatic voice giving a shade more hope. Within an hour of the news I had a transport ready for them at Havre, but the road was bombed and they could not get there.

The scenery and music are in a store at Haarlem. I am trying—what a hope!—to get it out.

Never mind—a good gesture—heads by no means bloody and haughtily unbowed.

BRIDGES

*Badingham Old Rectory,*
*Suffolk*
*September 18th 1940*

Trudy's welcome letter came today. Let there be no mistake about it: unless the BBC or the Council want you here, your job is to stay where you are and write music. There are few enough of us today who can do anything now but destroy. You are over age: you have 'kept' one Great War with distinction: moreover the composing of music should be as much entitled to a place in the schedule of reserved occupations as smelting or riveting. So much for the National aspect of the matter. But the hope of the world is in the Supernationalists. Very few of us can be that, but musicians can.

There are no two people Peg and I more miss than you and Trudy, For all that, we think of you both ten times a day and thank the gods you are out of it. So before irrevocably deciding to abandon your young and come back to join the elderly gentlemen in tin hats who are guarding railway bridges, reflect that you are quite possibly more useful where you are.

BRIDGES

*Badingham*
*November 2nd 1940*

A fly in the Amber, I doubt not. *You* feel a Fly in Amber because you are not here (one more mouth to feed: one more good man entangled). I feel a Fly in Amber because I am not staring grimly into the murk from a destroyer—like those dreadful advertisements of teetotal stimulants which the R.N. would rather die than touch: if I *were* on the bridge of a destroyer I should feel like a Fly in

Amber because I wasn't running the war (or, more important, thinking out the peace). You can go on for ever, because there is no limit to the human itch for self-immolation. My counsel to you is: make up your mind that you are a Musician, stay out of it and *work*.

You are in peril of the Action Neurosis, which has wrought more harm upon humanity from a desk or an easy chair than any that the poor smash-and-grabbers can do.

BRIDGES

I was too disturbed in my mind to write any music during these months, but finally, encouraged by Mrs. Coolidge, I composed a string quartet for the Pro Arte, resident in California, and this was given at Berkeley in April 1941 just before I eventually returned to England. Two of the original members of the Quartet were still with it, Laurent Halleux and Germain Prévost; Antonio Brosa led the ensemble and Warwick Evans was the cellist.

Then one day in April came a letter from Kenneth Wright, at that time Director of Overseas Music at the BBC, asking me to come and help in his department. The die was cast, indeed thrown by my own hand, and an unknown future suddenly and inexorably opened before my wife, my children and myself.

In old age I cannot bear to write much of the parting between my wife and myself; she came to New York to see me set off for Canada; it was the most anguished moment through which I have lived. Like some widower, bereft through his own action, I took the train to Toronto, Ottawa and on to Montreal to await the convoy that should take me across the Atlantic. The delay in Canada was much longer than I expected and the truest picture of my feelings and doings before sailing can be shown in some of the letters that I wrote to my family.

I have had some qualms about publishing the following extracts from the intimate letters that passed between me and my wife during the War years, but I remembered what Samuel Johnson wrote of his own personal letters: 'In a man's letters, his soul lies naked, his letters are the mirror of his breast; whatever passes within him is shown undisguised in its natural process. . . .'

During the month I was delayed in Canada before sailing many letters went to Trudy and to my two daughters, Barbara and Karen, and once in England a weekly letter went to California, and a weekly one came to London. In case one of my own letters went astray I also sent a weekly cable from the little Post Office next door to the BBC offices in Marylebone High Street, to say that all was well.

From these many hundred letters with some difficulty I have chosen a short selection with which to try to depict these tense years in my life. On re-reading them after many years I realise that I have given no idea whatever of life as endured in London during those times.

I have not mentioned the shabby battered state of the great city, the dismal wailing of the sirens, the fear of night bombing, the loss of friends, the depressive effect of winter 'blackout', the ersatz food and scarcity of goods, the grey monotony and sheer uncertainty of life. In front of me on the wall hangs a lithograph by Henry Moore. It depicts the ghostly groups which huddled in underground stations every night for the sake of shelter and safety. This picture by itself could have told much more of the unnatural life, feverish excitement alternating, because of fatigue, with 'couldn't-care-less' lethargy.

Perhaps it would appear from these letters that I myself lived quite a cosy life between office, club, and friends' houses. The truth was, of course, that my life was just like any other Londoner's of that time, but to emphasise it as such would not have brought much comfort to my wife. It was indeed a refreshment to me to exclude from these letters, as far as possible, all reference to the tragedies of the war, and to concentrate on trying to preserve the unity of my family.


Handed to Trudy in sealed envelope,
on parting in New York,
May 5th 1941.

*Hotel Roosevelt,*
*Madison Avenue at 45th Street,*
*New York, N.Y.*

Dearest love—Patience and Courage to us both. What we have between us is indestructible—so I defy anybody or anything to break it.

I shall write a *long* letter air mail immediately on arrival in Toronto I carry you and the 2 darlings with me.

A.


*King Edward Hotel,*
*Toronto, Canada.*
*Wednesday, May 7th 1941*

. . . Such a fine crop of letters fell into my box this morning. . . . You can't know what a fine glow I have inside me at the thought of the little core of love and beauty stationed in Berkeley. . . . You can rest *fully* assured I shall take *every* precaution I *should* from now onwards. I have you 3, I have important work to do, and I have much more to create. So do not rest anything but easy on that score, darling.

Spent a nice day at Niagara with the Hungarian partner of Boosey & Hawkes, Schulhuff. The falls still fall, the spray still sprays, the roar still roars, in spite of power stations, advertisements and bill boards and general commerciality. The drive lay through miles of orchards in blossom, and I enjoyed it.

I go to the CBC office every day and learn. Everyone is kind and hospitable and efficient—a thoroughly nice crowd.

*King Edward Hotel,*
*Toronto, Canada*
*Saturday May 10th 1941*

. . . I spent yesterday in Ottawa beginning my round of visits on the Canadian BC officials. Such a nice day—a certain Donald Manson took charge of me, led me round the Parliament buildings where I handed my Eva Gauthier letter to the secretary of the Prime Minister who told me the Prime Minister would be delighted to see me if I could stay over till the next day—was given lunch in the swanky Ottawa hotel where, summoned to meet me were a Canadian poet called Scott, the director of the Art Gallery, a young English musician, Naylor, and a fascinating man, bowed with sciatica, who was described to me as the 'shadow of the P.M.' and went by the name of Brocklington!

After lunch Manson, Brocklington and I drove down the Ottawa river while B-ton quoted T. S. Eliot, and hummed V.W., and spoke intimately about my own music, and altogether won my heart. Then off by train here (very like Manchester) where I arrived at 11.0, took a Seconal, and slept sound. This morning at 9.30 your grand cable came which lifted the Bliss optimism up—9.30–10 continual telephone calls from the press and the CBC here. Saw Bushnell at the CBC HQ (Excuse these awful initials but one must use them)— extremely kind and helpful. He has asked me to spend Sunday tomorrow with him and his family, as Sundays here are like provincial English Sundays!—He advises me to spend a few days here seeing musicians, then back to Ottawa, where they have the short wave service at its best, to hear a couple-of-days programmes from England, and then return here—My address always as above. Now— flying is out of the question—forbidden altogether—I am told I have a passage on a good swift boat in about two weeks' time—the BBC apparently look after their staff well. Bushnell has been back and forth twice—so you will be hearing from me for at least two more weeks from this side. To-night Schulhoff takes me to a string quartet concert in a Beethoven programme—so you see the days pass in friendly fashion. From a feeling of desolation on leaving my darling and beautiful wife my spirits are rising with active things to do and will continue to do so—and that is the only source of final triumph—to get through this separation with as little despair as possible, and I *know* we shall both do it, bless you. . . .

Your little note about the blank cheque and flying suit just sent up to me—lovely to see your handwriting.

One thing—I cannot find the little leather case and photos of my family. I have written to the Roosevelt about it. I have a pair of stockings of yours! Did you by any chance pack the photos in your bag?

Give B & K a great big hug and squeeze from me. I am so proud of them both, and all my thoughts for you, darling.

Shall write again on the heels of this.


*King Edward Hotel,*
*Toronto, Canada,*
*Sunday May 11th 1941*

Before going to bed I am going to write a few lines to my darling. . . . When I listened to the Hart House Quartet playing last night the very Beethoven quartet we listened to together years ago in the Lobero Theatre, score in hand, I realised that all these sweet and painful associations that will hit us hard in the next months must be faced and dealt with squarely. I am proud and grateful that so many things are dearer and more beautiful because *you* are mixed with them, and I am *not* going to be cast down by the loneliness (that you are not with me to share them) but carried forward by the thought that everything worthwhile is continually shared with you—the string quartet last night, and the wild trilliums seen from the train and perhaps above all, our common viewpoint on what is happening now—more and more I share your ideals of peace and happiness though the means are still obscure to me—one learns quickly when one passes from a country that is not at war to one that is—and *what* one learns is powerful proof of your vision. So on to the best constructive work I can do. I cannot tell you what a strength I feel to have you three together there in Berkeley. Do not let your imagination run riot. The reality is *far* less bad than what the imagination visualises.

P.S. (I am more and more convinced I have a job not only worth while but one that I alone can sense the size of.)

Darling, just to tell you I am moving in the most friendly and sympathetic circles. I arrived here late last night just before midnight, really sorry to say goodbye to Bushnell, who is a practical idealist, and whose opinion, by the way, of our C.G. in New York is guardedly annihilating (is that spelt wrong—it *looks* wrong?) I attended, as guest of Major Murray, (the boss of CBC) a luncheon yesterday of educators from U.S.A. and Canada—very fine speech made by the American organizer of radio education (Alan Cameron's position in England). He spoke of the need of clearing away tribal feeling, provincial feeling, even national feeling in favour of wide human feeling. You would have liked him. A full day to-day. Morning at the office!! Rest, and think this afternoon—Cocktail party given for me by some young musicians—6.45–11.30, listen *critically* to my first-heard short wave programme from London in the studios in this hotel.

To-morrow. Walk in the park—Ottawa is an attractive city, unlike Toronto—visit to Art Gallery in afternoon with director. He has just been entrusted by some French patrons with a fine collection of Renoirs that he *has* to keep in his cellars in cases, *unlooked* at, and is green with temptation—6.45–11.30, second critical listening.

*Ritz-Carlton Hotel,*
*Montreal*
*May 20th 1941*

I arrived here from Ottawa last night, having had a most welcoming time there with friends. To my joy I found 3 big envelopes from you. Telephoning the Mount Royal I unearthed a 4th letter, despatched a messenger for it, and sat down to dinner surrounded by loved things to read. I will first answer your points in turn. As yet I know neither the port nor date of leaving. I came here partly to see the CBC unit here, partly because it will be a good centre for any port (they give you about 24 hours' notice) and partly because it is far the most interesting town in Canada, a real French city with atmosphere. I *expect* to go in a week or so from to-day, but will put on my letter *LEAVING* which will give you the information. Ralph Hawkes arrived in New York from England yesterday, and I hope he is going to ring me up this evening and tell me all about it. . . .

I laughed over your letter about the arrival of my 3 special deliveries. *Whelpdale* Maxwell is *not* a puppy, but the head of Steinway & Co. and looks after my pianos! . . .

I just missed John Grierson in Ottawa. I think he did all the Post Office films in London—but to make up for it I expect to see Stephen Leacock here. Very beautiful 3 hours' journey from Ottawa to Montreal, large lakes, and flowering orchards. It reminded me (i.e. the lakes) of all our water trips from the lake at Cape Cod to Moosehead. Walking in the park at Ottawa I plucked a bunch of honeysuckle (unseen by anyone) the exact counterpart of the one growing over the toolhouse behind the Pen Pits cottage!

Well, my beauty, I must end for to-day and will continue adventures in my next.

All my love to my 3.

*Written at*
*University Club of Montreal*
*2.30 p.m., 23rd May 1941*

(really living at Ritz Carlton.)

. . . I got your telegram about 'listening in' just before my broadcast at 12.15 this morning. They have arranged to send you records from Ottawa, probably 2 double sided disks. You will have to play them inside out i.e. the reverse way of ordinary records—or they may be the large size which can only be played on a Broadcasting Station machine—I do hope you will like what I say, though I was a little nervous of the French (!) at the end, aimed at Montreal and Quebec. It is a real French town this, every sign in French as well as in English. I sat for a short time in Notre Dame here yesterday afternoon, remembering your face as you looked at the rose window in Notre Dame in Paris, and then you thrusting your head out of the window to look at Venice as we approached. I never forget these things.

Major Murray has given me the run of this Club for my stay—very nice indeed. I have just had a delicious Canadian salmon with egg-plant followed by strawberries and cream. I took my coffee and cigarettes in the small library and read a delicious article in the *Yale Review*, Spring 1941, by Osbert Sitwell called 'Pompey and the Peaches' a study of a painter (like Cézanne), and so to the desk to write to my darling. This evening I dine with a French conductor here, Baudet.

I shall want to know when you go to Mission Canyon and an address *after* you leave. I plan to cable you to Mission Canyon immediately on landing in England. I shall send for safety sake a similar cable to Eleanor at 43 Glendessary Lane, S.B. After that I shall cable you in Mission Canyon *every* Monday. It will be my 'love' or 'all well' so as to keep economical.—But it will mean much more. It will mean that I am well and happily doing my job. These weekly cables (and by the way try not to worry if a week goes by without one—because the cable communication is NOT infallible) will be supplemented by, I hope, weekly *written* letters, which may arrive in a bunch. Any letter containing important personal news I shall send in duplicate, one air mail, one sea mail. If there are any suggestions tell me. I should address all mail to me c/o BBC *London* until I make further arrangements, though letters addressed to me c/o Farquharsons, Heathside, Hampstead N.W.3 will also get me.

I feel no personal anxiety whatsoever, no more than you would in my case. What I *do* mind is that the strain is all on you—and I think one has just got to practise our slogan 'Relax is all' to its $n^{th}$ degree, hard enough it is for my more taut and sensitive little wife. I am hanging on to all the little permanent values of life for all I can (salmon, Sitwell, and Tuxedo!, so to speak) and if you can let that generous and sensitive imagination of yours *rest*, we shall all pull through the more easily.


To Karen

*Ritz Carlton,*
*Montreal*
*Sunday, May 25th 1941*

My darling Karen, I was so glad to get your letter and the bunch of photos—you on the horse, you in your best clothes with us all and Uncle B, you holding Nimbus* outside Elizabeth's house, Elizabeth herself looking terrifically big, as large as a house and twice as wide, and, finally, Nimbus herself looking as though she could not say boo to a goose. I carry them about with me and love looking at them, especially the one of you and the one of Barbara jumping, (and alas! knocking over the post—*no*, I think the hind legs have cleared it after all!).

I went for a walk in the fields close by here this afternoon and discovered a nest. Two young tree creepers peeping out of a hole in an old tree, with mouths wide open and yelling for food, and the mother bird flying up with a worm in her mouth and feeding them, and the male bird hovering about and saying to himself, 'Oh these greedy children, always wanting choc bars.'

I was very proud reading your report.

My love to you
Daddy

* Her kitten.

136

To Trudy

*University Club of Montreal*
*Wednesday, 28th May 1941*

To-morrow, I am going to the McGill University Convocation for conferring degrees, at which Dorothy Thompson is the speaker. All seats were given weeks ago—but did that deter me? No! I *have* one. Two other items. At lunch to-day a gold nugget fell from my mouth. Dashing to the dentist it was deftly replaced by a man who had seen me conduct *Things to Come* in England. Two—I visited just now the little art gallery, its smallness having distinct charm. As I wandered round, I came across so many things which bring you vividly to me, my darling—a Peruvian design with the kind of weird geometrical figures that you wove into your frock (blue) when we were just married, glasses with pontil marks and drops in their stems, lovely Brussels lace, Utamaro—Hokusai—and 2 little celadon plates—all precious and abiding memories.

*University Club of Montreal*
*June 4th 1941*

. . . I had a nice day yesterday. Douglas Clarke, who is the Albert Elkus of McGill University and a rough diamond if there ever was one (but a *distinct* diamond), took me out in his car along the shores of the St. Lawrence, and we sat and smoked and gossiped in the loveliest surroundings, lush trees, blackbirds singing and a slight haze over the water which is so wide at this point that it looks like a lake. There is always a serpent in Eden though, and *here* were mosquitoes large and hungry—and to-day we are both bitten piece-meal, but it was worth it to get away from the city into silence—except for water, birds and trees. We are going to take a picnic lunch to-day again somewhere—this will probably be my last day here, and, as I wrote before, I shall be glad to get a move on—this waiting around I could never abide. You will get another letter saying for certain though. I can imagine the Greek theatre the centre of B's life these days. I do hope the weather is on her side, and I long to know of my Karen's doings. I am writing to each of them this evening. I have investigated the small library in this club, and have been greatly entertained by the early letters of Lamb. What fun to have received one oneself, and then written a good savage one back! (as I write, outside the window stands a milk cart 'GEO. MOORE'). I shall copy Lamb's amusement and see myself in various stages of honourable notability:
Sir Arthur Bliss—Sir Arthur Bliss, Bart.—Baron Joy—The Marquis

of Felicity—The Duke of Bliss—King Glee—Pope Happiness. This is all nonsense but I love writing to you. . . .

LEAVING
*University Club of Montreal*
*June 4th 1941*
. . . Do not worry *overmuch* for the next 2 weeks. You will receive a cable about June 20th. It seems a *long* time but I shall be hanging about in port for a little before we go. . . .

I was finally ordered aboard a banana boat in a large convoy on June 5th.

*Canadian Legion*
*War Services*
*June 10th 1941*
. . . another pilot boat is ready to take mail off so I dash off a line to you at Santa Barbara. This is my 5th day on board at an Eastern Canadian port, and as I know nothing beyond the fact that we must sail soon, I cannot tell you much. I write in a comfortable cabin all to myself and have spent the last five days walking round the deck, reading your fine detective novel amongst other things, playing bridge and rummy with others on board.—There are six women amongst a crowd of men, and I sit for meals at self-chosen table for four, which includes the wife of an airman, a Canadian officer, a Lancashire business man and myself—all interesting and we get on well. I wish I could tell you the conditions under which I am sailing, but I can't.

You must know that they amuse and intrigue me and that in a little over two weeks I ought to be able to write you fully of my experiences. My love to you all. . . .

# Chapter XIV

# 1941

THE CONVOY WAS AN exceptionally large and slow one, and we did not put into Avonmouth until June 30th. We took a very northern route as the *Bismarck*, I think it was, was out prowling and we were a very vulnerable target. At night the convoy seemed to stretch from one horizon to the other. For a short time we were honoured with an escort from one of our own battleships which settled down in our midst like a bored greyhound; destroyers on each flank moved around like terriers.

On my Fyffe's banana boat was a contingent of young volunteer air pilots from the New World. They were a wild and gay lot and proceedings got really lively when a British Group Captain in uniform, who was also with us, tried to enforce a bit of old-fashioned discipline. His daily commands on the notice board and their replies could have got into any 'Beyond the Fringe' programme. A dramatic moment for me was about half way across when the Big Ben signal suddenly came over clear followed by the News, and of course the startling news of the voyage was the entry of Russia into the war as an unexpected ally. This was acclaimed in a very liberal way, and was one of the reasons that all worthwhile drink gave out long before we sighted the north of Ireland and sailed slowly down the Irish Channel in the direction of Bristol.

The BBC Orchestra had been stationed there, but due to the heavy bombing of the town had been removed to Bedford, so I travelled at once to London where I spent the first night in a bleak hotel: I felt I had wandered into some black nightmare.

To my joy next day, two of our closest friends, Maurice and Nancy Farquharson,* offered me the hospitality of their house: they had for many years been our next-door neighbours in Hampstead, and I had known Maurice long before that. When I first met him he was a fellow subaltern drilling on the square in Chelsea Barracks;

* A heart-warming cable 'Of course you must stay with us' had come to me from them before I left Berkeley.

139

he was now an experienced member of the Secretariat in Broadcasting House and so I was able to gain immediate knowledge of the jealously guarded procedures in that mysterious organisation. This was of great value to me, as I had never been behind an official desk before: my ignorance of paper work was incalculable as I found the first day when I went to my office in Bedford College and sat there attended by my allotted secretary, Ursula Elliott. I must write some words in praise of her, as in the years to follow she accompanied my rising footsteps, never allowing me to stumble or dislodge the dangerous bricks that I might ignorantly let fall. Her memory was remarkable; she never forgot for a second any telephone number or any name; her filing system was a work of art and in crises and moments of trouble she remained unflappable. The choice of her as a prop was one of the kindnesses that my immediate superior, Kenneth Wright, first did for me; there were many others.

With sympathetic understanding he wrote to Trudy immediately on my arrival.

> 17 *The Crossways,*
> *Wembley Park*
> *July 3rd 1941*

My dear Trudy,

I want you to know how very much I appreciate your generous attitude in sparing Arthur to us for this work he has come to do. What is more, we (*all* of us) do not fail to appreciate what Arthur himself has sacrificed in order to do it.

He looks well, and is his usual dynamic self. Never in my life will I have a greater thrill, nor a finer compliment, than his immediate cabled reply saying he would come. It made me very happy, for it set the crown on my hopes, and the Corporation itself did not underestimate the compliment he paid to all of us—and to me.

You know with what affection and regard I have long held him and how grand a friend he has been to me in the past. I see the great, the vital work we must do: the almost unlimited scope of the job: the great opportunities it will give to imagination, enterprise, and to youth: the future it must help to shape. Music can play such a role in this war as few people dream. I see all this: and knew that Arthur was the ideal colleague to help me—help us all—to carry it through.

Congratulations on the noteworthy attainments of your nice daughters by the way. Lucky parents—lucky kids!

> Yours ever
> KEN (A. Wright)

I was given an office in Bedford College, Regents Park and there, with Ursula attendant, I just waited to see what would happen. I did not have to wait long. The door suddenly opened and in came a messenger with an armful of memoranda and letters. They were all gibberish to me, mostly signed by inexplicable initials: the memos urged me to take notice of this or that, or to pass on this or that, or occasionally to take some urgent action on this or that, but not often in my first humble capacity. This was where Ursula proved invaluable, sorting all the papers out, putting some in a tray marked 'for future reference'—*they* answered themselves—others in a tray 'to be acknowledged', while I started a tray marked 'impending'— defined by the Oxford English Dictionary as 'hanging threateningly over one!'

I soon learnt that this ruthless machine never stopped; there *could* be no letting up night and day. It just had to be fed all the time. My colleagues, long experienced on this treadmill, had learnt how to deal with the BBC's demands without cracking up altogether, and gradually I patterned myself on the tempo at which they worked.

I continue with letters to Trudy from my office in Bedford College, Regent's Park.

To Trudy

*BBC*
*London*
*July 11th 1941*

. . . I have two lovely letters by me, yours dated June 25th, and the second June 29th with the snapshots taken at Hope Ranch Beach. How beautifully quick they have come! First to answer questions raised. I have never been so certain as I am to-day that the children should remain, & expand where they are. Here, everything necessarily is curtailed, from education & food to thought & space. *They* have relatively boundless horizons—and very many of their own age are blessedly in surroundings *just* as remote from the actual experiences of a wartime world.—Do not mull over it any more, my darling. I am *thankful* they are there. . . . *Their* consciousness of life & its value is far far more likely to go on deepening where they are. . . .

I want to give you a picture of what I do every day—to-day for instance. 7.45, awakened and given a cup of tea, breakfast with Maurice, Nancy, Phoebe.* Maurice takes 24 bus, Nancy goes to her canteen, Phoebe to her doctor's consulting room, I walk to Hampstead tube, buy *Daily Telegraph*,—Warren St., bus to Baker St., 100 yds. walk to Regent's Park, Bedford College—arrive 9.45. 'Good morning everybody'. In my room I find Rollo Myers & his secretary,

* Nancy Farquharson's sister.
141

& my indispensable Miss Elliott. 10 a.m., attend staff lecture on short wave transmission (very interesting)—11.30, see à Becket Williams about programmes he wants to give—kindly dissuade him —letters to answer—1.0, lunch in Bedford College—sort of cafeteria— fish salad & trifle—(quite good)—2.30, investigate light music rehearsal—4.30 see Benjamin Dale in R.A.M., and have tea— 5–5.30 with Miss Elliott—back to Hampstead—bath & dinner— Bridges rings up—Farqs go out—write to you—to-morrow I have Gerald Finzi for lunch & hope to get him into the BBC somehow. I enjoy the work because I am all out to get something done, but it is not so easy as in America—reactions are slower, & more timid—& without meaning it every one is a little frightened of being spontaneously friendly. *You* know exactly what I mean. I left out 5.30– 6.30—exercises with Hornibrook expert!! I went to Nancy's doctor (Eccles is not in London) & he overhauled me & pronounced me *absolutely A.1*—suggested, as I had a sedentary occupation, I should put in some scientific exercise—so twice a week I go close to Regent's Park & get put through the kind of exercises my darling did in the bathroom, occasionally falling over and giving her laugh, which I would give everything to hear again right now.

I loved the snapshots. How sweet they are—I could not tell whose BEE-hind was whose bending over scrabbling in the sand! Lovely to see B enjoying her chocolate (?) ice cream cone & K dancing on the sand. . . .

*BBC*
*London*
*Sunday July 27th 1941,*
. . . This has been a full and interesting week for me, as I have been doing a lot of varied work of all kinds. I have three times broadcast to North America & Canada, making records which are later at night or early in the morning broadcast, two were introducing programmes by Myra Hess and a jazz pianist (!), and the third was a half an hour broadcast answering questions cabled in by Americans & Canadians. There were four of us round the table, two members of Parliament both Labour, a professor of agriculture, & myself. I answered a question from Montreal about the condition of music in Cathedrals in England now. I have also been trying to arrange my first coup—the relay from the Albert Hall of a special American night in the Proms which I shall compère myself—(excuse word)—on Aug. 5th. Unless technical difficulties occur, I have won my way over this. I wish you could hear later one of these broadcasts in which I speak, because it would bring me closer to you. When I

can get one going to the *Pacific* I shall cable you the day & time & trust to luck there is a short wave set within reach. One meets friends sheerly by chance. I walked in yesterday to a studio in Broadcasting House & there was Scott Goddard, elegant with beard. He was delighted to see me, and over a coffee at that place close to Queen's Hall, I told him all the news of you and Les Girls. He thought I looked better than he'd ever seen me, and told me that he had heaps of work to do between BBC engagements & helping at the Ministry of Information. Most important—he sent you his love & meant it. I still stay with Maurice & Nancy, & take breakfast there. I lunch near my office, & have joined the Savile Club so that I can dine there (very well & cheaply) to avoid being too much in the way at Heathside. . . . You must think of me on my birthday being at Badingham with Peggy & Bridges & opening my 3 lovely looking 'not to be opened till August 2nd' letters. My fingers *itch*. They all came piling into my office one morning last week, and I was just going to open them when my Secretary said 'Oh, but you can't—it says you're not to'. Yours has an exciting bump in it. I do hope it will be something *very* family. These Sunday afternoons are very nice—not a soul in the house, and the garden looking lovely. I have just corrected the parts of my 4$^{tet}$ that Perry of Novello's has made and which goes to the Grillers next week. I have taken out a little of the 1st movement and improved it. Then I had a shot at a tune for a fine old Welsh hymn that Megan Lloyd George sent to me to have set, and here I am at Nancy's desk writing to my darling.

*Savile Club,*
*69, Brook Street, W.1.*
*August 31st 1941*

. . . I returned a week ago from a most varied trip. After seeing our place at Evesham and renewing ties with Leon Goossens and all the players down there (Leon's first words were 'How's Trudy?') I went on to Birmingham, saw Leslie Heward etc.—then Manchester—then to Buxton for the night to see the Wadsworths.* I walked over the downs, heather and blue bells—very lovely—then back to Manchester to rehearse my oboe 5$^{tet}$ with northern players—beautifully played—then back on the midnight sleeper from Manchester

---

* Edward and Fanny Wadsworth and their daughter Barbara had been close friends of mine for many years, and to see them again was to revive the happiness of pre-war times. They were wonderfully understanding and kind to me, and the snatched week-ends I managed to have with them in Buxton were a joyous release from the burdens of the BBC.

Edward had been doing a lot of painting, and I secured two of his large tempera canvases; one, entitled 'Bronze Ballet' (an exciting group of propellers spinning around on the deck of a ship) now hangs in the Tate Gallery.

to London in time for the office hour of 9.30. Several nice things in the future. I shall be broadcasting in a programme 'at your request' on October 2nd or 3rd or 4th on the *Pacific Transmission*, a message to the students (who can listen in) of the University of Cal. Berkeley!! I shall cable you the exact time and day at which *you* will be able to listen in on short wave, in case you can actually hear my voice. I have suggested to Adrian that I become Director of Music* and that he confines his duties to conductorship of the orchestra. I want more power as I have a lot to give which my comparatively minor post does not allow me to use fully. I had an interview with Ogilvie, the chief Pooh-Bah, but I doubt whether I rise to such sudden eminence immediately. . . . Your quotation from Spender, darling, is much much too flattering for me but I loved it. I enclose a letter from him. I sent him the Lawrence translation from the Odyssey & said 'get to it'—as Bridges can't tackle a libretto. It is nice to think this & kindred projects can still go on. News of you & B & K fills my days & keeps me optimistic & cheerful. You do not realise, not even you, how lovely it is to feel that there is such a reservoir of beauty & love to draw from, intimately connected with me. What a lucky man I am! . . .

*Savile Club,*
*69, Brook Street, W.1.*
*Oct. 27th 1941*

. . . I have had a most *enchanting* week-end with Stephen & Natasha Spender. . . . You would love them—sensitive, generous, modest.— But I had better begin at the beginning. You might—if you had been in the West End of London last Friday night—have seen your husband creeping in the dark about 8.0 p.m. towards a West End Theatre. He was about to meet Alan Bush & a Labour Chorus who were to rehearse Soviet Russian Songs. At 9.0 the rehearsal being over, Alan Bush, myself, & a Miss Kallin, a Russian who was to announce the broadcast, had a bite & drink nearby.

10 o'clock saw the three of us + the chorus settling down on mattresses in the theatre, men in the pit, women in the dress circle! 11.0 a jazz band suddenly arrived and broadcast in the theatre—I hiding my ears under the blankets. 3.30 a.m. we were all awakened. A cup of coffee and at 4.30 a.m. the chorus was singing to North America & Canada—and most inspiring it was. . . . I was *thrilled* by this small choir of shopkeepers, carpenters, typists, etc.—5.30 a.m. tube (the 1st) to Hampstead.

6.30 a.m.–10. Sleep. Breakfast & a completely blithe I went to

* Until now I had been working in the Overseas Music Department of the BBC.

the station, met the Spenders & journeyed down to Rye near where Robert & Norah Nichols lived. We were joined by two other men, one who edits a modern monthly, *Horizon*, & one who keeps a fruit orchard—& then a rational quiet refreshing week-end. Natasha Spender is a good pianist & I was awakened on Sunday morning by her practising a Mozart concerto. In this atmosphere with Stephen correcting his new poems & Natasha practising, & the well known landscape I was overcome &—frankly—burst into my first tears.* They were so understanding that I felt a friendship had been formed. If there is this kind of value in human beings let us set it against the horrors & *know* that it has infinitely *more* power. They took some snapshots of me that I will send you. Spender came dressed in his fire fighting uniform. He confessed to a dread of heights & loathed the practice of jumping from a high ladder! He also said he had once had a letter from *you. See* how everyone you encounter remembers— & so they *might*! . . .

*The British Broadcasting Corporation,*
*Broadcasting House, London, W.1.*
*Nov. 6th 1941*

. . . I welcome this night of fire-watching because I get a chance of writing to you, and I have not got off a letter to you for 10 days, which worries me. To-day was a *great* day. Every morning at regular intervals (in my office) the door opens, a boy appears, and slams down a wodge of papers to be answered. At 11 a.m. the post appears mixed with additional memoranda,—and *this* morning your long letter of Oct. 18th (No. 20) came, telling me of the opera—how *right* you are about minkery!—but preserve balance—everything is not bad that glitters—life *must* flow on and the adornments of existence have their place—otherwise *all* is drab. (You can see le chic at the Berkeley here any day in uniform, & without—& *it doesn't offend*). . . . By the way tell Barbara that Bridges Adams is writing to her about Macbeth. It is a great compliment to her, and even if it arrives *after* her performance she must treasure his remarks & write him back *about her views.* All goes well here. Next week I go on my travels again north. I conduct my Concerto in Scotland with a young Russian pupil of Solomon—Shulamith Shafir, remarkable player—then a Hallé Concert with Solomon playing the Concerto—then the Song Cycle! (I now call it *Music to 7 American Poems*) in the Wigmore Hall with William Parsons, then to Scotland again for *Things to Come*—later to Cambridge to conduct *Introduction & Allegro* & *Colour Symphony* & to Oxford to hear Watson Forbes & Irene

---

* Not from unhappiness but from the force of memories.

Kohler play Viola Sonata.—I shall almost certainly step up into Deputy Director of Music soon with Thatcher as my temporary Superior & *then*—we shall see!! . . . All goes well here. I keep well up on the crest of the wave because I *know* all will go well. . . .


*December 21st 1941*

. . . Your letters up to date are written *before* Japan's attack. You can well imagine my mind has been full of problems (1) What is the immediate effect on you three and those close to you? I am hoping that after the first alarms and emergency decrees you will all stay where you are and not have to move. It is the universal belief here that you are out of any real *danger* zone. This is where our honest letters come in and I know you will tell me. (2) Is this going to prolong the war and our separation? Opinion very divided on this— official utterances always talk of a *long* war for policy reasons. We can but hope and hope. I am glad I was not selfish and persuaded you to return—you and I would not have felt we had done right, and I *know* we have our future together. You will have something to live for (apart from me and them) now, as there will be so many ways of helping others and you are so beautifully generous in this, and that brings me to Pauline—she must be feeling very desperate, and I dread the possible news that something has happened to Walter.* We have to steel ourselves to a lot of things, but the anxiety over those whom we love with all our hearts is the only one really unbearable thing.

I had such a grand two days at Cambridge with Paddy Hadley; he put me up in Caius, while I conducted the *Colour Symphony* & *Introduction & Allegro*, with Walton taking the second half of the programme. You try & imagine Walton, Lambert, Alan Rawsthorne, Paddy & myself sitting in his room till the early hours, arguing and laughing and having a real grand set to—it did me good—Christmas will have come and gone when I next write. It will be a busy working Xmas with little time to think—and then into the New Year! May it bring *peace*! . . . Morale is high and confident. . . .


*at Badingham Old Rectory,*
*Woodbridge, Suffolk*
*Dec. 29th 1941*

. . . I have four lovely letters of yours propped up in front of me to answer—first the Christmas letter which I opened so eagerly on Christmas morning. It moved me so that *you* should thank *me*. Why?

* Trudy's brother in Hong Kong.

146

I owe everything to *you*—any inspiration to write these last 15 years has come from you—and how it has flowed sometimes! I should never have thought myself capable of it. To-day it all lies asleep again and that part of me hibernates. . . . Then a little note of Dec. 9th after the new war had broken out, with your reassuring tone, and finally a long letter of Dec. 11th. . . . I too am glad that the girls have had these years in America. They have grown magnificently in every way and they will never forget their widening experiences. That is all on the plus side—you are right too about peace and war. There has been no inner peace in the world ever since 1939 and before—much better to get it all over and done with quickly, horrible as the operation is. . . . I listened in to Churchill's speech from Congress with Bridges & Peggy—for me the ominous thing was 1943—as it is to you—but I am not going to be daunted even by *that*. Many things may happen to shorten the world's misery. . . .

*Presents.* Those were lovely & *practical* presents. I am well stocked with clothes, including a thick winter ulster which keeps me beautifully warm, but one is rationed sufficiently to make it difficult to get lovely frivolous ties—socks too wear out in spite of my keeping my friends like Nancy & Peggy darning! So you beautifully did the right thing. Sweet of you to send something for Ursula Elliott, my quiet competent secretary. Her family (naval) are scattered over the world in dangerous places, and she has a good deal, I feel sure, to worry about. . . . One must not reduce life to a colourless grey just because the world boils over with war. For that reason I buy ludicrously expensive flowers (1st violets, 2/6 a bunch) to put on my desk in the office—get a book every week end to read—*Grey Eminence —Byron in Italy*—& lastly, *Goethe & Hellenism*—books you can read slowly & enjoy sentence by sentence. I have not been to a theatre or cinema (except Noel Coward's silly play about spiritualism, . . . in July) because I don't want to, & there is no time; but I laugh like anything at the Savile. . . .

On Boxing Day I came down to Badingham and am having a glorious slack few days—I can't tell you how deeply grateful I am to Nancy & Peggy—Nancy will not have me live anywhere else in London at any price. I have tried, because I can't believe you always want a guest in your house—but she just gets in a rage & says 'No!' Maurice told me that when they wanted the children to come up for a few nights in the Christmas holidays, Nancy waited five days before she could bring herself to ask me 'did I mind moving out for a few days to the Savile', which I did most comfortably!! She & Maurice *very* pleased with your gifts & message. Peggy & Bridges too, v. *real* friends. This is the third long week end I have come down, and nothing could be more generous & understanding. I take a 5 mile

147

walk with the dog, in the morning. I have just come in now—a heavy white frost, lovely sun close to the horizon, & the ploughed fields a vivid lilac—just outside the window a perky robin—very red. The seasons in England are really most magical, and I look forward to a *whole year* sometime with you in Pen Pits—see how I have changed!—but the emphasis is as always on the words— *with you.* I shall go back to-morrow invigorated and calmed. It has begun gently to snow. Last night Bridges read two M. R. James ghost stories I did not know—so went to bed pleasantly shuddering! . . .

# Chapter XV

# 1942

I HAD BY NOW fully taken the measure of the music policy in the BBC, and in order to set down my own thoughts as to what, in certain aspects, I felt to be utterly misguided, and to formulate what I myself should like to do if ever I had the authority, I drew up a short statement of policy which I sent to the Director General and to those most responsible for the music programmes. As it has a certain historical flavour I reprint it below:

## MUSIC POLICY

*30th December 1941*

*Truism*

A sense of music is a primal thing in mankind, and a tremendous force, either for good or evil.

*Threefold Function of Broadcast Music*

1. Inexorably to continue and expand the principle of great music as an ultimate value, indeed a justification of life.

2. Faithfully to enrich leisure hours with entertainment.

3. Physically and mentally to stimulate tired bodies and worn nerves.

N.B. It betrays its trust if it debases spiritual value of music, acts as a narcotic or drug, or bores by sheer inanity.

*Coaxing Caliban*

The danger of the theory of the maximum audience for music is that it can so soon degenerate into wooing the lowest common denominator of that audience. We are apt to be a timid nation, aesthetically and intellectually, and a bit shame-faced when appealing to the finer instincts of people. Just as the pace of a convoy is determined by the slowest ship, so often is the level of a programme determined by consideration for the lowest common intelligence.

149

You cannot coax Caliban without losing the interest and respect of Ferdinand and Miranda. It is to the Brave New World that future programmes must inevitably appeal.

## Popular Rising Values

There are two ways in which you can no more popularise great music than you can popularise Christianity.

(a) The cinema organ. The delight Caliban takes in this, is in its evocative power to recall the holding-hands atmosphere of a cinema, where he can enjoy, suffer and live vicariously. Certain successions of chords free the tear glands, the music starts a physical sensation of a cloying kind, offensive to a vigorous mind. The cinema organ exploits with skill its red plush quality. The Germans prohibit what they know is a depressant and not a stimulant. It is a dope as insidious as opium, it is certainly not educative, winning the masses over to fine music.

Your policy as regards the cinema organ is not comparable with that of Sir Henry Wood in the early Promenade programmes, in which he included separate movements of classical symphonies in an otherwise light entertaining programme—because—those symphonic movements truly reproduced the composer's genius, while the cinema organ only exudes 'Ersatz'. This has no more relation to, say, Beethoven, than has a highly coloured copy of Titian, done by a pavement artist, to the real achievement. All the cinema organ does when it grasps the classics is to prettify and debase values, and can never justify means when that end is crippled and dwarfed by the very means employed.

(b) Jazzing J.S.B. What applies to the cinema organ, applies even more strongly to the jazz band. 'Mr Christ comes to town' will win no more adherents to the Sermon on the Mount. The missionary aim is defeated by the vulgarity of the Hollywood setting. When you hear a messenger boy whistling the first eight bars of Mozart's Piano Sonata in C Major, he is not necessarily a convert to Mozart, but simply a convert to swing. After hearing the *Unfinished* Symphony magnificently swung by a prize jazz band at the top of the St. Regis Hotel in New York, I cannot easily listen to the original Schubert, the former sounds so much more contemporary and exciting. I have had a dose of Benzedrine, and naturally want some more. The jazz band can be used for artificial excitement and aphrodisiac purposes, but not for spreading eternal truths.

## Transcriptions

The above criticisms do not apply to transcription of well-known classics. Liszt and Busoni have transcribed masterpieces from one medium to another, and enlarged the scope of appreciation. Present-

150

day arrangers for military bands are doing a similar service. This is not simpering at classical music, like the cinema organ, or like the jazz band, but is an honest translation, and as such, is commendable. *Note.* But there *is* a place for both cinema organ and the jazz band in our programmes to provide entertainment, and your suggestion that they should be included in the policy of Music Department is the right one.

### Condensed Opera

Due to the 'vision limitation' there is a valid case for some adjustment and compression in performance of broadcast opera, and the finely rehearsed and spirited performances I have heard will justify the experiment, but I should like it remembered:

1. That a whole opera is relayed throughout the U.S.A. from the Metropolitan Opera House in New York every week, and that the audience that listens to this is one of the largest in the States. Ergo, broadcasting limitations *may* be overcome.

2. That in many cases an alternative to mangling the form of an opera is to give one act at a time complete. Opera is an art form that cannot stand much mutilation, and sometimes the effect produced is not unlike that of the Lyon's Popular Café 2/6d. dinner, masquerading as a Ritz Carlton one.

### Crush the Girlish Male Crooner

This is obviously a case for the application of 'peine forte et dure'. Has this actually been done?

### Let the Air Breathe

In war time the BBC must be kept on the air, but in peace time its breathing moments of silence are indispensable for life. These pauses would avoid such frequent instances as:

Announcer: 'I think we just have time to play you the beautiful sonata by Scarlatti', etc. etc.

After thirty seconds the beautiful sonata of Scarlatti is faded out, one more bleeding chunk from the knacker's yard.

Announcer: 'I am sorry we have no time to finish the beautiful sonata by Scarlatti, etc. etc.

### Music and Defeatism

A certain type of music I believe to be debilitating, e.g. the recent plugging of such songs as 'Russian Rose' and 'My Sister and I'. Their appeal is mawkish and forced.

*Scrappy-Mindedness*

A glance at the *Radio Times* is like looking at a jigsaw puzzle. A paper like the *Daily Mail* will give the same impression to the eye. The Harmsworth Press years ago decided that sensationalism sold a paper. To induce love of sensationalism, a reader must be prevented from concentrating his attention on any one subject for more than a minute or so. Hence the birth of paragraph technique, and headline announcements. A word to the wise!

*A Fantasy*

The ideal method of broadcasting throughout this country would be to have three separate channels. Available for all citizens that are worth fighting for would be two contrasting services, so that at any minute of the day he or she could draw on two of the three categories mentioned in my note on functions. For the Calibans, there would be a third service, 'the dirt track', a continual stream of noise and nonsense put on by untouchables with the use of records.

\*     \*     \*     \*     \*

At this time my daughters were aged fifteen and nine respectively. I had told them that when they had finally made up their minds what career they wished to pursue, I would be one hundred per cent behind them. Barbara had chosen the stage as her first wish, and Karen was already taking ballet lessons. Two years before in the San Francisco Opera House I had introduced Karen to Massine, who was dancing there, telling him that she wished to study ballet. 'How old is she?' he asked; 'Seven,' I said. '*Too* old,' he replied. 'I started at five!' In spite of this depressing drawback of old age, Karen persisted, and in eight years' time could be seen dancing at Covent Garden in the second act of my Opera, *The Olympians*.

Barbara later went for a short time to R.A.D.A. in London, and then did her toilsome round of 'Weekly rep'. But these doings were still in the far and cloudy future, and I only mention them to explain references in the following letters to the two daughters' special activities.

To Barbara

*Savile Club,*
*69, Brook Street, W.1.*
*Jan. 7th 1942*

You do not know how much pleasure that lovely long eight-sided letter gave me, telling me so much about yourself, what you were reading, all about your friends—what a nicely critical mind you have and what sharp eyes!—your friends must fear you as much as they admire you—and then the exciting adventure on the way to the *Doctor's Dilemma*. Very few get the thrill of being in danger alongside somebody they admire very much, and finding the danger evaporate altogether, leaving the mind dancing with glee—& you have had the experience. I miss you very much and hate to think of these months passing without being able proudly to watch your growth—but your letters make up for a lot. You know, you ought to grow into a remarkable person, inheriting a touch of genius from me, & from your mother something better than genius—i.e. extreme sensitiveness to beauty & to other people's feelings, which in itself produces beauty. If you had seen Mummy when, for instance, she first saw the great windows in Notre Dame in Paris, or could see her when she hears something beautiful, or learning about a fine deed, you would realise how beautiful *she* can be—so I expect great things of *you*.

To Barbara

*BBC*
*London.*
*Feb. 8th 1942*
. . . I am so glad you have been devouring so many different books. You have an A1 imagination and it is a good thing to feed it. I enjoyed the *Forsyte Saga* immensely—his best book—but in spite of the interest, it seems a kind of life absolutely gone—a life rather like my childhood, where everything seemed settled & there was heaps of leisure to go round. I remember being very depressed by Tess. It all seemed so unfair, and I disliked the idea that something called fate could go dealing out blows at random whatever we do. I believe we make our own fate very largely. Yes, Dickens isn't for everyone. I read aloud *Bleak House* to Mummy during the winter evenings one year in Hampstead, & it is probably his best, but I should not think he fits into your scheme very much. I am glad you read *Emma*. Jane Austen must have had an eye like a hawk. While she was sitting sewing in the drawing room, the others little knew that she was observing them like specimens with the keen eye of the dissector, summing them up & remembering every little detail until she got up to her own room & could put it all down.—Rather like you, I believe, my pet—a friendly hawk's eye! Do let me have a copy of your essay 'On Music'. I should love to see it. You are a good daughter to write to me so often, and I always get a thrill when I see that handwriting on my desk.
Did you see the Katharine Cornell rehearsal—I hope so as she is a

good actress & Bernstein always has something personal to say in his plays. I had a long talk with Leslie Banks yesterday. One of his daughters (older than you), with a mop of yellowish hair, was at Ottaway's school. He says the whole secret of acting is in *'timing'*— *when* & *where* to make a gesture, *what* word in a sentence to lay emphasis on, use of pauses etc.—My love to my elder daughter.

To Barbara

*Broadcasting House,*
*London, W.1.*
*March 21st 1942*

I am glad about the Mozart. In one letter soon I will tell you what to look for in the G minor Symphony that is so wonderful. What fun it will be going about to things with you!, with your quick incisive and slightly caustic mind.

To Trudy

*Savile Club,*
*69, Brook Street, W.1.*
*March 29th 1942*

. . . March 8th is the last date of 3 grand family letters, grand because *you* have done the right thing and got a hat, shoes, coat, dress —this is important—do not let us all go corpse-grey. It is so easy to be got down, and I am going off to-morrow to buy a brand new hat & other things besides. Good! Grand also because B is looking forward to her trip south, & K has found a kindred ballerina in Kay to work with. The three letters made me very happy. . . .

You have now my cable about the Directorship of Music. I have taken the whole thing over and am touched by the response to leadership. My salary is double what I got before, so you need have no qualms about the financial side. In the contract are the words:— 'The terms of notice are 3 months on *either* side, and the BBC will not stand on unnecessary formality in the event of any change of plan, such as your resignation'. That is the result of my making it *quite* clear that I feel my first & foremost duty is to you & my 2 other darlings. . . .

*Savile Club,*
*69, Brook Street, W.1.*
*Sunday, April 12th 1942*

. . . Well! I have been in the saddle now for just over ten days, a nice birthday present.* I am establishing a H.Q. in London with Kenneth

* Trudy's birthday is April 2nd.

Wright & his department & Julian Herbage & W. W. Thompson, representing the Home Service programme planners. Tuesdays, Wednesdays and Thursdays, I shall spend near London with the main music department at Bedford. On my first official visit there as D.M. I got all the staff together, about 50 of them, and gave them a pep talk—that's what I am at present, a combination of vitamin producer to a tired but good bunch, father confessor to individual round pegs in square holes, and manipulator of committees (you don't know how subtle, and tactful—yes, *tactful*, my darling, I am becoming . . .) It comes quite easily and you would be pleased with me, which is my great and constant stimulus. I think of you all the available time but mostly over the week-ends when I am by myself. Saturday afternoon, for instance, I strolled off through St. James' Park after a siesta in my room here (for the time being Heathside is full with the family)—sat down in a nice deck chair in the sun and started reading Proust—a grand sedative—watched the first migrants —my friend the Pochard looking superb—forsythia all out and almond too. How I welcome these details after this long cold grim winter!—then off to the National Gallery to see an exhibition of recently acquired Tate Gallery pictures—3 magnificent Sickerts, a Gertler I often saw in his studio—a violin case with flowers in it— Matthew Smith, Paul Nash, and more Blake drawings which I dislike. To-day (beautiful-April-sky-after-rain) bus to Queen's Road —walk along the Broad Walk (I remember *so clearly* our first together)—Dutch Garden and a whisk round the Round Pond—still the yahct (damn!—yacht) enthusiasts—back across Hyde Park, very peaceful and natural, back to the club for lunch.—

Sat next Clarence Elliott—famous botanist authority on Alpines. . . . So to the writing table, & my darling. It is nearly a year now— it will never come again—how glad I am! perhaps this next year will bring peace & you & happiness. . . .


To Barbara

*Savile Club,*
*69, Brook Street, W.1.*
*Sunday, April 19th 1942*

Thanks for your sweet letter of congratulation on my becoming Director of Music, known officially as D.M. on memoranda. Your idea of a vast office, with me stalking up and down between rows of awestruck and adoring secretaries playing on their typewriters, must *immediately* be put into effect. At the moment I have only one secretary, neither awe-stricken or languishing for me, who performs on a machine so old and loud—like a tractor—that I have to beg her to stop whenever my telephone bell wrings (sorry rings) so that I can hear myself speak. Sorry about the bruised eye, but it will add eccentricity to your beauty, like someone, beautiful, who has eyes of different colours, or whose nose just slants a bit.


To Karen

*Savile Club,*
*69, Brook Street, W.1.*
*April 21st 1942*

I've just received two lovely letters from you—one tells me all your weekly routine, everything you do from the time you are dragged out of bed on Monday morning to the moment on Sunday night when you are listening to the Quiz Kids in bed with Nimbus—Lovely! Then the other one is a lesson in ballet with all the important positions clearly marked. Arnold Haskell, whom Mummy knows, . . . came to see me the other day. He is a real balletomane and knows all about the technical side. I showed him photos of you dancing and he said 'she has very good points indeed'. I felt very proud. I told Mummy in my last letter how I had been down to see Pen Pits, and how lovely it all looked there. The cuckoos were hard at practising, the pheasants honking, an adder was seen and quickly despatched, bluebells were just coming out, and I felt somehow that before very long we shall all be happily playing about there. You are a good daughter to sit down and write so regularly to me, and I love getting your letters. . . .


To Trudy

*Angel Hotel, Cardiff,*
*May 9th 1942*

. . . I have spent such a nice three nights in Bristol. I am visiting the scattered forces in my domain, and I thought I would take in the week's very sporting musical festival at the same time. Bristol looked lovely in the warm May weather, cloudless blue sky. I sat out in College Green in the morning just having a slack, with the grey Cathedral on my right and young green leaves all around—enchanting! I began to re-read *The American* by H.J. In Francis Edwards book shop just opposite my London office in Marylebone High St., I found a set of old Tauchnitz editions 1889 nicely bound in calf belonging to 'Margerita Louise', whoever she may have been. Among them were clean copies of *The American* in 2 volumes by Henry James Junior! In spite of my determination not to collect I bought them for 4/– each; & enjoyed them in the sun of Bristol. In the evening I con-

ducted excellently (!) the two *Morning Heroes* excerpts—introduced by
Henry Wood in a charming 'Cockney' speech. . . . Then instead of a
drink & long post mortem with you, supper with Henry. Next day I
interviewed all our staff & discussed problems—& saw the XVIIIth
century Theatre Royal—a perfect gem. I wish Barbara could have seen
it. Ellen Terry made her first appearance in it. The original benches are
still there—the gallery for melodrama still costs 4d. (on certain nights
2d.)—& women bring their babies & suckle them—so I am told—all
quite Hogarthian. I visited one of the churches & saw the organist who
showed me outside, a little stone tablet to 'The Church Cat' 1917–29.
Tell Karen that a kitten used to come in every day & sit in the organ loft,
& when it died they had a short organ recital, and buried it close by!


To Trudy

*Savile Club,*
*69, Brook Street, W.1.*
*May 26th 1942*

. . . 4 *superb* letters in a bunch, just when I was grousing that the air
mail let me down.

(1) April 25th—Of *course* you stay at No. 76—financial plans will
be arranged somehow and you are *not* to worry about L.S.D.—I shall
see to that and be proud to do it from this distance. So sleep in your
comfortable big bed. Oh golly!—and weed the garden. Thanks for
the bergamot, which smells even at this distance. I love your 15
minute Radio programme, & have looked critically at the outline of
the 13 radio programmes. Isn't it funny? You are doing in Berkeley
*exactly* what technically we do here—the play or interlude, the
sound effects, the music, the script. How I wish I could help you with
my professional knowledge (!) OR YOU HELP ME. Good for you! I
think of you going through at 10.20 exactly the same qualms that *we*
do over programmes. I am DELIGHTED with the news of B & K.
B waitressing at the Maison Française (just like *all* the girls here) &
K the girl scout. I do not mind these months of absence knowing that
they are developing so grandly with you to help. My God! how
different it might be in different quarters of the globe! *May 2nd.*
A photo of me is on the way, taken for 'a tribute to Russia' book.
I do hope I have not changed too much. I feel *just* the same—thinner
but in perfect condition! . . .

I have just visited my dept. at Manchester, conducted the Hallé
in *Things to Come* & spent Whitsuntide in Buxton with the Wadsworths. I went crazy & bought a new picture of his—a lovely
seascape with fascinating objects—pipes, yachting fixtures, anaes-
thetic tubes (!), darts intermixed. I adore it. In a few days we shall

have been married 17 years—lovely years! The Grillers play our 4$^{te}$ that evening. No gloom. Keep a good heart—this is only an interim. . . .

To Karen

*Savile Club,*
*69, Brook Street, W.1.*
*May 30th*

I have such a lovely bundle of letters from you, some typed and some written in your own queer fist. First about Nimbus and the two cloudlets, how exciting! I can just see those funny little grey balls waiting for *me* to come, with my handkerchief and stir them into fury. What lashings of tails under sofas and quick leaps and dashes! Then I want to hear more about Elizabeth Millar and how she is getting on in ballet. I expect you are a good teacher and *very* strict. You have been working very well and hard and I hope you are having a really good laughing holiday. Congratulations on becoming a girl scout. Troup 17 is it? I looked hard at the excellent drawing (in ink) you made for me in your uniform, and thought what a grand and enthusiastic scout you would make. I want to know *all* about the camp, and cannot wait till I get a letter telling me of all the adventures. You are a *good* daughter, as I've said before, for writing to me so often. When I feel I want to feel extra happy, I just take up the large bundles of your letters and read them through. I loved the snapshots of you too—just the same K, a little taller, a little older, but the same unique zooming ballerina. I would call the two kittens Cirrhus and Cumulus* (ask Mummy what these 2 clouds are). Twitch the three tails from me!

I hope all colds are over, my pet, when you get this, & that you are in your usual good form. . . .

To Trudy

*Savile Club,*
*69, Brook Street, W.1.*
*June 14th 1942*

. . . I have now a 'personal assistant' as well as my Miss Elliott!— Peter Montgomery, the perfect screen between me and crashing

---

* Subsequent references, in letters of mine and once in a telegram, to Nimbus, Cirrhus, Cumulus, and to a fourth kitten, Pluvex, brought an agent from the American Federal Bureau of Investigation to Albert Elkus in Berkeley to enquire about Trudy. Did these cloud names in our correspondence form a possible code? Did they conceal information about the movement of troops or imminent military operations? Whether he was immediately satisfied or not I do not know, but I thought it safer to drop any further meteorological terms.

prima-donnas, insistent composers and bores of all description. He used to be in the BBC in Belfast doing an assistant conductor's job—you may have met him the time you came over with me (we went to a zoo—am I right?) I am sure B would fall for him—tall, elegant, perfect manners, nice blue Irish eyes, & slightly mysterious— he has telephone calls with a Persian Princess!—so I can relax a little and, instead of signing a memorandum every 8 minutes, stir the huge department imaginatively. *Your* broadcasts have all the professional ring to me. We could use you at once—and I am so *proud* of a wife that refuses to let events sweep her away into loneliness and boredom, but on the contrary says 'I have 2 beautiful daughters, who are the future, & I am not so dusty myself—so here goes'. . . . On Wednesday I am going to see the private showing of a new film from Russia at which my *Fanfare for Heroes* is used. . . .

*Savile Club,*
*69, Brook Street, W.1.*
*June 21st 1942*

. . . I took part in such an impressive demonstration yesterday evening. . . . I was asked to send greetings in the name of music to Russian musicians, and to limit my speech to 3 minutes, at the Empress Rooms, Earls Court. I did not know what I was in for, and was appalled to find it was a stadium as big as the Albert Hall in the centre of which was a floodlit platform on which the speakers sat. They all seemed very distinguished though I knew no one except Laurence Olivier, who spoke for the stage. Tell B I sat next him and I spoke of our both seeing Vivien Leigh in *Romeo & Juliet* in San Francisco. I spoke into a microphone, & felt quite free from nerves, but it is an ordeal I do not want to face again. The proceedings started at 6—and ended at 10. I went to Le Perroquet still in Leicester Square for old times' sake and had supper with myself. Hours by myself are precious—as during the week personalities press on me from all sides—but it is only for the war—and then back to my darlings and quiet and thinking and creating and happiness. I came across 4 lines from Spenser that hit my mood often—

> *Ah when will this long weary day have end,*
> *And lend me leave to come unto my love?*
> *How slowly do the hours their numbers spend?*
> *How slowly does sad Time his feathers move?*

But it's only in those hours that I feel absolutely tired, that I am not on top of myself, and in command of just proportions—then, as with you, a good sound sleep does the trick and I am my optimistic self

159

again. I had a lovely slack day to-day, Sunday. I was going to tea with H on his birthday but he is away. Breakfast at 10 a.m.,—a stroll to Kenwood,—read the first volume of Proust, sitting in front of the house in the sun—lots of young children frolicking around, mostly foreign,—spoke to Emmie Bass who sent you her love—delicious cold lunch—ate your lovely dates—snoozed on a sofa—played a little—walked down the hill at 5.30 took 24 bus—changed at Tottenham Court Road—bus to Bond St.—Savile Club where I am writing to my precious one before going up to dinner. . . .

To Barbara

*Savile Club,*
*69, Brook Street, W.1.*
*July 5th 1942*

In front of me are 3 delicious letters from you, full of charm—and indeed as Miss C. said of your French prose poem—'*beaucoup* de charme et de poésie'. How goes *Le Mariage Forcé*? Breathe deeply several times before you go on, & your voice will not shake—just as well known a trick to professionals as pausing for a few seconds after the curtain has gone up 'to let the dust settle' before you speak.

I *wish* you had been older when Mummy & I went to Paris & saw a Molière play, with a lovely stage setting, which changed in full view of the audience from a street scene to an interior. Madeleine Milhaud will teach you a lot about 'timing'. I am not going to write you a very intellectual letter *now* because it is too late ( I *will* do soon, so help me God!)—but I must at least cross swords with you for saying 'rattle up a few conservative (sic) views that I can argue radically about.' Cripes! *I* was always l'enfant terrible & I am still I hope '*papa terrible*'—and believe my views are *well* in advance of yours, & *will give them to you later*. I like Tessimond, and hope to send you some modern verse soon from the Times Book Shop to grit those teeth of yours on.

I read with great pleasure your Shelley & Baudelaire essays. Some one called Shelley 'an ineffectual angel' with the accent on ineffectual— he is particularly the poet of the young, though the image of the giant Titan nailed to the rock & defying Jupiter is vivid to-day for all, with Prometheus Europe & Jupiter Nazism.

Baudelaire is, as you said, at the hub of the problem of evil. Why is it? Is this planet some other planet's hell, or is it a wondrously & most variedly beautiful heaven?—One's own experience day by day supplies an answer.

I want, my darling, to know *all* about La Maison Française. Is it worth while?—What do you think of the boys? Remember they are

Head in clay modelled
by Alma Mahler, 1938

*Edith Tudor Hart*

The Bliss family on holiday
at Moosehead Lake, Maine, just
prior to the outbreak of War, 1939

*Miracle
in the Gorbals*, 1944
*(from left to right)*
The Lovers:
Moira Shearer and
Alexis Rassine;
The Official:
David Paltenghi;
The Stranger:
Robert Helpmann;
*(below The Stranger)*
The Suicide:
Pauline Clayden;
A Beggar:
Leslie Edwards;
A Street Urchin:
Gordon Hamilton

*Edward Mandinian*

much *'gaucher'* and younger in outlook & mind than girls at the same age.

Your reading matter is grand. It will fill your horizon when experience in life has caught up with all the subtle events & emotions you have read. Preserve your own personality at all costs. To be Barbara Bliss & no one else is IMPORTANT.


To Trudy

*Badingham Old Rectory,*
*Badingham,*
*Woodbridge, Suffolk.*
*July 12th 1942*

. . . This heading tells its own story—a lovely Friday to Tuesday week-end spent with Bridges, Peggy, Unity, a young Captain from Oxford, who has just published a book of poems with Faber & Faber, called F. T. Prince, +Hoover & Harvey. The last two have just come in with tongues hanging out, as I took them on a long walk—country looking lovely after a heavy rain—lots of flowers whose names I did not know and *shall* not know until you walk with me again. After lunch I shall curl up on the sofa, and continue *The Tragic Muse.* Tea in the garden. I shall then help Peggy feed the rabbits, & do a spice of gardening—a bath—dinner in Bridges' study, and afterwards Unity is going to read her play on Milton.—Last evening Prince read some of his poems, very difficult in the Tessimond-Empson manner,—but as he said 'I can only write poems when they explode with difficulty'. This is such a relief from the constant responsibility of the London office. I relax just as I did when I used to come out to Carpinteria in the early days of the *Beggar on Horseback* and you told me 'Relax!'—and it is very important that *you* get the same feeling *now*.—On Wednesday I go to Scotland for a few days to look after certain BBC matters there, and conduct the Military Band in a programme of *Things to Come*, dances from *Checkmate*—which will sound very odd for Military Band—& a group of *Fanfares* I did years ago for the Jubilee broadcast. I have a bowl of sweet peas on my table a few inches from my nose, which reminds me I loved the scented geranium leaf in a recent letter. It smelt just as fragrant as when you picked it. . . . I was very intrigued with your recorded script. I see you have caught the right broadcast technique, but how I should love to hear the voice too!—although, generally, one's voice sounds absolutely different—mine is just like an affected plum—too Oxford for words—and I used to think I had such a personal accent. . . .

To Barbara

*Savile Club,*
*69, Brook Street, W.1.*
*Aug. 15th 1942*

How enchanted I was to hear your voice on the record with the fine
poems by Tessimond, Hardy, and Baudelaire!—a bit fast in the two
English ones I thought, your besetting sin on the stage—we shall
always have to book front row stalls to hear you—but the French—
golly, how you have got on! I *was* proud listening to you—absolutely delicious. Mummy tells me everyone was enthusiastic over
your part in *Le Mariage Forcé.*

Sorry you went down with a cold at Mills. I laughed over Miss C's
bedside manner and the bug crawling up your screen. Your minute
description reminded me of a scene in Hardy's early novel, *A Pair
of Blue Eyes*, which I read years ago & in which the young man,
trying to get something for his girl, falls over the edge of a cliff—
and as he hangs precariously between heaven and earth he notices a
few inches from his eyes a little fossil, which he describes in detail,
as if it were the last thing in life he was ever to see.

I have just come back from Buxton in Derbyshire where I have
been taking six days leave with the Wadsworths and filling my
lungs with fine hill air. I took them up your essay on Baudelaire to
see, as I have talked so much about you to them.


To Barbara

*Savile Club,*
*69, Brook Street, W.1.*
*Aug. 29th 1942*

The last letter I got from you was the bottle of port one 'the stuff
drunk out of tea cups'. Gosh! the barbarity of Mills College!, when
delicate glasses should have appeared, should be lifted slowly to the
nose—then, a drop of port tilted *under* the tongue, close the eyes
seraphically, throw the port elegantly *on* to the tongue, and let it
gently slide down the throat—this operation to be repeated till the
glass is empty—conversation in between time. What fun you had
there! I am so glad. . . .

# Chapter XVI

## 1943–1945

DURING THE EARLY PART OF 1943 I was buoyed up by the hope that I might be sent on an official visit to America, and that while there I could devise some means of bringing back my family to England. But though this visit had the backing of the BBC and of the British Council it came to nothing: my request was disallowed. At this time of disappointment I had a strange meeting with Lady Cunard who from some source or other must have learnt of my efforts to get across the Atlantic.

I had never met her and was therefore surprised to receive a telephone call from her at my office in Marylebone High Street. She wanted me to come and see her as soon as possible and discuss a matter that was, she said, as urgent to me as it was to her. I could not have been more curious and went that very afternoon to her suite of rooms. After a little anxious skirmishing she made her purpose clear. Sir Thomas Beecham, it seemed, while he was in America, had become emotionally involved and it was important to persuade him to return to England. I knew nothing of Beecham's private life, and, being totally uninterested, wondered where on earth I came into this domestic affair. My role was soon made clear to me. I was to urge the Director-General of the BBC to invite Beecham to supersede me as Director of Music, and in return for the success of this scheme she, Lady Cunard, would use all her influence to see that I could rejoin my family in California.

My first impulse was to laugh outright at the thought of Beecham sitting behind my desk, administering a large department, punctiliously answering memos, attending conferences, interviewing would-be broadcasters etc. etc., but this soon turned to anger at the unwarranted presumption behind this absurd deal, and after advising her to write direct to the Director-General herself, putting forward clearly all the reasons and facts, we parted very coldly.

My wife had for some time been convinced that she and our two daughters should be in England sharing my life and after what seemed an endless battle against regulations and travel difficulties, she managed to secure a passage for herself and the two daughters on a Portuguese boat sailing from Philadelphia to Lisbon. So, late September, with many other English children and parents aboard, the *Serpa Pinto* set out, with all lights blazing, across the Atlantic. I heard nothing for some time, and then came letters from Estoril: they were back in Europe. Another long wait ensued, for there were too many high-ranking priorities for the planes available. Then some indication reached me that the flight was near: my loyal secretary remained at the telephone, having alerted the exchange at Broadcasting House, and on November 5th 1943 my wife rang up from Poole, where she had just landed, and I heard her voice for the first time in two and a half years. That evening I dived into the black obscurity of Waterloo Station—and found them.

I had managed to get a flat in Cavendish Square, and this was to be our home for the next three years or so, buzz bombs or no. I continued my work at the BBC for six months longer, but then took advantage of the terms in my contract and resigned. I was glad to shake off such a restricting administrative position, but it was with real regret that I said 'good bye' to my colleagues. We had been through many crises together and firm friendships had been formed.


Although I myself had cut loose from the BBC, the family still maintained a thread with it, for my wife contributed occasionally to the early morning programmes called 'The Kitchen Front' in which she offered various American recipes, with sometimes such strange sounding names as 'Hush Puppies', and 'Fried Cats'. Very soon she was invited to give weekly broadcasts on the North American Service to New Orleans, Cincinnati, Sioux Falls and stations in California. She spoke on any aspects of British life and events that she thought might interest American audiences: she kept these programmes going for ten years.

In 1946 she revisited America and had the satisfaction of seeing her opposite numbers on the other side who were responsible for handling these broadcasts, and receiving their suggestions. She had a natural gift for broadcasting and certainly enjoyed exploring the special possibilities that radio programmes offer. I remember two favourites that she wrote for the Home Service—'Trains of Thought' and 'Flights of Fancy', each of which was a delicious montage of sounds and words. She was later to collaborate with me in a drama entitled *Memorial Concert* in which specially written music had an integral part.

I should add here something about what my two daughters were doing at this time. Barbara always wanted to be an actress, and had the mercurial personality for this; so, shortly after returning to England in 1943, she entered the Royal Academy of Dramatic Art. However, after six months there, she volunteered for the W.R.N.S. and was drafted to H.M.S. Collingwood Barracks at Portsmouth. Knowing her temperament I found it hard to realise her as an exemplary and disciplined member of the service! I believe that as Christmas 1944 came round, and her task was to send out some general orders, she added the words 'Happy Christmas, Barbara' to each one—a delightfully festive note but an unusual one on an official form. Luckily she had a chance to act as well. It was here she met her future husband, Richard Gatehouse, who had come to England from Victoria, British Columbia, in 1939, and who joined the Royal Navy when war broke out. He had been appointed Entertainment Officer at Portsmouth and on hearing that a WREN, Barbara Bliss, had been to R.A.D.A. he sought her out and enlisted her in a theatrical company formed from Southern Command to give performances to the navy personnel. Their first venture was a production of *Night Must Fall*, followed by one of *Hay Fever*, with Barbara and Richard in the leading roles.

It is a strange family coincidence that these two should first have encountered each other in the theatre, in the same chance way as Trudy and I had met, in Santa Barbara, nineteen years before. They were married in London in January 1948.

At the same time Karen, with her usual determination, was pursuing her ambition to be a ballet dancer. In 1943 she was eleven, and before returning to England in that year had been working in Lew Christensen's classes in San Francisco, and later in the ballet school founded by Ruth St. Denis and Ted Shawn at Jacob's Pillow in the Berkshires. While we were living in the flat in Cavendish Square for the remainder of the war, Karen went three mornings a week to the ballet class at Sadler's Wells—a concession from Queen's College in Harley Street, where she was a day pupil. After the war Barbara was to undergo the rigours of 'Weekly Rep'; and Karen was to enter the disciplined training of the Sadler's Wells Theatre Ballet.

I had composed nothing since my return, and now free of public responsibility I could turn to my own work again. Robert Helpmann was anxious for a new ballet, and he brought me a theme that appealed to me very much. It was a contemporary story about the slum area of Glasgow called the Gorbals. In the melodramatic action a young girl commits suicide by drowning and is miraculously

165

raised to life again by a Christ-like figure who mysteriously appears in the sordid street. His very powers arouse jealousy and fear, and he is ultimately done to death by a gang of young hooligans. The scenario by Michael Benthall gave the Sadler's Wells Ballet a great chance to show their powers of characterisation and realistic acting. Pauline Clayden as the pathetic suicide, Celia Franca as a prostitute, Leslie Edwards as a beggar, Robert Helpmann himself as the saint-like stranger, and David Paltenghi as the official who opposes him, all gave life-like and moving performances, and the colours with which Edward Burra portrayed the scene and decked the dancers gave the ballet a sombre beauty. *Miracle in the Gorbals* remained for long in the repertory, and whenever I saw it I was moved at the tense portrayal of tragedy given by these young artists. The score bears the inscription 'To Trudy, Barbara and Karen—thanksgiving for November 5th 1943'.

The first performance was given in the Prince's Theatre, London on October 26th 1944 and was conducted by Constant Lambert.


Quite a different subject had been occupying my mind while I was writing this score, and that was a film version of Shaw's *Caesar and Cleopatra*. Shaw had asked me to provide the music for this venture, and in two letters gave me his advice; in the first he writes as a clear-headed business man, in the second as a quondam music critic. I give these below:

*4 Whitehall Court,*
*London S.W.1.*
*30/4/1944*

Dear Arthur Bliss

Are you a copyright expert and a good man of business? If you are, read no further and tear this up. If not, be careful not to let yourself be placed in the position of an employee of Pascal or of the film company, as anything you compose for them in that capacity will belong to them and not to you.

If I were a composer writing for a film I should make a skeleton piano score of an orchestral suite consisting of overture, nocturne, barcarolle, intermezzo, and finale. I should copyright this in my own name in England and America. Then, being in an impregnable position as sole owner of the music, I should license the film people to use the material as an accompaniment to their film for a stated period on stated terms, giving them no *rights* whatever.

I gathered from Pascal that he was dealing with your publishers. That is usually the very devil: they naturally look after rights for themselves, which you should never allow. Always hold on to your rights like grim death; and license publishers and performers.

Do you belong to the Society of Authors, Playwrights, and Composers, Brierlea House, Mortimer, Reading, Berks? You should.

Forgive this impertinent interference in your business. But I served ten years on the committee of the Society, and learned that all artists, hating business as much as I do myself, are in danger of being plundered by publishers, who, being all gamblers by the nature of their business, cannot be blamed for playing 'with the advantages'.

Remember that an orchestral suite by you will long survive Pascal's film and become a standard concert piece quite independently of my play, like Grieg's *Peer Gynt* music. Let no parasites fasten on it.

faithfully

G. BERNARD SHAW

4 *Whitehall Court,*
*London S.W.1.*
*7th May 1944*

Dear Maestro,

In Heaven's name, no Egyptian music. It must not even be sham Egyptian: it would be sham *Aida*. It must all be Blissful and British. If you feel tempted, think of what *Messiah* would have been if Handel had felt bound to compose Jewish and Syrian music for it, and what *Figaro* and *Don Giovanni* would have been if Mozart had gone Spanish, or *The Magic Flute* if he had gone Egyptian. Or even what my play would have been if I had Latinized Caesar's dialogue.

Of course, if Pascal wants a ballet for the banquet scene, you can amuse yourself by giving it a fanciful turn in the direction of the Nile as you conceive the Nile, just as Mozart and Beethoven composed 'Turkish' marches with *grosse caisse*, cymbals, triangle and piccolo; or Gounod did a lively farandole, Bizet a real Spanish song and dance, and Meyerbeer some Russian short rhythms in *L'Etoile du Nord*. These larks are jolly and harmless. But Holst's quite serious Sanscrit music! No: damn it, no.

Write your Blissfullest, and your imagination will give the music the necessary cast without knowing it. After all, there is a complete difference of atmosphere between *Figaro* and *Zauberflöte* which I am sure was automatic.

This letter is quite unnecessary; it wont alter a single demisemiquaver; but as you mentioned the matter and may possibly be led to think that I want my play *Aida*-ized, I must disclaim any such folly. Let yourself rip in your own way and it will all come right. Pascal

167

will be Schickaneder, of course; and there will be sub-Schicks all over the place, each believing that he knows better than you what is needful; but you are master of the situation.

Pascal runs after every new notion; but he always comes back to the right thing in the end.

I suggested to him an ophicleide for the Roman bucina partly because my uncle played it, but also because it has the peculiar tone that made Berlioz call it a chromatic bullock, quite different from the tuba. The tuba is only a bass saxhorn. The ophicleide is a monster keyed bugle.

Bach trumpets, which are keyed posthorns, have also a different and rather pleasant difference from the ordinary orchestral trumpet and can reach higher notes. But military bugles have their points too. And cavalry trumpets.

All of which you know better than I do.

Dont bother to answer. In fact I should have begun with Dont trouble to read.

G.B.S.

Taking Shaw's advice I started on a 'skeleton piano score', but then I ran into the director of the film. One look at him made it self-evident that he would never be a sympathetic collaborator, and I withdrew from the assignment.

A much more rewarding film venture came in the following year, 1945, with a picture called *Men of Two Worlds*. The Director, Thorold Dickinson, was a man of imagination, sensitive to music, and serious in aim. It was an interesting subject. What would happen to a young African, a concert pianist and composer who has been subjected to a European training, when he felt it his duty to return to his primitive remote tribe, and try to convert its members from the superstition and ignorant belief in black magic by which their lives were governed? Thorold not only brought back from Africa records of native drummers and singers, but a whole cast of natives whose natural acting never failed to astonish. The colour photography, mostly done in Africa, was beautiful, and it was a pity that the subject of the film debarred its showing in certain countries.

My mind during these years was engrossed with the theatre and with the possibility of writing my first opera. I was continually casting around for the right librettist and the right subject. During the war I had often talked with Stephen Spender about episodes from the *Odyssey*, but he was too busy with his own medium of poetry and with public obligations to be able to give the time, and also he did not, I think, react enthusiastically to the excitement of the theatre. A year or so later I was to find in J. B. Priestley the man for whom the theatre was a natural home, who could shape a drama as easily as an architect designs a complex building, and with whom I could work with contentment.

Towards the end of 1945 I collaborated with Robert Helpmann and Michael Benthall in yet another ballet. It was scenically the most ambitious of my three works for the stage. and was entitled *Adam Zero*. It was an allegory of the cycle of man's life: his birth, his passage through the spring, summer, autumn and winter of his existence, and his death. The world in which he lives was represented by a stage on which a ballet was being created. Adam was cast for the principal dancer's role: Omnipotence was represented by the Stage Director, and Adam's Fates by the Designer, Wardrobe Mistress and Dresser. The Woman in this allegory, under the symbol of the Choreographer, was both the creator and destroyer of Adam: his first love, his wife, his mistress, and finally the figure of beneficent Death.

There was an unexpected moment at the raising of the curtain when Adam's birth was depicted: the audience saw the whole of the huge Covent Garden stage right back to the far wall, completely empty except for the protagonists. Then as Adam grew in manhood the stage was gradually filled with scenery, only to empty again, bit by bit, as he approached old age until finally he was left alone, with the figure of Death, on the bare boards. It was a splendid role for Helpmann, and might have had a long run if an early accident had not sent him from the cast. Early in his life cycle he had literally to leap into life, hurling himself from a height into the supporting arms of his friends. After a few performances there was a miscalculation, and he was sufficiently hurt to have to retire. As I consider this my most varied and exciting ballet score, I am disappointed that it has fallen into oblivion. It was given its première at the Royal Opera House in April 1946 and, again, Constant Lambert was the conductor.

In May of that same year I conducted the Vienna Philharmonic in my *Checkmate* Suite and Piano Concerto, with Shulamith Shafir playing the solo part. After so many years' absence it was a shock to see post-war Vienna, the proud city, brought so low, and its people looking so impoverished and under-nourished. Watching the players in the orchestra I just could not bring myself to make them sustain long rehearsals, though the music was completely strange to them: it was sufficient pleasure for me just to work briefly with this famous orchestra.

# Chapter XVII

# 1945–1949

THE SEED OF MY OPERA, later to be known as *The Olympians* was sown during a talk I had with Priestley at the Cheltenham Festival of 1945. I could not have chosen a better collaborator. He is a quick thinker, prolific of ideas, and with an enviable experience of the theatre. I can never understand why his importance as a dramatist is so underestimated, and why there are even plays of his that have never been staged in London.

As in the case of Elgar, Priestley's public image and the private man, as I know him, have little in common. In working with him on our opera I found him both generous and sensitive, and though it would make more of a story to pretend that we had plenty of rows, the truth is that we got along remarkably smoothly, he deferring to my opinion as the musician, as I did to him where stage matters were concerned. As a subject for the opera he suggested a variation of the ancient legend, that after the advent of Christianity the classical gods and goddesses lived on, but in humble disguise. It was assumed that they formed a troupe of strolling players, travelling the roads of Europe, century after century, but that every hundred years, on Midsummer Night, they found themselves again in possession of divine powers. The action was to take place in a Provençal village in the days of Louis Philippe.

To compose a full-length opera is a long and fatiguing task, and it took me the best part of the next two and a half years to complete the three-act score. Most of it was composed in the quiet remote music-room that had been built for me in the woods of Pen Pits. Frequent adjustments had always to be made, by both composer and librettist. Most of these were done face to face, either in London or at Priestley's house in the Isle of Wight, but many letters too were exchanged, and I quote from some of them.

as from Billingham Manor,
Chillerton, Isle of Wight
August 1st 1945

Dear Arthur,

I enclose a very rough synopsis of the opera plot. I don't want to work out the story in any greater detail until you feel fairly satisfied about the rough outline. I am still uncertain about the exact form of the finales to Acts I & III, and it is possible that you might have a musical idea you favour that would help me to find the kind of 'curtain' you need musically. As it stands there is quite a good Act III here, on a smaller scale than Act II of course, but full of comedy and good dramatic value. Already of course I see a great deal more in these scenes than I have put down here, but I want to get the rough outline right first, particularly as I dislike typing out synopses and have no secretary here.

It is important that you should feel the chief characters musically as I do dramatically. For instance, a character like the half-barmy old beggar-woman, Margot, who doesn't give a damn for anybody and has a kind of second-sight, is useful for me dramatically, but she may be, for all I know, a mere headache musically. If so, then we can if necessary scrap her. And so on. Then Act II has to be worked out very much in terms of a musical build-up, also in terms of broad movement, almost like a ballet. The other two acts are more ordinarily dramatic in structure, like a play. Anyhow, send me your observations. I shall be down here probably until about the 20th or so. . . .

Pen Pits,
Pen Selwood,
Somerset
August 18th 1945

Dear Jack,

Here are some thoughts about the sequence of events. Act I— I feel the players must be more important in this than they appear in your first synopsis (two of our principals are among them!). Instead of their being discovered on the stage, I should much prefer a good entrance a little later on, and a scene (short) to themselves where they feel excited about the coming anniversary and, in their rags, show a slightly mysterious side to the audience, as if the coming transformation were casting a shadow before.

This Act might commence with Lavatte telling the landlady of 'The Golden Duck' (and, incidentally, the audience!) his troubles about money, Madeleine etc. What do *you* think?

I believe the final laughing chorus excellent, if well led up to,

171

and the curtain might come down on them unconsciously grouping themselves as a classical frieze, the scene mysteriously lit.

Act II—This is a grand opportunity for *me*—balletic, as you say! Why cannot Venus enter with her train, and Bacchus with his rout, rather like a Rubens picture?

Act III—I feel this is too complicated for Opera e.g. Madeleine's telling the Curé what the audience has already seen and surmised in Act II *might* be cut out—and the ending (especially in a romantic comedy) musically needs a full choral ensemble—everything! The lovers are subsidiary singers and the end might fall flat if they were left alone singing, as the curtain falls. When the Curé starts to discover 'the moral', the action must grow and grow and grow. Lavatte feels he must endow the church, the lovers sing like turtle doves, the Olympians, now full of vitality (not half-dreaming), get ready to move to the next town, coins in their pockets, wine in their flasks, and the satisfaction that in time they will have these experiences all over again. There must be a glorious burst of sound and movement to bring the curtain down.

I am back in London September 1st. If by any chance you go to Russia earlier, wire me, and I will come up to London for a couple of hours' discussion before you go. I think it is important that we meet before you get filled with new visions inspired by the Bolshoi theatre!

ARTHUR

*Billingham Manor,*
*Chillerton,*
*Isle of Wight*
*August 20th 1945*

Dear Arthur,

Many thanks for your letter of the 18th. I am keeping it and considering carefully the points you make.

We must be careful, however, with so many characters, not to disperse the interest. In my view, which I am certain is dramatically sound, the emphasis must be on the ordinary human beings first, and the actor-gods, no matter how tremendous they are in Act II, must be subsidiary. We must get this straight. Either the piece is about what happens to gods when they find themselves actors among human beings, or it must be about what happens to human beings when actor-gods come amongst them. One or the other. Any hesitation here, I swear, will be fatal to the dramatic interest. And I plump outright at once for the second—what happens to human beings when actor-gods arrive. Therefore—if you accept this view, as I'm sure you will, then the four chief characters, the real principals are

Lavatte
Florac
Madeleine
Curé

with Acts I and III concentrating on their affairs, and even Act II shown as affecting them. You can if you like add Jupiter and Venus to these principals, though as Venus ought to be really beautiful in Act II, I'm rather afraid of giving her too much to do, for casting reasons. I should like you to think this over musically before I re-draft the synopsis, which is easy enough. De Craval could if necessary be left out, and as we have so many characters, I think this should be considered. I agree with you about the finale to Act III, and will reconsider this, but while it must have a big ensemble it needs some small dramatic twist to it. Possibly that while the god-actors want to stay, everybody else is damned anxious they should go, and urges them, promises them wonderful engagements elsewhere, showers parting gifts on them, all to get them away. I fancy that when they are actors the gods must not be too conscious of their godhood —and the night's events oughtn't to be completely clear to them. This bit is rather tricky. Again, while there are hints and nudges, too much mustn't be anticipated in Act I. I'd like to keep Act III musically rather quiet but dramatically interesting until the big finale. About Madeleine's piece—she will not tell what the audience knows, because Act II is clearly only the beginning of the night's orgy and madhouse, and the audience will want to know the situation several hours later, when Act III opens. But there are ways of doing this, of course, without a long narrative from one person, which I never like. I'll go over all this before we meet. No exact dates yet for Russia, but I'll let you know as soon as I can. You might find it better, if there's time, to slip down here for a day or two instead of going to town.

JACK

*Pen Pits,*
*Pen Selwood,*
*Somerset*
*August 24th 1945*

Dear Jack,

Yes,—you are quite right!—let us put the *main* emphasis on the humans, and make them creatures of flesh and blood (not opera singers)—and let the Olympians play *dei ex machina*. I am with

173

you in cutting out de Craval. This character has appeared (arm-in-arm with a rascally old lawyer) in many operas from Mozart to our own day: also, a penniless poet who drinks with vagabond actors is sufficiently untrustworthy(?) to warrant Lavatte's opposition, without a rich rival for his daughter.

ARTHUR

During the next few months the plot of the opera was finally agreed on, and dialogue from Priestley began to arive.

*Pen Pits,*
*Pen Selwood,*
*Somerset*
*April 1946*

Dear Jack,

I am down here hard at work on the opera. I have already sketched the music from the rise of the curtain to the entrance of the players—also Diana's lyrical outburst, Jupiter's impressive advice, and, later, Hector's warning to Lavatte.

Early in autumn we will have a run through of the Act and see what is the general effect.

I have played most of it to Trudy and she . . . But perhaps she is not quite an objective critic!

ARTHUR

*Billingham Manor,*
*Chillerton,*
*Isle of Wight*
*April 24th 1946*

Dear Arthur,

Thanks for your letter. I am delighted you have made such an enthusiastic start, and are finding the words easy to work with. Where any scene or aria refuses to come to life musically in your mind, because my treatment and rhythm do not help you, then don't hesitate to say so—and we'll go over the passage together and I'll find different words.

I enclose the rest of the act. You will notice that this time I have padded out the recit. speeches to the kind of length you need. If you find them too long, then cut, of course. I am pleased with Diana's aria. You may or may not want something from Mars and Bacchus there, and I have merely sketched in some possible words for them. You may consider Jupiter's speech too long and on the dull side. I have written it in blank verse to give it a certain dignity and weight. It is rather humourless but the situation is difficult for humour. If this

174

speech worries you, I will have another crack at it. I am pleased with the little Catch in verse, and it ought to give you a chance to do something that will be sung very frequently outside the Opera. I feel of course that this quintet ought to be a definite detached number. I am pleased too with Hector's warning to Lavatte. The finale of course really must be left to you—that is to decide its length and what voices you want—and I can easily supply extra short bits for any particular character to sing. Here I have merely indicated the kind of thing that ought to be going on then. In your place I'd be inclined to write a finale, from the exit of Lavatte to the fall of the Curtain, that was complete in itself musically, and I will fit words to it. The Act as it is seems to be about the right length, from my point of view.

JACK

*as from B4 Albany, Piccadilly,*
*W.1.*
*19th July 1946*

Dear Arthur,

I have now finished Act II and my secretary is making a copy for you. . . . All this has not made for calm and easy creation, but I am quite pleased with what I have done, and the classical arias and choruses are in keeping with their subjects and have dramatic rhythm. Wherever one of them conflicts with your own musical ideas, you must of course tell me and I will shorten or lengthen the lines and change the rhythm. Naturally much of the stage action needs to be worked out in much greater detail than I have given here, but that can come later, if necessary to fit your musical treatment of the various scenes. What I have tried to give you is all the necessary verbal material—and a sketch of the main action—you will require to complete the act.

I keep thinking about the title. *Jupiter Tonans* is probably better than anything we have had yet, but it still seems to me to be too classical and gloomy and perhaps to give too much emphasis to Jupiter instead of to the troupe of god-players. . . .

*Pen Pits,*
*Pen Selwood,*
*Somerset*
*August 29th 1946*

Dear Jack,

I think, after the rapid sequence of events in Act I, and the exciting balletic scenes *later* in Act II, that the opening of this second act should

175

be in the nature of a quiet Intermezzo, a link between two ground swells. If you agree, I should like the Watchman's song to be slowish and ruminative (about the length of Jupiter's first rebuke to Diana). During this song (probably sung, sitting) applause will be heard from Lavatte's house; perhaps the flitting of a servant or two, or late guest, will be seen so as to keep this soliloquy from being too static. Lavatte will break the moonlight quiet with his outburst, but Madeleine will recapture this meditative nocturne mood with her song, and the love scene with Hector will also be a murmured one.

I think that the mood of this human scene, before the gods appear, should be affected by the light. We all talk, sing, think a bit differently under a full moon, and, except for Lavatte's jagged and irritable intrusion, I feel the first quarter of an hour or so could well be labelled 'Nocturne in F minor'!

When Diana addresses the moon, it is a very different thing. It is *hers*!

ARTHUR

*Billingham Manor,*
*Chillerton,*
*Isle of Wight*
*January 11th 1947*

Dear Arthur,

Thanks for your telegram. No letter yet. I suggested your coming here next week as I shall be starting Act III, and we would be alone. But it doesn't matter if you can't manage it. I hope the enclosed additions to Act I, and the new material for II is what you want. The Jupiter speech was far from easy, and though of course I cannot tell how suitable the new version is for setting to music, it seems to me a good massive speech about paganism etc., picturesque enough but done in terms of modern psychology. Don't hesitate to change phrases, reverse words etc. to suit yourself, but I wouldn't cut anything without referring to me or make any great changes as the speech is fairly complicated in thought, a kind of sketch of our mental history during the last two thousand years. In the Mars stuff I have toughened it up. I must leave the chorus to you, and have just put in 'War'!

JACK

*Novello*

Manuscript page from the full score of the opera *The Olympians*, 1949

Alfredo Campoli and myself in Moscow, April 1956, after the
performance of my Violin Concerto

Rehearsing with the American Wind Symphony Orchestra
(conductor, Robert Austin Boudreau) on the Thames, June 1961

*The Sport and General Press Agency*

Dear Jack,

Many thanks for the material which is *fine*—the Jupiter speech gives me plenty of excellent material. I rather like the idea of him carrying the large majority of guests gradually with him, so that I can help in magnificence with a choral background. I feel musically this is important, and will greatly help the 'build-up' before the final explosion. Perhaps you could think of some sentences in which they could, in keeping with his serious mood, show their allegiance to his power. Also at the start of Act II, I would like the impatient guests to be 'heard off' *expressing* their impatience and gradual bewilderment as well as clapping etc. Their ejaculatory musical phrases should break in on the quiet of the garden, I feel. The Second Act is going to be fun for me.

with many thanks,
A.B.

*Billingham Manor,*
*Chillerton,*
*Isle of Wight*
*15th January 1947*

Dear Arthur,

I am now working at III, but I am finding it pretty hard going, as I imagined that I would without having heard some of the earlier parts or without any direct co-operation with you. There is a certain amount of absolutely essential and rather cumbersome 'business' in this Act, but I think I can manage it all right.

I have done Jupiter's long speech which I think very good indeed but it has turned out to be serious and not humorous, and I have also done the quartet which I have found very worrying simply because this is a purely musical rather than a dramatic passage and it would be almost better if the words were written to the music rather than the music to the words.

I am now leading up to the exorcising scene and in order to make this humorous and to avoid offence I am not using any religious phrases in it but will make the Curé say a number of quite appropriate things in Latin.

The Marriage Scene I think ought to be in formal verse. I may have a rough sketch of this Act ready by the week-end, when I shall be in London.

JACK

*Billingham Manor,*
*Chillerton,*
*Isle of Wight*
*April 8th 1947*

Dear Arthur,

I have now had time to do, as best I could, without your guidance, the bits and pieces you suggested should be tidied up. If, as is possible, they are not what you had in mind, we can improve them next time we meet.

I am still worrying about the title. *The Gods Grow Old* has much to recommend it, as a title, particularly in sound and shape and neatness. But, as one or two people (notably Peters) have pointed out, it has a rather melancholy ring that in fact does not suit our piece. I have spent a good part of this morning with dictionaries of synonyms and the like, trying to improve on it: *Gods in Exile* (this was the name of Heine's piece, and is an exact description of our plot) *The Gods Go By, Passing Gods, Banished Gods*, but I am not satisfied yet with any of these alternatives. I have spent so much time— an unusual thing with me, by the way—on this title, that I seem to have gone stale on it, and perhaps we need some fresh minds on the problem. . . .

Yours ever,
J.B.P.

*Pen Pits,*
*Pen Selwood, Wincanton,*
*Somerset*
*April 9th 1947*

Dear Jack,

Many thanks—now I am all set. I have made great strides into Act II which is going well. Early in May Novello's will inform Covent Garden that our opera will be available for their summer season 1948, and that the first two Acts can be seen and heard this summer. Trudy & I both like *The Gods Go By* better than the more melancholy twilight of the *Gods Grow Old*. I like the feeling of passing across the Stage. . . . I think we ought *now* to have a designer in mind & move the pieces about. Is there anyone at Stratford (Shakespeare's). I don't know that side of it, I'm afraid.

Yours ever,
ARTHUR

A year of hard work went by, and then—

*Pen Pits,*
*Pen Selwood, Wincanton,*
*Somerset*
*May 5th 1948*

Dear Jack,

Today at 2.30 I brought down the final slow Curtain on a beautifully poised A major chord. I am very pleased with this last Act. Now we have only to be clear of how soon we want to plunge in medias res in Act I, and then find, at the end of Act II, the right re-entry for Mars. If you have the first draft (the more sober one) of Mars' War Song in Act II, can I have it? I cannot find the earlier version.

I am going up to London for a week on Monday next, and after that re-immerse myself in the orchestral scoring. I am determined to cut nothing from Acts II and III, and am with you over all the love scenes.

Perhaps shortly I could spend a couple of days at Billingham, or you come here, for a final appraisement.

ARTHUR

The opera was accepted by Covent Garden in 1947, but preparations for its production did not start till two years later. One early stroke of luck Priestley and I had was in securing Peter Brook as our producer. He was not very experienced in opera production, but we knew that his vivid imagination and keen sense of theatrical effect would be of great use in a romantic opera such as ours.

When the work was advertised for future performances I received a cable from America, signed by Benjamin Britten and Peter Pears, wishing me 'Good Luck' and intimating that I should probably need it. In truth I did. Two factors began to weigh heavily against a successful début. Early on, in rehearsal, there arose a clash of temperament between Peter Brook and the conductor, Karl Rankl, which increased to such an extent that they even avoided speaking to each other. How could an opera be brought to performance standard in such a hostile atmosphere?

Secondly, there were too-late decisions on the choice of singers: I did not get my principal tenor until ten days before the opening night—and then he had no time to ease himself into the role of a Byronic young poet. Not realising the difficulties that attend the birth of a new opera I had urged that the final dress rehearsal should be open to the critics. This was disastrous. What they saw was a well rehearsed and produced first Act, even an exciting one, a second Act that obviously needed a few more days' polish, and then a third Act which looked exactly, in its raw state, like some village charade.

179

Difficulties in this final Act were not lessened by the mysterious absence of the scene designer.

I knew we were lost, and on the first night sat gloomily in the Garrick Club, only going to the Opera House in time to thank those to whom, under difficult conditions, genuine thanks were due.

Seventeen years later Priestley, in greeting my 75th Birthday with a published article* (referring to *The Olympians*) wrote 'This production was no shambles, but from the very first rehearsal to the very last performance, it always had the makings of one. The truth is, conditions at Covent Garden in 1949 were not favourable to the production of any big new work. For example, the producer of that work and the conductor should be close and friendly collaborators. Ample time should be allowed for the study and the subsequent rehearsal of it. Whatever in reason the libretto calls for should be adequately provided. And of course stage staff must be able to cope, promptly and efficiently, with any demands made upon it.'

*The Olympians* was understandably greeted with very mixed criticisms. Among the letters I have preserved is a long one from Edward Dent, which heartened me.

> 17 Cromwell Place,
> London S.W.7.
> 3 November 1949

Dear Arthur,

I was sorry not to get more than a glimpse of you at Covent Garden the other night; I saw Priestley and had a few words with him—he was delightfully friendly and cordial. I have now seen your opera three times and I can honestly say that I have enjoyed it more each time. The actual performance seems to have improved a great deal, and I fancy it has been a little cut and speeded up, which was also an advantage.

I was sorry to see such poor audiences, but those who came were certainly enthusiastic, and I have seen the same situation for *Così fan tutte* and other operas at various times. And I have read and heard a good many criticisms, most of which I thought foolish and unintelligent. At the last performance I met severa¹ friends who were seeing it for the first time, and enjoying it more than they expected; they had either heard it on the BBC or had heard from other wireless listeners that it was poor stuff. Webster told me yesterday that the first broadcast was very inadequate and that the BBC people had not taken sufficient trouble over the technical business. . . .

I met Forster in the foyer, keenly interested; but he said he was unable to buy a libretto at the bookstall. I have had the same trouble

* I *Composer*, Summer 1966.
180

over the sale of my translations, so I advise you to make trouble about this.

Everybody has fallen foul of Priestley's libretto, even if they did not fall foul of your music; but I thought it extremely good, and after reading it very carefully more than once I have the greatest admiration for it. It is just idiotic to say that it is too colloquial and commonplace; look at Da Ponte or the authors of *Carmen*! Priestley has merely used the right words in the right situations. Some of it is deeply poetical, with far-reaching thoughts and ideas which don't always come through in the music. One might, after very careful analysis, find places where the libretto is not well laid out for the stage and for musical composition, but I cannot at this moment lay my finger on them.

I think it important to insist on this, because I should not like you to feel the least bit nervous about Priestley's share or his competence as an opera librettist, and I told him myself that I had nothing but praise for it. After translating some two dozen operas of all periods and styles I think I know a little more about librettos than the critics, though I am quite incapable of writing an original one.

I enjoyed the music thoroughly; some people found a lot of reminiscences, and I certainly was hit full in the chest by Lavatte's familiarity with *The Bartered Bride*, but don't worry about that. The famous operas of the past are full of reminiscences of older composers, but the critics don't know that, because many of the 'remembered' operas are now completely forgotten and only known to musicologists like myself. What I enjoyed in your music was its immense (and characteristic) vitality and continuity. . . .

I liked the first Act best, and also the third; the weak spot is the scene of the gods in Act II, which becomes a series of allegorical 'entries' like a 17th century masque. The gods appear and tell us who they are, but there is no drama, until the very brief moment when Hector finds Venus more attractive then Madeleine—I wish more had been made of that. Priestley's words in this scene have much food for thought as well as beauty of language, but it does not get through on the stage.

Act III has a great deal of fine music and stage effect, but is rather confusing, mainly owing to the semi-darkness of the stage. I got more from reading the libretto than from trying to 'see' the opera. I would suggest that the bogus exorcism ought to have been made much more of. The stage business is very difficult to see and understand (if you have not read the libretto). . . .

The real trouble about the opera is that like Mozart, Busoni and others, you have put everything you had into it, and there is too much stuff—it makes the opera feel very long and rather exhausting

181

though never tedious. I think it is all much too 'grand' and I should have preferred it treated more as opéra comique, even at the cost of a throw-back to Offenbach on Olympus.

I remembered your determination to use the resources of C.G. to the full, to write really big parts for big singers and give that excellent chorus every opportunity. The chorus is of course magnificent. But the result is that your choruses are all on the long side, and very much on the massive side, rather slow in movement. When I read the libretto I felt I wanted to set them in much livelier rhythms and lighter in texture. The same with your love for music; it has too many opportunities for the singers to show off their voices (but only their *voices*, not their phrasing and style) in successions of ecstatic pauses. . . .

Your orchestration is needless to say masterly, and never drowns the voices; and it is Rankl's great virtue that he never lets that happen, even in much heavier operas. . . .

Yours

EDWARD DENT

# Chapter XVIII

# 1947–1950 (continued)

In the winter of 1947 I had interrupted work on *The Olympians* to go to Budapest and conduct a performance of my Piano Concerto. I had often wished to visit this city, but on the way thither had always so enjoyed Vienna that, with pockets depleted, I had been compelled to turn back. It seemed a difficult city ever to reach. This journey in 1947 might likewise have been abortive; Budapest was held by the Russians, and to get there I had to acquire a specially stamped visa from the Russian authority in Vienna. This was obtained for me by the British Council, and with one of their representatives I motored to the frontier. It was a bleak spot in its snowy aspect, with a barred obstacle across the road guarded by Mongolian sentries in their sheepskin coats. Some way ahead on the Hungarian side waited a car to take me on to Budapest. But could I get permission to pass the frontier? No! My visa was scrutinised with curiosity (I wondered whether the guard could read) and their bayonets barred the way. There was nothing else to do (the telephone wires were down) but ignominiously to return to Vienna, concert or no concert. From Vienna communication was made with Budapest, and the British Council representative, not to be daunted, suggested that we should try again. And here occurred one of those tiny little coincidences that can have a disproportionate result!

One of my fellow members in the Savile Club during the war had been Peter Chalmers-Mitchell, a fervent admirer of Russia and its ideology. When Russia came into the war against Germany he had distributed to his friends some little pins carrying the red five-pointed star. I had stuck one in my wallet and forgotten all about it. It was still there when I arrived in Vienna. I pinned it to the lapel of my coat, and started for the frontier once more.

The same sentry greeted us, gave us a grin, and shook his head. I went up to him, smiling broadly, and displayed my pin. Whether he could read or not, he certainly understood this friendly symbol. It acted as a talisman—this is sober fact, not a film fantasy—the barrier was lifted, and I was through. I got to Budapest just in time for rehearsal, and managed to secure a splendid performance, thanks to the soloist Béla Böszormenyi-Nagy. Later, on the same visit, I was taken to the University town of Szeged, where the British Council had staged an exhibition of photographs dealing with many varied facets of life in Great Britain. My being there coincided with a concert of British music given by an amateur group who sang folk songs and madrigals. In the middle of the programme two very young players came on to the platform and to my amazement plunged into the Furiant movement from my own Viola Sonata. The audience appeared equally flabbergasted!

Everyone I met on this short first visit treated me so generously and kindly that I came away with feelings of great affection for the people of Hungary, and of admiration for the courage displayed at this terrible cross-roads in their history.

Before I left Budapest I thought I had found a possible Venus for *The Olympians*. After all, in the opera she did not have to sing, only to pose as a veritable symbol of sex. Taken to (I believe) the only cabaret in Budapest at that time, I saw a 'strip-tease artiste' with a figure similar to the voluptuous outlines of the Venus de Milo. The girl was of course vastly entertained by the possibility of a part on the London stage and, indeed, her picture and that of the statue mysteriously appeared side by side in a London paper. Back, however, in the atmosphere of the Royal Opera House the thought of bringing her over 'on spec' struck us as entailing too many responsibilities!

In the spring of 1948 George Weldon the conductor, Noel Mewton-Wood and I went to Ankara, at the invitation of the British Council, to give the opening concert in the recently built Opera House there. The representatives of the British Council, here as elsewhere, were of invaluable help; all their arrangements worked smoothly, and we found the Turkish musicians eager to rehearse the unfamiliar scores. My first impression of the orchestra was that it was a bit dispirited. I learnt from the musician in the British Council, Thomas Eastwood, a young and forward looking composer, that the players had recently been under the direction of a German conductor who used the methods of a Prussian drill sergeant. However, the genial personality of George Weldon soon encouraged confidence, and at the end of our series of concerts the orchestra gave us an uproarious party which culminated in some of the principals carrying him, Mewton-Wood and me—though certainly capable of walking—half-way back to the Embassy.

One of the side-interests of these foreign visits is the unexpected meetings with friends with whom, for varied reasons, one has lost contact. I had not been long in Ankara before I re-met Julian Huxley, then on a mission for Unesco. I had first seen him some twenty years before, when Trudy and I had attended some lectures of his in London, and later he and his wife, Juliette, had on several occasions been fellow guests with us at Priestley's house in the Isle of Wight. You cannot be long in Huxley's company without being enriched by some learning; indeed his superior intellect shows up one's own deficient education only too vividly. It was probably this sense of inferiority that led me, on the only occasion that I served on the Brains Trust, to dispute hotly with him. I was duly rapped over the knuckles for this later, by receiving an anonymous postcard: 'How *dare* you interrupt Professor Huxley, you insignificant little person!'

One sight in Ankara that particularly interested Huxley was a pile of storks' nests that had accumulated during the years on the top of a column near the centre of the city. I remember him expressing a hope that one day the figure at present dominating the Duke of York's column in London would be removed to provide a happy site for some visiting White Storks.

Another renowned person was also in Ankara. I had never actually met her, but had so enjoyed her company during, for example, long train journeys or on wakeful nights, that I felt I knew her well— Agatha Christie. She had an impressive manner, with a Queen-Mother charm, and at a reception given in our Embassy she sat as though enthroned among the other guests who like me must have owed to her many hours of relaxed pleasure. I certainly thank her for her books: they are my literary Soneryls.

Whilst I was in Turkey, Karen on the advice of Ninette de Valois went to Paris for further training in ballet, and during her three months there I kept in touch with her by letters.

Barbara by this time had married, and my wife and I had moved to a house in Kensington.

To Karen aged 16

*15 Cottesmore Gardens,*
*W.8.*
*Sat. April 24th 1948*

. . . I arrived back from Turkey last Sunday. . . . The first person I saw in Istanbul on arrival was Joy Newton, who is running a ballet school for 12 year old Turkish girls and boys there. She was most interested to hear about you & said a Paris schooling would be ideal. I saw her class at work—one little girl quite good. It was in a fine large light room in a school perched on the edge of the Sea of Marmora—so they could all bathe without going more than 50 yards. The Festival was a great experience, & the piano concerto went well.

I brought back a pair of nylons for you (I almost bought a green and a blue pair, but I was told they made the legs look a terrible colour.) . . . We are just off to Pen Pits together for 2 weeks—lovely!

To free myself from brooding over all the hopes and subsequent frustrations associated with *The Olympians* I retreated into the intimate and private world of chamber music. Four old friends of mine, the members of the Griller Quartet, were celebrating in 1950 the twentieth anniversary of their coming together. To give them a birthday present which they could acknowledge at the Edinburgh Festival that year, I wrote during that spring and summer a new string quartet for them; it grew into the most substantial chamber work that I had attempted.

On my seventy-fifth birthday the Amici String Quartet broadcast a splendid performance of this difficult work, and on rehearing it I captured once again the excitement with which, sixteen years previously, I had started work on it. When the Griller Quartet later recorded it I wrote an analysis of the music, but this would convey little without the many musical quotations. I still think that the slow movement reveals a new side of my musical personality, and where the Scherzo is concerned, I am pretty certain that I have never written more brilliantly for strings. The Griller Quartet used sometimes to play this third movement separately, at recitals in American Universities and Schools, just to show the outrageous demands which contemporary composers make on their instrumentalists!

That autumn of 1950 Trudy was on a visit to her family in Santa Barbara, and I attended an International Conference on Musical Copyright in Madrid, as one of the delegates from our own Performing Right Society. If from my mother I inherited a creative gift, from my father I acquired the need to do some practical administrative work, to organise and plan, to see theories put into practice. In the lulls between the times when music takes hold of me, and temporarily I lie becalmed, I find it necessary to occupy myself with alternative activities. I know the rhythm of my musical life very well, and can judge the intervals during which my extrovert side must exert itself. At these times it must be the American strain in me which causes me to rage at relatively unimportant details such as telephone delays, or the necessity of writing two or more letters to extract one reply, or at certain evasive answers, and the impression that the other person, through sheer lack of interest, would rather say 'No' than 'Yes'. I find myself then, to my own surprise, bursting into uncontrollable anger out of all proportion to the incident that has

186

caused it. When the introspective self is in command, I only feel such frustrations as comic intervals in life.

I remember one such time when my wife, Karen and I were visiting Peggy and Bridges Adams on Garmish, the beautiful garden island in Bantry Bay. As our day for leaving came we found there was difficulty in returning to England because of a strike. We determined to ring up a steamship company in Cork and find out if a boat might be sailing that day or the next. The telephone line from the island to the mainland was rather primitive, and it was delightful to hear a pretty Irish voice suggest that we should all say 'Hullo' together to attract attention. Attention *was* attracted, and after a little while we were connected with the Cork Steamship Company. On enquiring whether it *was* the Cork Steamship Company, another pretty voice unexpectedly said 'I'll go and see!' We waited quite a time while we imagined the young telephonist going out into the street and gazing at the sign or board in front of the building; finally, we heard her surprised voice saying 'Yes, it *is!*' Such an enchanting waste of time caused no irritation.

But to return to Madrid in 1950—here, I have to admit, there *was* an instant explosion. The hotel at which I had been booked, with the booking confirmed, strongly denied any knowledge of me—besides, I was told, the hotel was absolutely full—indeed, all Madrid was full. With rising anger, I took myself off to Madrid's best hotel, the Ritz, and enquired there—'No, not a chance of a room'. I generally carry some credentials with me on these visits, as a safeguard against such misadventures, and, luckily the Spanish Ambassador in London had been kind enough to give me a few letters of introduction. Banging the reception desk with fury I laid the Ambassador's letter in front of the man who appeared to be in charge. How ridiculous the subterfuge of officials! The hotel was *not* full, and I obtained a splendidly quiet suite for my stay.

I have never attended any meetings of the United Nations or similar World Conferences, but I somehow feel that the meetings of all these copyright protection societies, such as I have attended in Madrid, Rome, Amsterdam, Paris, London, Bergen, etc. must be a microcosm of those larger and more important organisations. They probably start off with some function, perhaps called 'Séance solennelle d'ouverture du Congrès au Palais du Sénat'; thirty or more countries have sent delegates, the official language is French; all begins in amity and glass-raising fraternity. Then, bit by bit, at the long wearisome meetings, with endless speeches, many of which are on the table before us in print, there is sensed a slow rising discord. This is almost always occasioned by a jockeying for position, an argument as to who should hold what post, the priority of one faction over another. At our conferences music is rarely mentioned, for the delegates are mostly fiercely engaged in legal arguments. From the mountain of papers set before us, what emerges? I dare not hazard a guess: my feeling is that real practical decisions are made off-stage.

In Madrid, as in other capitals, there were relaxations to arouse the mind numbed by hours of sitting in resonant halls listening to amplified speeches. There was, for instance, the pleasure of meeting Walter Starkie who, if any foreigner did, knew the real Spain and was persona grata wherever he went. As I wrote to my wife in California, 'Most of my fun here I owe to the Starkie family. Walter Starkie is head of the British Institute here, a resplendent character, Irish to the core, who knows every inch of old Madrid. I think his wife is Argentinian, and he has a daughter who most kindly went around with me, and helped me shop. Through Starkie I have heard some real Spanish singing, and seen some real Spanish dancing: most of it for the tourists is quite phoney.'

One of the letters of introduction from a friend of mine at the Savile Club also brought me an evening of gaiety. This letter was to a popular and talented dancer, and in due course I asked her out to dinner. She called for me at my hotel in a smart little car and drove me to the restaurant of her choice. Luckily she spoke excellent English. Friends kept coming to our table to greet her, and as we had started our dinner at a fashionably late hour, it was approaching midnight when a note was brought to her. On reading it she suddenly turned to me, and in a beguiling tone said 'I have to go and rescue a friend, and *you* must come with me'. I thought that at fifty-nine I was rather old to act d'Artagnan, but, of course, there could be no refusal, especially in Spain! But who and where was her friend, and why must she (he?) be rescued? She said nothing about it while she drove me through the old parts of Madrid, and finally we arrived at what looked like a large garage, with a roll-up metal door. She hammered on this, and a man opened it. It wasn't a garage but a kind of patio, with a spiral iron staircase up which I followed her. It led to a room in which three persons were finishing a meal, two women and a man, one of the former obviously being the 'friend to be rescued'. The three of them gazed at me in astonishment, never said a word to me, nor asked me to sit down. All the time a rapid altercation was taking place. Suddenly my dancer friend seized *her* friend's hand, muttered 'Quick' to me and then—we were clattering down the spiral staircase and out to the car. We ended the evening, or rather early morning, in some other haunt of my friend's, and I was delighted to be told that I was 'most sympathetic'. But *what* it was all about, and *who* the far from sinister pair were who had been left behind, I never learnt. It was at any rate a diverting change from the protocol of the Conference.

# Chapter XIX

## 1951–1955

THE MOST COLOURFUL EVENT for me in 1951 was the celebration of the Quincentenary of the founding of Glasgow University. Trudy and I motored up there to stay with Ernest and Marjorie Bullock (he was at that time Professor of Music at the University and Principal of the Royal Scottish Academy of Music). The Scots organise such ceremonial occasions impeccably, and several thousand representatives were taking part in the pageantry. A great many foreign universities had sent delegates, and their strange robes and stranger headgear transported us straight back into the Middle Ages. Official dress, even from early morning, meant a white tie, and a visual memory remains of many such ties ironed by Marjorie and Trudy for Ernest, myself and other guests in the house, continually hanging over the fireguard in their living-room. I received an Honorary LL.D. degree, and the brilliant red gown that goes with it is the one I always wear if I have to dress up, peacock fashion, for any function.

My wife already had a close connection with Scotland. In 1947, she had started compiling a selection of the letters of Jane Welsh Carlyle, interspersing them with biographical comments. This task meant visits to the National Library of Scotland, and a good deal of intensive research elsewhere. The large volume of letters, running to 350 pages, was published by Victor Gollancz in 1949, and it was a special delight to me that her scholarly selection and comments met with such favourable reviews, for the title page of the book bears the dedication 'To A.B.'

Jane Welsh Carlyle's own letters are a joy to read. Who would not want to continue after sighting that first sentence quoted in my wife's selection?

'Allons, ma chère—let us talk of the *"goosish"* man, my quondam lover.'

At the time of the Glasgow celebrations Trudy had already started a companion volume, dealing with most of the letters written by Thomas Carlyle to his wife. This was published two years later in

1953. While we were in Scotland she took me to see Craigenputtock, that remote farm north-west of Dumfries, the heritage of the Welsh family, where the Carlyles were to live for six years early in their married life. To reach it 'the road winds up from Dunscore' (these are my wife's words) 'through treeless pastures, grey stone walls flung across them like a wide meshed net. A line of firs on the horizon, a plantation of larches down the slope, and there, across the burn, lies Craigenputtock. Remote it certainly is, but very beautiful, and it had space and comfort beyond the ordinary moorland farmhouse. The best rooms face north-east, but the study in which they sat of an evening and read *Don Quixote* together, and where Carlyle wrote during the day, was snug and sunny.'

My wife's sympathy with Jane Carlyle was very sincere; as a young girl brought up in the New England traditions, she had a feeling of kinship with the young Jane nurtured on the plain living and high thinking of Scotland, and both faced in early marriage the contrasting impact of London.

While we were in Scotland we planned to see one or two of the fine private gardens within easy motoring distance. Ever since our purchase of the wood at Pen Pits and the making of a wild garden there, I had felt the fascination of growing shrubs and plants myself. There is the same pleasure to be had from seeing plants looking happy in their surroundings as there is in seeing children growing in the right environment or works of art placed with affectionate precision.

Trudy knows a good deal more of botany and gardening than I do—I confess to never getting past the amateur stage—but neither of us has sufficient knowledge to talk to the true professional. Nevertheless, we wrote off to the owner of the famous gardens at Inverewe in Wester Ross, created by Osgood MacKenzie, and received permission to visit them.

We arrived on a pouring wet day but, notwithstanding, in the drive was a figure clad in gum boots, mackintosh, and large hat, bending over a border, trowel in hand. It was of course, Mrs. Sawyer, the owner of Inverewe herself, and she immediately suggested a tour of her large woodland garden. This contained a famous collection of rhododendrons and azaleas, and gardeners come from all over the world to examine the rare species among them, brought from China, Turkestan and Northern Burma.

I should say here that we had come at the completely wrong season; not one bloom was showing—but, of course, that is a detail hardly considered by the real connoisseur. Rain poured down, dripped from every tree, shook on us from every bush. It was soon apparent to our hostess that I could hardly tell the difference between the ordinary *R. ponticum* and (say, to take a majestic name) *R. serpylli-*

*folium*. But with Scottish thoroughness she was not going to let us miss a single shrub. We had come to see Inverewe, had perhaps detained her from her some important planting, and *see it we should*. Relentlessly she went forward, and like two drowned rats we plodded after her. With the sight of the house at last again in view, I had to beg for a room to make a complete change. Having completed this, my wife and I were treated to one of the finest tea-spreads that I ever remember, while the portrait of our hostess's father, a commanding Highland Laird with patriarchal beard, benignly approved from over the mantelpiece. She was a splendid personality, and if I did not thank her warmly enough for the experience of that afternoon, I do so now.

Towards the end of 1951 I was occupied in writing an extended scena for Kathleen Ferrier. For help in the text I sought the aid of the poet Henry Reed. I had met him many years earlier on a holiday that Trudy and I spent in that part of Cornwall which forms the landscape of Hardy's novel, *A Pair of Blue Eyes*. We followed up our acquaintance by motoring with him to Birmingham, and seeing the Birmingham Repertory Company, then in its prime, perform *Timon of Athens* in modern costume. The production was completely convincing, and I was further impressed by hearing a pianist, between the Acts, play movements from the *Waldstein* Sonata as Interludes!

Henry Reed is the most elusive of my friends. He has the faculty of sudden appearance and sudden disappearance, with long periods of invisibility between, so it was a lucky throw in 1951 that caught him long enough to enable him to complete the script for my scena. He proposed the 'Second Idyll' of Theocritus, in which a proud Syracusan lady, Simaetha, has been deserted by her lover, Delphis, and resorts, in despair, to sorcery to charm him back. His free adaptation was a perfect vehicle for dramatic music. I scored the work for an orchestra without clarinets or bassoons, relying on the nasal tone of oboe and cor anglais, and the sardonic sound of muted brass.

It was a delight to go up to Hampstead and start rehearsing with Kathleen Ferrier: everyone who ever met her was struck with her joyous vitality and goodness. It was indeed her goodness that made it *impossible* for me to imagine her using black magic with evil intent, and, in the person of Simaetha, calling on Hecate for revenge, and burning in the fire the wax image of her lover. I told her so, but she only laughed—and went on singing gloriously. With Charles Groves and the BBC orchestra in Manchester she gave the first performance the following April. Between rehearsals we visited the Art Gallery;

191

Kathleen was a keen amateur painter in a style I thought far too academic, and I remember trying to get her, with much laughter between us, to choose one of the most avant-garde painters, on exhibition there, as her future model. Our encounter was brief, but to me unforgettable.

Another artist at this time gave me great pleasure to work with, the young pianist Noel Mewton-Wood. He had already played my Concerto with me on a number of occasions, and to show my appreciation, early in 1952 I wrote a piano sonata, dedicated to him. When with his characteristic fire and sensitivity he played this for the first time, I little thought that within two years he was to meet a tragic death at his own hands. I have a photo of him, given me by his mother who taught him when a child, showing the young Noel rehearsing a Mozart Concerto with the Melbourne Symphony Orchestra. He was twelve and a half at the time, and looks the very image of happy gifted boyhood. For the 'In Memoriam' concert, given in the Wigmore Hall by his friends, I set an elegiac sonnet, to which Cecil Day Lewis contributed the poem. After a lengthy piano prelude, the singer begins

'A fountain plays no more: those pure cascades
And diamond plumes now sleep within their source'.


In the autumn of 1953 Arnold Bax died, and I was appointed to succeed him in the post of Master of the Queen's Musick. The rapidity with which one musical fashion succeeds another has for the moment relegated Bax's music to some lumber-room, where it lies awaiting a new generation that will admire its uninhibited musical flow and romantic expression. During my seventy-five years I have seen many reputations rise and sink, and some which before my birth seemed buried for ever now exhumed with full honours. Musical reputations seem to move around like the slats on a water mill, first ascending to a peak of admiration, then descending to a depth of neglect, before once more climbing the ascent towards renewed appreciation. There will always be the constant ever-shining stars, and also the constellations that in rhythmic order dip below the horizon only to return; in the musical heavens there are also comets that flare up and disappear for ever. Of what magnitude is the star of Arnold Bax? Only time will tell what all his innate musical sensitivity and technical facility has left, to blaze for others.


The first years of the 1950's seem now to have taken on the indeterminate vision of a 'montage'; without diaries or letters to help me I find it difficult to sort out a clear sequence. My elder daughter Barbara had been happily married for some years, but my younger daughter Karen, dancing in the Sadler's Wells Ballet, was still living with us in our house in Kensington. We still kept on our Somerset house, Pen Pits, but it was gradually becoming too great a responsibility, and when in 1955 we moved to our present home in St. John's Wood, with great regret we gave it up. We have however revisited it several times since and were grateful to see that its present owners have preserved the beauty of the woods and improved the wild garden we tried to lay out. Only the secluded little music-room, in which I wrote so much, has taken on a wan, ghostlike and rather sad appearance.

A memorable family occasion in May of that year was the birth of our first grandchild, Barbara and Richard giving her the name of Susan. They were to have two more children in the years following, Michael and Carol. Susan was to show an innate love for music, Michael for acting, and Carol for dancing.

My half-sister, Enid, was only a small child when Trudy and I were married in 1925; she was a bridesmaid at our wedding, and clutching a posy followed Trudy through the garden of the Old Mission in Santa Barbara. Since that year she has continued to make her home in California, but both she and her mother remained devoted to London, and in the 1950's Enid began to come to England every summer, sometimes with her mother and sometimes by herself. In these yearly visits the ties between the far-off members of the Bliss family are drawn close.

Enid resembles our father in many ways; she has the same zest for life, the same ability to deal with practical affairs, the same keenness in collecting works of art, relying solely on her own taste. I have never seen her studio in Carpinteria where she displays her finds, but I know that every year she encourages what local creative talent there is by organising a competition for painting and sculpture. For her amusement I wrote a short fanfare for piano and trumpet with which she and a friend can 'open' these yearly exhibitions.

Between 1953 and 1955 I was engaged on three quite different commissions—a musical edition of *The Beggar's Opera* for the film, produced jointly by Laurence Olivier (who both acted and sang the part of Macheath) and Herbert Wilcox, with Peter Brook as director. Then there was an invitation from the BBC to write a violin concerto for Alfredo Campoli, and finally a commission from the Feeney Trust to compose a major work for the City of Birmingham Symphony Orchestra. I took my time over the Concerto, and found working with Campoli a most rewarding experience. His talents are manifold. In addition to his prowess as a violinist, he is a skilled tennis player, billiards player, bridge player, and driver, both daring and safe. He is also expert with his movie camera. When later he played my concerto with me in Russia, he took many pictures on tour, including the very colourful May Day procession in Kiev. On his return home he arranged a musical accompaniment for the film, and gave a showing of it at his house in north London.

I learnt a lot about violin technique from him. As each section of the concerto was sketched I would take it to his house, and we would play it through together. If a passage seemed to him ineffective, he would exaggerate its difficulty, distorting his face in anguish. He would suggest an alteration, and then play it through again, murmuring 'beautiful, beautiful'! I was always amused by this play-acting, but the result of his persuasive cajoling was that, whether the concerto be liked or not, it certainly is apt for the instrument.

I have played it with him on many occasions, and there is only one place where we have different views. The argument concerns the joining of the cadenza (in the last movement) to the final coda. After rising to his high notes at the end of this long cadenza Campoli wishes to plunge straight into the *animato* which carries the finale to its quick brilliant close. I quite see the soloist's point of view; he feels he has now said his say, and so wants promptly to say 'goodbye'. But before he can do so I have delayed this with a twenty-four bar passage of mysterious half light, which, as a composer, I find a beautiful bridge passage. Which of us is right? By now, I myself am not sure. So, in future performances, I shall adopt an aleatory attitude, and allow the soloist to decide for himself.


When the commission came to write a work for the City of Birmingham Symphony Orchestra, as always, before starting to write, I had to await the moment when some lucky find or incident would fire my imagination. This came almost immediately in the form of a present from Anthony Lewis, Professor of Music at the University of Birmingham—a copy of the *Coronation Anthems with Strings* by John Blow, recently published in the collection of *Musica Britannica*. As John Blow held the office of Composer in Ordinary to James the Second, perhaps Anthony Lewis thought it would be a good thing for me to see what a predecessor in that official position had achieved! Playing over these Anthems I was greatly struck by the beautiful tune in the Sinfonia for strings which precedes the verse anthem 'The Lord is my Shepherd'. At once I felt compelled to write a set of variations on it. When I read through Psalm xxiii I saw that each variation could illustrate one of the verses, and that as the Psalmist does not reach the joy of 'The House of the Lord' until the end of his song, I could keep, as in the *Istar* Variations of Vincent D'Indy, the full version of Blow's tune until the finale.

This half-hour symphonic work *Meditations on a Theme by John Blow* starts with an Introduction in which the pastoral scene hides the presence of evil and danger. The succeeding variations, founded mostly on segments of Blow's melody, convey the imagery of the Psalmist's words. 'He leadeth me beside the still waters'—'Thy rod and thy staff they comfort me.'—'He restoreth my soul'—'In green pastures' —'Through the valley of the shadow of death'—'In the house of the Lord'. Each of these longish pieces represents a meditation on the mood of the corresponding verse: hence my title, and between Meditations II and III, I have inserted a lightly scored scherzo entitled simply 'Lambs'. This work was given a fine first performance in December 1955 by the City of Birmingham Orchestra under its then conductor, Rudolf Schwarz, and the same orchestra has just, at the time of writing, made an authoritative recording with its present conductor, Hugo Rignold. If I were to be asked for a few works that might represent my life's music, this would certainly be one of them.

# Chapter XX

## 1956–1957

EARLY IN 1956 I WAS ASKED by the British Council to take a party of British musicians to the U.S.S.R. and give concerts in Moscow, Leningrad, Kiev and Kharkov. Our best musicians are kept extremely busy, often with long-promised engagements, and it was no easy task to gather together a group who happened to be free at the same time. I was lucky to get, for nearly three weeks in April, the services of Alfredo Campoli, Leon Goossens, Gerald Moore, Clarence Raybould, Phyllis Sellick, Cyril Smith and Jennifer Vyvyan; these seven, my wife and myself, left London on April 14th by air for Moscow via Copenhagen and Helsinki. Flying over Finland with its network of lakes, its fir forests, its mists and snows, was like experiencing a Sibelius tone poem. We arrived at Moscow airport just before midnight, to be welcomed in the traditional Russian manner. Strong lights were thrown on us, moving cameras levelled, and a gathering of musicians headed by the composers Kabalevsky and Khatchaturyan, together with representatives from the Ministry of Culture and the Philharmonic Society, advanced with bouquets. Kabalevsky, President of the Union of Soviet Composers, welcomed us over the microphone, incidentally telling us that every seat for our sixteen concerts had been taken, and I replied briefly for our party, throwing somewhat rashly on the air my few Russian phrases of thanks. We were the first British musicians to visit Russia since the war.

My first impression of Moscow was of size: I felt Lilliputian in the great squares and streets, and indeed in our hotel suite, which consisted of a large bedroom, dining-room, reception room and bathroom. In the suite were a piano, enormous pieces of furniture, television, radio, and several life-sized statues of draped nymphs. We arrived in it about 2 a.m., and my wife, a devotee of fresh air, immediately noticed that the double windows were still 'puttied up' against the severe winter cold. Climbing up on a pedestal and using a poker, she hacked away until a window could be opened and the icy blast let in. When I peered through the window, I could see propped up against a wall opposite life-sized pictures of Stalin, Krushchev,

Bulganin and other members of the Praesidium, waiting to be hoisted and carried in procession on May 1st next. The need for a new yardstick for judging size never left me throughout the tour. When the time came to fly back home and I gazed from the plane on mile after mile of this seemingly endless country of Russia, I felt that would-be conquerors must be mad indeed to imagine that their armies could encompass and hold it.

After size the next strangeness related to time. It was imagined either as capable of great prolongation or of sudden excision. We had either to accept a static interval (forty minutes, for example, to get an egg boiled) or be ready for instant action. Once it was realised that time is a purely relative concept, that the need for punctuality, for instance, was not pressing, the relaxed responsibility brought with it an ease and charm, at least it did to me, though not quite so much to an important American businessman with whom I made friends, and who went about muttering in despair 'Why *can't* they just sign right *now* on the dotted line?'

I could have given him an answer some days later when we attended a meeting of 'The Club of Art Workers', an association of writers, painters, musicians, actors and technicians connected with films and television. The evening was devoted to a discussion of the influence of English literature and art on the Russian mind, and actors declaimed Russian translations of poems by Byron, Burns and Dylan Thomas. At the end we were invited to put questions to the audience, and I asked 'What do you feel that Russia has contributed to the world that no other nation has?' A tall bearded young student immediately got up and said one word—'Patience'.

Russia to the visitor must always seem to be in a state of change, however slight the new angle may seem; but a constant puzzle to me was the juxtaposition of the traditional old and the revolutionary new conspicuously side by side. On our very first day we saw the Novo-Dievitchy Monastery, the scene of the first act of *Boris Godounov*, still deep in snow, and the Cathedral of St. Basil with its coloured domes, pineapple and bulb shaped, as pictured in the opera *Khovanstchina*. The powerful personality of Boris Godounov haunted us again in the Kremlin, an imaginative setting for *Coq d'Or* or *Kitesh*. There to be seen was his coronation throne in gold and precious stones, his gold saddle decorated with lion heads, his breast-plate of 2,000 links, each engraved with the motto 'God with us, and nobody against us'. Every country has of course its past and present interwoven, but in Russia the mood of the past seems less dead than in other countries: I kept on feeling that Boris Godounov and his times were not totally inconceivable even today, in spite of the triumphs of astronauts.

197

I had a striking example of this Janus side of the Russian character in Kiev. On the morning of May 1st several of our party were given seats on a dais overlooking the great new avenue down which the May Day procession was to pass. Just opposite to us was one of the largest military bands that I have seen. I counted in the first rank sixteen cymbal players, whose highly polished disks caught the sun as they clashed.

The start of the proceedings was suitably dramatic; between troops lining the broad thoroughfare two cars slowly approached from opposite directions; one contained the Commander of the Kiev forces, the other the defender of Stalingrad, Marshal Chuvikov. As a salute of guns was fired, the Ukranian flag (of immense size) floated up to a barrage balloon moored high in the air. A military march past followed, the pattern made familiar by films taken of the Red Square parade in Moscow. In succession came detachments (some twenty-four abreast) of cadets from the Suvorov School, of the Air Force, Liaison, Infantry, Tanks, Medical Corps, Naval forces from the Dnieper and Artillery. The step was quick, similar to that of our own light infantry regiments, and the method of marching resembled the goose-step. It was disciplined and precise from start to finish.

Then for three hours came, in continual waves, what looked like the whole population of Kiev. Actually there were about 350,000 I was told, men, women and children, many of the latter carried on the shoulders of their parents. Everyone carried something, flags, banners, slogans, pictures of the Soviet leaders, artificial flowers. Every activity of the city was represented. Among these civilian marchers were representative students of the University. Some of them recognised Trudy, who had visited the University the day before and spoken with them, as they strolled around in the breaks of study. In the friendly fashion of the Russians they smiled and waved to her in passing, and shouted greetings. At the end a magnificent march of athletes, boys and girls, galvanised us into attention, and finally the heroic band opposite us, who had been on duty from 10.30 to 2.00 wheeled into position, and marched away, still playing. We had witnessed a pagan Spring Festival.

The next day we saw a glimpse of the old 'Holy Russia', the monastery or *lavra*, the most revered convent in Russia. It was mined by the Germans, but survives as a glorious ruin, still showing many traces of its frescoes and paintings. Near by are the eleventh-century catacombs in which are buried saintly persons who spent their lives underground in these cells and chapels, and whose shrunken mummified figures, in glass cases, are shown to visitors. Tapers in hand we felt our way round this underground labyrinth and learnt that, shortly before our coming, a group of pilgrims had walked all the way from the Volga to pay their tribute at these shrines. To show their reverence they had refrained on the long journey from lying comfortably down to sleep. The contrast between this day and the previous one could not have been more pointedly marked.

Both in Moscow and in Leningrad the orchestras were fairly responsive to the new British music; the rehearsals normally took four hours, and on one occasion the players themselves asked for an extra hour. I had an expert linguist as interpreter, and though she knew next to nothing about music she set herself to learn the commoner musical terms so as to help me. At my first rehearsal in Moscow the orchestra made rather heavy weather of my suite from *Checkmate*, so, in the half-an-hour interval between rehearsals I challenged any player who was willing, to have a game of chess with me. A board was produced in the artists' room, the orchestra gathered round it and pushed forward their best chess player to meet my challenge. He proved far too good for me and, to the delight of the orchestra, at the end of the half hour I had to acknowledge myself well and truly beaten. After that they played like angels.

We all found the Russians a warm friendly people. The young would come up to us in the street, and try their English on us, though in that year they showed a certain diffidence in coming to our hotels when invited. They did not seem to have much curiosity about England and our way of living: they were too anxious to find out what *we* thought of *them*. Showing an interest in *their* plans and ideals was the surest way to a quick friendship, and no musicians could wish for a warmer reception than we got from the concert audiences, consisting mostly of young Russians. Looking from the platform at them was exactly like facing one of our own Promenade Concert audiences.

Before leaving Moscow for Leningrad I had the pleasure of meeting Shostakovich. He came to the hotel in which I was staying, and spent two hours with me. I had asked him to bring sketches of the new symphony he was then writing, but he said they were not sufficiently advanced to be seen. So we discussed various musical subjects— the problems of symphonic finales, the unconscious influence of audiences on composers, atonality, and that inevitable topic when composers meet, the role of the critic. When Shostakovich left me, to lay a commemorative wreath on the grave of his master Miaskovsky, I felt affection for this shy, modest, sensitive and highly gifted musician.

We had quite a historic encounter in Leningrad, where we were taken to see the cruiser *Aurora*, moored in the Neva; this was the warship which fired the signal shot, in the direction of the Winter Palace, to start the rising on October 25th 1917. In the gunroom of the cruiser were photos of two young seamen. One, we were told, had broadcast Lenin's slogans from the primitive radio apparatus, the other, under orders, had fired the gun. We asked what had become of these two. The former, we were told, was dead but the latter, now a Lieutenant-Colonel, was actually in command of the boat. Would we like to meet him? In due course he appeared, and through his interpreter said that he *did* know one word of English; it was the name of the port to which he had once sailed—Portsmouth. I told him that at our concert that night we were playing a work entitled *Portsmouth Point*. Would he like to come? Indeed he would— and then we all shook hands, feeling that we had touched history!

Leningrad looked beautiful in the early spring when the snow was just melting and the ice cracking; great blocks of ice floated down the Neva, some with little fir trees embedded in them, on their way to the gulf of Finland. We walked through the city seeing places made famous by Pushkin and Tchaikovsky in *The Queen of Spades*— the saloon where Hermann gambled, the bridge from which Lisa threw herself into the river. In Leningrad as in Moscow I had to get used to a new scale of dimension. Everything looked more than life size, the streets, the squares, the new buildings, the river, the stadiums. Only the modest house of Peter the Great seemed of normal size and he himself was a giant.

On May 3rd we flew to Kharkov for concerts, and it was on the way there that a tragic shadow fell on our little group. Cyril Smith, who had been playing brilliantly throughout the tour, was taken seriously ill with a stroke during the flight, and we had to leave him behind in the hospital at Kharkov, with Phyllis, his wife, staying to look after him. My wife quite rightly felt that she too should remain and keep Phyllis company in her anxiety. The courageous story of Cyril's recovery and eventual return to the concert platform is admirably told by Phyllis in their joint book of reminiscences *Duet for Three Hands*.

In spite of this sad setback, we others gave two concerts on the stage of the Opera House in Kharkov, and then by 7.30 a.m. on the morning of May 6th were on the plane back to Moscow. Even at this early hour many members of the Kharkov Symphony Orchestra were at the airport to give us a friendly send-off. We had offered to give an additional farewell concert in Moscow before finally leaving for England, and the Moscow State Symphony Orchestra, though it was officially their free day, volunteered their services. The hall was decorated with Union Jacks and Red Flags, and Mr. Krushchev sat with our Ambassador in a box. The evening ended, with characteristic Russian hospitality, at a banquet where innumerable toasts were given.

On our return home I received on behalf of us all the following letter from our Foreign Office.

*June 5th 1956*

Dear Bliss,
I have followed with interest the progress of the tour of British musicians led by yourself in the Soviet Union. From Sir William Hayter's enthusiastic report, it is clear that the visit made a great impression and that you have left much goodwill behind you in the Soviet Union.

I should like to express to you Her Majesty's Government's appreciation for this outstanding service in improving Anglo-Soviet cultural relations.

Yours sincerely
READING

I appreciated the unexpected gesture that life sometimes enjoys making, for this was the first letter I had received from the writer since I had sat next to him day after day at our Infants' School in Orme Square, Bayswater. On my other side sat an equally small Philip Guedalla.

Two years later, again in early spring, I received another invitation to visit Moscow, this time from Shostakovich, to serve on the jury of the Tchaikovsky International Competition for Pianists. I eagerly accepted this chance of renewing friendships with Soviet musicians; I only stipulated that I might be relieved from attending the pre-liminary sessions. In an article for the *Moscow News* I wrote some of my impressions of this Competition.

A huge portrait of Tchaikovsky gazes benignly across the hall of the Conservatoire in Moscow. His presence presides over these musical festivals in his honour. For the last ten days the adjudication for the prizes has been continuing. At the moment of writing, out of thirty competitors from many countries nine are engaged in the finals; three pianists from the Soviet Union, two from the U.S.A., one Chinese, one Japanese, one Bulgarian and one French. It is an ordeal for these young players. As they enter the hall, ablaze with television lights, they see directly facing them in the stalls the seventeen members of the jury; under the chairmanship of Emil Gilels, these award points according to an agreed schedule. Behind the jury sit the public, rows and rows of them. The hall has been packed for each session; often those who cannot obtain seats overflow into the aisles on either side, and stand.

There are obviously many music students in this huge audience, but the types are very varied, and many nations are represented. They are attentive and critical, and, after any specially fine performance, wildly enthusiastic.

For example, the American pianist Van Cliburn got an ovation lasting eight minutes when his recital in the second round finished. The playing of these finalists has been of a high order. It has been especially interesting to me to hear the music of Prokofiev, Shostakovich, and Kabalevsky played by their compatriots. The latter has written a special Rondo which, by the rules, all finalists have to play between the two Concertos. . . .

I wrote again, two days later, immediately after the judges had taken their final decision:

We deliberated for two hours, and it was not till well after midnight that agreement had been reached. Even at this late hour groups of eager young students were still waiting outside the Conservatoire on the chance of getting information as to the first prize-winners.

There is in Russia a huge new public, composed mostly of young people, who are eager for the stimulation of fine music, and who only within living memory have been granted the opportunity to satisfy this need. The music of Tchaikovsky probably remains their ideal, with its beauty of melody, its brilliance of colour, its rhythmic zest and Russian character.

I once said to a Russian friend that I thought European audiences were on the whole more sophisticated than those in Russia. 'Sophisticated?' she asked, 'what does *that* mean?' If I had brought the Oxford Dictionary with me I should have had to confess that it was defined as 'deprived of simplicity' or 'made artificial'. One habitually uses the word in a less pejorative sense, but I found it difficult to explain my meaning to her without appearing insufferably snobbish. Russian audiences are, I believe, more directly 'simple', in the sense that they do not crave for the type of music that appears on the programmes of any International Festival of Contemporary Music. Their composers on the other hand naturally feel the need to keep in touch with the works of their foreign contemporaries, just for the possible stimulation that they may derive for their own music. Hence there is a conflict in the minds of many Soviet artists, anxious to keep loyal to their audiences, which can lead to much strain and distress.

On this second visit to Moscow Shostakovich who was the President of this year's International Competition asked my wife and me to dinner at his apartment. We were the first guests to arrive and Shostakovich was feverishly playing an elaborate game of patience with two packs—to calm his nerves, Madame Shostakovich told us. Some other musicians arrived, including Kabalevsky and Khatchaturyan, and we sat down to a splendid meal cooked by our hostess. During it many toasts were proposed and the time flew by. We were just in the middle of this glorious spread, when our host and hostess remembered that we ought to have been at a reception given in the Kremlin by Krushchev for all the participants in the Tchaikovsky Competition. Leaving with the feelings of Tantalus, so much good food untasted, we had hurriedly to pack into cars and drive off. The reception was held in the hall of St. George, and if there is a larger or more imposing setting for a great banquet anywhere else in the world I have yet to see it.

Two immensely long tables laden with food and drink were set out the whole length of the room beneath the glittering chandeliers with their three thousand candles, and at the end behind a low railing, guarded by a Red Army soldier, were gathered members of the Praesidium and Deputies to the U.S.S.R. Supreme Soviet. My wife and I were summoned there to be greeted by Kruschchev, and as at that very moment dancers from the Bolshoi Ballet entered to entertain the guests, and everyone quickly took a chair; Trudy found herself sitting next to Krushchev, and I found a seat next to Vladimir Davidov, the favourite nephew of Tchaikovsky, to whom the *Pathetic Symphony* is dedicated. He spoke excellent English, and was then in charge of the house at Klin, where the relics and documents of the composer are preserved. It was enthralling to hear him talk about Tchaikovsky, as I had been familiar for many years with the letters edited by Rosa Newmarch, in which Davidov's name appears so often

A year or so later Shostakovich paid a visit to London and Trudy and I were naturally anxious to repay his kindness to us. He came to dinner at our house with a Counsellor from the Soviet Embassy, and then we took him to a concert of English madrigals sung by the Golden Age Singers, and given in the chapel of the Royal Hospital, Chelsea.

It was a very stormy night and he saw little of the Wren architecture, but he enjoyed the music immensely. He told me he had never heard our sixteenth-century music, and he followed the scores that I had brought for him with keen interest, occasionally nudging me when typical 'false relations' struck him as novel. Some years later at a concert of his works the Royal Philharmonic Society gave me the privilege of handing him their Gold Medal. It was a great disappointment that his illness in Russia at the time prevented him from being present in the Royal Festival Hall to receive it.

# Chapter XXI

# 1958—1959

SOON AFTER RETURNING to London from Moscow I had the pleasure of joining the Belgian conductor, Edouard van Remoortel, in a concert at the Royal Festival Hall, the orchestra being the London Symphony. I took the first half, conducting Tippett's Concerto for Double String Orchestra and my own *Meditations on a Theme by John Blow*, and Mr. Remoortel the second half, with a Sinfonia Concertante of Mozart and the *Dance Suite* of Bartók.

This was, as it were, a dress rehearsal for the repeat of the programme next day in the Grand Auditorium of the Brussels International Exhibition. Grand it may have been, but acoustically it was poor, and set in very unsympathetic surroundings. It was not a concert I enjoyed. However, the short visit to Belgium was wholly redeemed by a visit to the new Cloth Hall of Ypres with the orchestra, all of whom offered their services for a concert there before an invited audience.

It was moving to be on that historic spot, and the Burgomaster of Ypres welcomed us all in an affecting speech, ending with the words: 'Therefore we commemorate tonight those who have never returned but gave their lives to win peace for us, while we pray that a better peace than ours may be theirs.'

After the concert we all walked down to the Menin Gate, on which the names of the many thousands who fell in the Salient are inscribed, and heard the 'Last Post' sounded, as indeed it had been on every night since the First World War.

As I stood there I could not help thinking of the last time I ever saw the trenches on the Western Front. It was shortly after the Armistice. A friend and I made a pilgrimage to the places in the front line which we had known during the war. We set off in France on bicycles. I was not drawn to return by any morbid desire such as murderers are said to have in haunting the scene of their crime, but I wanted to satisfy the craving to know what was 'beyond'—what I had never been able to reach or see all those months of trench warfare—a glimpse of the dark side of the moon as it were. *What* lay further than the stumps of those battered trees in that minefield? *What* did that sinister looking mound hide? Where *exactly* was the road up which at night we heard German transport moving? It was an eerie sensation to step out of a familiar trench into no man's land, and meet absolute silence instead of machine gun fire, macabre to visit the dugouts of our fellow troglodytes opposite, and look back at our own parapets through their eyes. A year or so later, and all this terrain was to heal over and grow fresh and green, but at that time it still depicted utter desolation. That bugle call at the Menin Gate in 1958 saluting the dead as dusk fell, seemed not only a poignant reminder, but a dark warning as well.

Another memory of the year 1958 comes back to me. It was the last occasion on which I was present at one of those private run-throughs of a new work that Vaughan Williams liked to arrange. He used to gather together in his house a few of his friends of the younger generation, have the music played on the piano while they sat round the full score—and then ask them for criticisms. In this way fellow composers like Howells, Rubbra, Finzi, myself and others were given the honour of a pre-audition. He insisted that we spoke out boldly—before doing so we generally demanded a repeat, while he himself would sit back, quietly listening, and showing remarkable forbearance, for we were often at variance among ourselves! On this occasion it was the eighth symphony that we were to discuss, the symphony which John Barbirolli has since made his own.

I must have been in some doubt about certain passages because I remember sitting down at my desk immediately I returned home, and writing a long letter to Vaughan Williams, partly to dispel the woolliness of any remarks I may have made to him at the time, and partly from the knowledge that, though he listened patiently enough, he seldom veered from his original point of view.

I print his reply because it is so characteristic of his personality.

> *The White Gates,*
> *Westcott Road,*
> *Dorking*
> *November 6th 1958*

Dear Arthur,

Thank you very much for your letter—as a matter of fact what you said set me thinking hard, with the result that I have already made an alteration. *I can't cut out* the recapitulation of the second subject (*slow*) at the end, but I have led up to it differently. I realise now that the 'scrabble' which I thought would sound brilliant was merely fussy, and the *sudden pp* was wrong. Now I have made a more emotional climax, and a gradual diminuendo to the soft end.

So now we have the second subject the first time vigorous, led up to by the 'scrabble', and the second time soft and slow, led *down* by the dim.

I believe this will be all right.

I am going to alter the end of the scherzo, but cannot yet see the right way to do it.

I have cut about ten bars out of the slow movement. I *cannot* yet see my way to alter the finale and at present it seems all right to me.

You mustn't think that your advice has not been valuable because I have not exactly followed it. When I give advice to *my* pupils, I tell them they can do one of three things:

(a) accept it blindly—bad!

(b) reject it blindly—bad, but not so bad!

(c) think over a third course for themselves—good!

Yours with much gratitude<br>R. VAUGHAN WILLIAMS

By this time Christopher Hassall had become a close friend of ours, and began collaborating with me in a series of dramatic works. A poet, the author of two weighty biographies, an actor, a keen musician, he was inevitably a man that composers would look to for libretti, and indeed, many did. He often referred to himself as 'the composers' moll'!

We used to have what we termed 'inspirational evenings' together, when we would shoot ideas into the air until one hit a target that interested us both. From these evenings of argument and discussion came first a ballet, *The Lady of Shalott*, then an opera for television, *Tobias and the Angel*, next, the cantata, *The Beatitudes* and, finally, the cantata, *Mary of Magdala*. Christopher Hassall's sudden death at a comparatively early age left a great gap in my musical life, and deprived me both of an inspiring mind and of a generous friend. I should add that among his other gifts was a beautiful voice for reading poetry, which many can hear still on the records that he made. I recall too with pleasure his performances as the orator in *Morning Heroes*, for which his training as an actor and reciter made him a perfect choice.

The writing of *The Lady of Shalott*, my fourth ballet, came about through an invitation from the University of California to provide a new work for the Music Festival celebrating the opening of the May T. Morrison Hall and the Alfred Hertz Memorial Hall of Music on the Berkeley Campus in the spring of 1958. It was Christopher Hassall who suggested Tennyson's poem as a basis, and the figure of

'The Lady', living her emotional life vicariously and unable to survive when at last compelled to face reality (a true Henry James heroine, in fact) appealed to me.

The ballet seems to have satisfied the requirements, for in the *San Francisco Chronicle* of May 4th 1958 the music critic Alfred Frankenstein wrote that 'the score is very brilliant, wonderfully orchestrated and finely shaped, and the composer had had the best possible collaboration from Lew Christensen, the choreographer, from Tony Duquette, who designed the set and the costumes, from the dancers of the San Francisco Ballet Company, and from the musicians, headed by Earl Murray'.

The next project on which Christopher Hassall and I collaborated in 1959, was a more ambitious one, an opera especially devised for television. I cannot think that we could have chosen a more suitable subject than the astonishing story of *Tobias and the Angel*, taken from the Book of Tobit in the *Apocrypha*.

Starting in the slave market in Nineveh where the youth Tobias hires the manservant who turns out to be none other than the Archangel Raphael, thence to the river Tigris where the monstrous fish is caught, and so to Ecbatane and the house of Raguel, whose daughter, Sara, is possessed by the devil, the story goes from one dramatic scene to another. The ensuing battle for the soul of Sara between the Archangel and the Devil, and the subsequent miraculous healing of Tobias's blind father, Tobit, give plenty of scope for film presentation.

Composing for television was a new experience for me, and I had to learn as I went along. Here my film experience came in useful, as the 'duration of time' factor conditions the writing; conciseness is all. What might be lengthened to twenty minutes in the theatre (a quarrel between two people for example) would have to be shortened to (say) ten minutes in the opera house, and, when the medium is the screen, to very much less. I had the good fortune to have the experienced Rudolph Cartier to produce the opera, and in our first discussions the question of the duration of each scene came up. 'Take your watch out', he said, 'and see the second hand do its minute circle.' I did so, and the time seemed endless; much could happen on the screen during those sixty seconds; I saw his point clearly.

Christopher Hassall's libretto was rightly praised; it is a model of its kind, in which every line in this supernatural fantasy seems a natural utterance. I had a fine cast of singers, who looked their roles, and Norman del Mar was in charge of the whole musical performance. No one who has not seen the preparations necessary for an elaborate television opera like *Tobias and the Angel* can have any idea of the technical difficulties involved. With his cool head, his acute ear, and his quick grasp of what was needed, Norman del Mar was the ideal interpreter.

The opera was shown on BBC Television in May 1960, and later was fortunate enough to win an award of Merit when repeated at a Festival in Salzburg. Television opera is an ephemeral form, and after all the work I put into it, I decided to publish an adaptation for the stage, on the chance that one day some enterprising opera company might attempt it.

# Chapter XXII

# 1960–1963

THIS WOULD SEEM a fitting place to mention the composition of *The Beatitudes*. As soon as I had received the invitation to contribute a work for the opening of the new Cathedral at Coventry—to be celebrated in May 1962—I asked Christopher Hassall to come to London (he was then living in Canterbury), and talk over possible subjects that would suit the occasion. It was *his* suggestion that the Nine Beatitudes should be the theme.

As far as I knew there had been only three previous settings, by Liszt, by César Franck, and the episode in Elgar's *Apostles*. I saw at once that I must guard against one obvious danger—monotony—for each Beatitude shines with the same clear silver gleam, and little contrast of light is possible without deliberately using a distorting mirror. So Christopher and I chose a sequence of mystical poems which could provide interludes, and comment on the Beatitudes that preceded them. Even these did not afford me sufficient contrast, so in addition I planned to express a mood of violence (force opposing the beatific vision) at four places in this hour-long cantata.

I decided to start the work with one of these outbursts, and appealed to Christopher for some quotation that would explain my purpose to the hearers. His letter to me early in 1961 showed that he had taken much trouble to help me find what I needed:

*Tonford Manor,*
*Canterbury*
(undated)

Dear Arthur

About the Prelude to the Beatitudes and the Quotation. I have gone through Donne and Vaughan, also Beddoes. In the latter (in an unfinished poem called 'Doomsday') comes this line:—

> 'World, wilt thou yield thy spirit up and be
> convulsed and die?'

In 'The Storm' (Donne) comes:

'All things are one, and that one none can be,
. . . so that we, except God say
Another *Fiat*, shall have no more day.'

The Donne is a good piece, and the first line is worth considering as standing on its own without the rest, though I think 'except God say another *Fiat*' applies excellently. The only other possible lines in Donne come from 'The First Anniversary':

'. . . And freely men confess that this world's spent
When in the Planets, and the Firmament
They seek so many new; they see that this
Is crumbled out again to his Atomies.
'Tis all in pieces, all coherence gone;
All just supply, and all Relation.'

(lines 209–214)

But this is rather obscure, out of context, and refers to the advance of scientific research, etc., in a way that you don't really mean yourself in the Prelude.

The first Donne piece, though, written about the effects of a storm at sea when it seems as if the world itself will be destroyed, does appear to me to be worth considering seriously. I can find nothing in Vaughan.

Yours ever
CHRISTOPHER

P.S. later: The shorter quotation 'so that we, except God say etc.,' now seems very striking, so long as one has read into it the sense of a future possibility rather than a present situation, which, on the surface, the words mean. I wonder what Trudy's opinion is? I am inclined to offer her a casting vote.

Visiting scenes of the past has never appealed to me much; by temperament I live in the present and, as far as I can, into the near future. But now in my seventieth year I found myself without design recalling much earlier years. There was, for instance, a performance of *Morning Heroes* in Norwich, a city associated in my mind with the première of the work conducted by me thirty-one years before. This time, just as then, Heathcote Statham, the Cathedral organist and choir master for so many years, helped to prepare the chorus, and Basil Maine, the first of many 'Orators', again declaimed with moving effect the passage from the *Iliad*, and the poem of Wilfred Owen.

Then there was a performance of my *Pastoral* in King's College, Cambridge, where I had walked so often with my brother Kennard fifty years before. I realised once more the immense change, since my time there, in musical conditions; this performance showed so clearly the transition from amateur enthusiasm to professional skill. Of course David Willcocks was the responsible agent on this occasion, and the work with him, the hospitality of the Provost, and Cambridge itself in June composed a happily coloured picture, untinged with any regret for time past.

One more association with my youth during this year I should like to recall, and that is a birthday concert given me by the students of the Royal College of Music, where for a brief time I had studied and later taught. This concert shortly after my seventieth birthday was made memorable by a splendid performance of my violin concerto. It was played by a young student, José Luis Garcia, a pupil of Antonio Brosa. As far as I knew, no violinist except Campoli had ventured on learning the concerto, and the technical mastery of this young Spanish boy came all the more as a thrilling surprise.

Earlier that year I received an unusual commission: it came from the American Wind Symphony Orchestra of Pittsburgh. What interested me was that this orchestra specialised in giving concerts on *rivers*, hardly a good sounding-board one would think. In its three years of existence it had played on the rivers of its own country, the Alleghany, the Monongahela, and the Mississippi, and it was now making its first overseas tour and was to play on the Thames. For the performance a barge some 120 feet in length had been designed with a revolving deck-house at each end, providing a stage for the soloists and storage room for instruments; the main orchestral platform was backed and roofed by adjustable sounding panels. The orchestra consisted of some sixty young professional wind players drawn from universities and musical conservatoires (on this tour they came from China, Great Britain, Japan, Mexico and the U.S.A.), and they were conducted by the founder and musical director of the scheme, Robert Austin Boudreau from the Juilliard School of Music. For him I wrote a short piece to exploit the antiphonal effects of two separately placed brass choirs, and named it *Greetings to a City*.

The orchestra and the barge duly arrived, and one morning in July I went to their moorings off Battersea Park to hear them rehearse. As luck would have it there was a brisk wind blowing, and as I went out to the players in a motor boat, I saw the barge rolling quite a lot, while the breeze was blowing the orchestral parts from the stands. In spite of the unsteadiness of this strange concert platform the young players blew their best, undismayed by the fact that the wind off-shore carried their sound away from any audience that might line the banks. Their future itinerary was to be Henley-on-Thames, Reading, Oxford, Abingdon, Marlow, Maidenhead, Eton, Greenwich, Richmond, and the South Bank Promenade, London; their repertoire was almost exclusively contemporary. I am glad that this gallant enterprise was, when weather permitted, warmly acclaimed en route.

I finished the score of *The Beatitudes* towards the end of this year 1961, and it was ready for the Festival Chorus at Coventry to begin to study it. This Chorus was formed by bringing together many small choirs in the district, and was expertly rehearsed by Meredith Davies, who was also responsible for preparing Britten's great *War Requiem*.

As the day for the première in May drew near, I realised I was in for a major disappointment. I had been led to believe that the performance was to take place in the majestic surroundings of the new Cathedral, but alas! the Cathedral was needed for services and the concert was relegated to the Coventry Theatre, a maladjustment most unfortunate to me. Instead of the ecclesiastical grandeur which I had imagined, there was the ugly theatre whose stage could not properly contain both large orchestra and chorus. The latter could not be placed where their voices would tell, and some of them acknowledged that from where they were wedged in they could not see my beat. Also I had written an important part for the Cathedral organ. What effect could one possibly obtain from an imported small Hammond organ? We had to do the best we could. This is not the first occasion on which conditions, unrelated to musical problems, have deprived me of a reasonably successful première.

The reviews commenting on the work hoped that a performance would be given in the Cathedral, its rightful place, on 'the earliest possible occasion after the Festival'. As I write six years later, this expectancy remains unfulfilled.

The year 1963 opened happily for me with the award of the Gold Medal of the Royal Philharmonic Society. On four previous occasions I had been privileged to present this to other musicians, to Vaughan Williams, to Stravinsky, to Malcolm Sargent, and to Shostakovich (in absentia). To receive it now myself and join the long list of famous recipients gave me great delight. The occasion was the celebration of the Society's one hundred and fiftieth birthday and was solely a social function. I should have liked, as is the traditional custom, to have expressed my thanks in music, but this being impossible I had to substitute words for notes, to the best of my ability.

I have written that the year 1963 opened happily for me, and so it did in musical terms, but it also brought a personal sense of loss to my wife and myself. My younger daughter Karen and her husband Christopher Sellick decided that Australia could offer them a rosier future than seemed possible in England, a healthier life for their three little girls, and a wider scope for Chris's talents.

So early in the year he flew out to Australia, ahead of his family, to investigate possibilities, and then, in March, Karen with her small daughters left to join him. They decided to try their luck in Perth, surely the most isolated big city in the world, and some twelve thousand miles away from us. We felt the wrench very much, and could not feel satisfied until we should see for ourselves the kind of life they were living, and how successfully they were adapting themselves to an environment so different.

We therefore planned to keep 1964 as free as possible from engagements here, and in that year make a flying trip to Australia to see them.

During 1963 I was occupied with two works of widely differing character. The first, a song cycle, originated in my seeing in *The Listener* a number of translations made by Kevin Crossley-Holland, of old English riddles from the Exeter Book. These Anglo-Saxon puzzles were chosen from some hundreds that can be found in the library of Exeter Cathedral, and may date back to the eighth century. The subjects are drawn from nature, from animal and bird life, and from such objects as were in familiar use at the time: they were probably recited as part of the entertainment customary at feasts.

I chose seven of these riddles. The singer first gives the clues (often as obscure as a Torquemada Crossword) and then announces the solutions. The correct answers to these seven show the variety that can be found in the collection: Fish in River, Swallows, An Oyster, A Weather Cock, A Book Worm, A Cross of Wood, and Sun and Moon.

The finding of these poems came in very handy for me, as I had accepted an invitation from the BBC to write a new work for the Cheltenham Festival and, as usual, I was waiting for the needed impetus. The texts gave plenty of opportunity for musical realism (an additional help, perhaps, to the verbal clues) and seemed to demand a chamber orchestra with a solo baritone. So I scored the music for a string quintet, a wind quintet and harp, and under its title of *A Knot of Riddles* it was first given at Cheltenham in July 1963. It had a perfect première, as my colleagues were the singer John Shirley-Quirk, and the famous Melos Ensemble of instrumentalists. I could not forbear putting the words 'Hommage modeste à Maurice Ravel' at the top of the fifth riddle 'A Book Worm', for in imagining the grub boring its way, without benefit, through some classic masterpiece I thought of the quotation with which Ravel heads his own *Valses nobles et sentimentales*—'Le plaisir délicieux et toujours nouveau d'une occupation inutile'.

The other work completed that year, for the Worcester Festival

213

in September, was of a very different character. It was a sacred cantata, whose subject comes from the twentieth chapter of the Gospel of St. John, and describes how Mary Magdalene goes to the sepulchre and meets the risen Christ. This work carries a memory of sadness for me, for it proved to be the last time on which I could call on the advice and help of Christopher Hassall. Soon after he completed the libretto he died, and never heard the result of our last happy collaboration.

The whole imaginative text is his, starting first with the description of early morning on 'the third Day'.

> *Ashen the sky, uncertain, grey,*
> *The hour is neither night nor day.*
> *Darkness and dawn are midway met,*
> *And a mist hangs over Olivet.*

The librettist then describes Mary's thoughts as she hurries to the sepulchre, and her recalling the feast where the guests mocked her and Christ showed his compassion. Arriving at the grave she sees the two Angels, and then the man whom she supposes to be the gardener, and finally there is the sudden recognition of His Presence.

Into his dramatic text Christopher Hassall wove two seventeenth-century poems, one by Edward Sherburne (1651), which parallels in feeling the scene of Mary at the feast.

> *The proud Aegyptian Queen, her Roman Guest,*
> *(To express her Love in height of State and Pleasure)*
> *With Pearl dissolved in gold, did feast,*
> *Both Food and Treasure.*

> *And now, dear Lord, thy Lover, on the fair*
> *And silver Tables of thy Feet, behold!—*
> *Pearl in her Tears, and in her Hair*
> *Offers thee Gold.*

The second poem is a free adaptation from 'The Gardener' by Rowland Watkins (1662) and has, as a refrain, this couplet:

> *He is the Gardener still, and knoweth how*
> *To make the Lilies and the Roses to grow.*

With this quiet chorus, the work ends.

I needed a contralto for the role of the Magdalene, and was lucky enough to interest Norma Proctor whose lovely voice has something of the timbre of Kathleen Ferrier's. The initial performance took place in Worcester Cathedral, with John Carol Case singing the part of Christus, and later the Cantata was given in Hull, in Norma's own part of England. I remember this particular concert vividly, for shortly afterwards Norma appeared on our doorstep in London bearing a present of fish, straight from the sea at Grimsby. Never had fish tasted so fresh and delicious; it is lucky that we have the faculty of remembering gastronomic delights years after the meal has been enjoyed and digested.

The mention of fish recalls that a particularly large specimen led to my first meeting with Edith Sitwell. She was then living in Moscow Road, off the Bayswater Road. I had forgotten the number of her flat and stopped at a fishmonger's shop near by on the chance that I could learn it. I was not only told, but asked if I would take a fish to her for which she had just telephoned. So, like Tobias, whose story I set to music later, I toiled up the staircase with my offering, and gave it into the long shapely hands of Edith Sitwell. She welcomed me and it without surprise, and leading me into her flat began to talk about *Les Illuminations* of Rimbaud, the prose poems of which her friend, Helen Rootham, was putting into English. I had long admired Edith Sitwell not only for her great poetical gift, but for the spirit in which she crusaded against what was evil and ugly. Like most artists she was very sensitive to adverse criticism. A little later, after reading a malicious reference to her poems, I wrote to her, paraphrasing a couplet of Goethe's to the effect that when curs are snapping at your heels, it is a sure sign that you are on horseback. In reply I received the following letter from Renishaw Hall:

(undated)

Dear Arthur Bliss,

I cannot tell you what pleasure your most kind and charming letter has given me. It would delight me anyhow, but it delights me especially, naturally, coming from you. I am most happy that you like those poems. Actually your letter arrived at what seemed a most hopeless moment and it made me persevere with my work. I was just crawling inside and then outside a long poem, and my struggle had reached almost the proportions of a physical one.

I really *do* thank you for your letter. I feel if the fellow artists whom one admires like one's work, I don't mind about anyone else, and what you said gave me great happiness.

I have almost finished a book on Shakespeare—almost, but not quite. When, in the dim future, it appears, I will send it to you.

With very grateful thanks and best wishes

Yours sincerely

Edith Sitwell

Praise is a necessary tonic; during my long life I doubt whether I

215

have met anyone who is so filled with self-confidence that he can afford to do without it; creative artists particularly need it. Even the greatest have confessed in letters and conversations that there are times when their belief in their powers has faded, when through fatigue or ill health or discouragement they have felt impotent to create any more. As for lesser artists they tend to fluctuate continually between the two poles of buoyant hope and deep despair: only in extreme youth perhaps is there an absolute confidence in future power. Hence the importance of praise, and when it comes from someone, a fellow artist perhaps, who really knows the difficulty of bringing *any* work of art to successful completion, the resulting glow is all the warmer.

There is one other incident in the year 1963 which I should like to mention for the special pleasure it gave me. On July 24th I was privileged to lay the foundation stone of a house in Lindfield, Sussex, to be called the 'Arthur Bliss House'. This unexpected compliment was the result of a meeting seven years before. I had taken part in a Gala Concert at the Royal Festival Hall, to celebrate an important tercentenary in Anglo-Jewish relations, at which I conducted my *Meditations on a Theme by John Blow*. The Chairman of the Concert Committee was Mr. Daniel Schonfield, who was also chairman of a non-profit housing association pledged to provide homes for old people where they could be in close touch with their families, and so ward off the dread of loneliness at the close of their lives: this is the Samaritan Housing Association. Mr. Schonfield planned to name each house, as it was built, after a living British musician, and he chose my name to be the first, saying in a letter that it was 'to show some small appreciation for your assistance in this particular concert and for your general contribution to the world of music'.

I thought the appreciation shown anything but small when on the afternoon of July 24th my wife and I with Mr. and Mrs. Schonfield motored down to Lindfield and I duly put the foundation stone in place, tapped it with a silver trowel, and expressed the hope that all who should live in that house might find happiness and serenity. This short ceremony gave me the same sense of pleasure that planting a tree does, in the knowledge that with skilful care it will grow to a great height and enjoy long life—*more* pleasure, in fact, for builders can work quicker wonders than arboriculturists. In just over a year the house, with its independent flats, was built and, in our absence in Australia, opened by the then Minister of Housing and Local Government, Sir Keith Joseph. When Trudy and I returned from Australia, we went to Lindfield, just after my seventy-fifth birthday, to meet all those who were living in the house and, at a party in the residents' lounge, express thanks for the compliment paid us. Since then two similar houses have been planned by the same Association; they bear the names of Yehudi Menuhin and Malcolm Sargent.

While on the subject of names, I have often wondered why we in England have never honoured our past musicians on our postage stamps. I believe we are now the only musical country that has not issued stamps to celebrate musical anniversaries, say, in our case, the centenaries, or longer, of the birth of Purcell, Handel, Elgar, and some of the Elizabethan composers. A friend of mine, an ardent philatelist, recently brought me a design for an Elgar stamp, complete with musical quotation; this I submitted to the Postmaster General, but in vain.

# Chapter XXIII

# 1964

AN UNUSUAL MUSICAL ANNIVERSARY was celebrated at Cambridge early in 1964. The first degree in music to be given anywhere in the world was awarded by Cambridge University in 1464, and to mark the quincentenary Thurston Dart (then professor of music at the University) and his colleagues decided to commission music for a special concert by the University Musical Society.

Thurston Dart came to see me, as I was a Cambridge musician, and with his dynamic enthusiasm and drive easily persuaded me to attempt a new work for the occasion. I felt this must be a collaboration between a Cambridge composer and a Cambridge poet, and, after reviewing possible names, to my delight we decided on approaching Kathleen Raine, whose poems I admired, and indeed, in the past had marked for setting to music—but they were as fragile as shells, and as delicate as flowers, and I had refrained.

Now, however, there was a chance to get her to write a cycle of poems especially with music in mind. I went to see her in Chelsea, and found her at first very diffident of her ability to write for a special occasion; it was a long time, she said, since she had written any poetry and in any case what could she write suitable to this quincentenary? I liked her sensitive approach to poetry so much that I was determined to secure her help, and badgered both by me and by Thurston Dart she finally consented to try. As I have said Thurston Dart is decidedly persuasive; his talk is like a succession of champagne corks popping, and his letter-writing has the same characteristic.

*Jesus College,*
*Cambridge*
*1:iv:63*

Dear Arthur Bliss,

Hooray. It's like making tea: 1st, set the table (i.e. arrange for a convenient quincentenary); next, find the teapot (i.e. consider what are usually called 'Ways & Means'—about which more in my next— and find a body like CUMS who'll perform); now for the Ty (you)

218

and the Phoo (La Belle Raine) and the bringing-to-the-boil. The essence of this last process is, of course, time. May I also ask David Willcocks to be in touch with you for the remaining stages? The only cooks who really need to be involved from now on are you and Miss Raine and he, or (some prefer) him.

'Occasional' verse may well be a problem. I think all that matters, you know, is to *know* what occasion is sparking off all this, rather than to honour—in so many words—an abstraction like music, which cannot be tasted, or touched, or seen. This is one of the several features distinguishing it from tea. I mistrust (as a historian) Odes to Music since they've produced some awful disasters in their time. I won't list 'em, but you can think of some for yourself. . . .

Ty and Phoo, between them, may decide on some quite different topic, and it doesn't seem to me that this would in the least matter. What we want, as Paddy Hadley would say, Is An Op.

More later. I've been away, and have a mountain of bumf on my desk. This letter is no more than a potboiler . . . and, as someone pointed out to me long ago, it is revelatory that *all* my metaphors are culinary ones. Belgian steaks and wines are excellent, & have bounced me back into being.

Yours ever,<br>BOB DART

The other Cambridge composer to be asked to contribute a work for the occasion was quite rightly Patrick Hadley, Dart's predecessor as Professor of Music at Cambridge.

Kathleen Raine finally wrote a sequence of eight poems for me to set; in her own words 'the sequence attempts to suggest the evolution of music and how this follows the evolution of the world itself, first of articulate life, then of consciousness and finally of Orphic utterance'. She is not an easy poet to comprehend and I found her shift of thought from poem to poem difficult. To help the singers in a chorus to a comprehension of her theme, I have ventured to put an interpretation in my own words.

'This poem cycle is An Ode on Sound, starting from the sound of the wind ("voices of empty air") and then passing to the cries of gulls ("wind's cry takes wings") who in Poem III are seen as a symbol of the soul ("phoenix-like') trying to break free. As a contrast to the screams of the gulls, the poet takes the frail reed-warbler's song ("delicate reed notes") which leads her to human song.

'There is first, in Poem V, the child's song, and then in Poem VI, the mature human being's experience of joy and sorrow. Poem VII tells how only by *Art* can life's experience be fully expressed and

Poem VIII is an Ode to Music ("the golden form") and to its inspirer, Orpheus.'

Kathleen Raine and I were working at this *Golden Cantata*, as it was finally named, through the summer of 1963. Apart from meetings to elucidate this point and that, we corresponded, and I have kept the letters of the poet as they are indications of how her mind was working. They also show her generous attitude to the composer, who so often has to break the sensitive web of words for his own selfish musical purposes.

All her letters are characteristically undated—she stands a little outside time, I always feel—but they were written sometime during that spring and summer.

*47 Paulton's Square,*
*S.W.3.*

Dear Sir Arthur,

I won't take up time and space with explanations and apologies for my silence—I have been and still am taken up with my family—parents and grandchildren. But in a brief intermission I have returned to the poems, meditated upon your letter, and written in some haste today the enclosed poem which may do as a link, following the Eden poem. In this, the Pilgrim of Eternity does take on human, even Orphic form, though still bird-winged. He takes a turn down into the long shadows of the journey through the underworld, seeking for Eurydice. In the next, which tomorrow I plan to attempt, I hope to grasp the human a little more firmly; even though I was, so an astrological friend told me, born when the moon is full and am therefore, according to Yeats' calculations, scarcely human. I certainly find it hard to leave the cosmic for the mortal, but I promise to try, and tomorrow is the day it shall be attempted. I shall ask, in the poem, 'Pilgrim of eternity, as you travel through the underworld, what is this music you are playing? And where did you find the lyre that you carry on your journey, and who taught you to play upon it? And why do all creatures, as you sound its harmony, bow themselves before you, even the souls in Hades and the power that rules the underworld?' Leaving the question unanswered, don't you think?—or rather I know you do think so, from your reception of my heavenly Choir!

You may not find the enclosed poem any use at all: but as I wrote it it seemed to flow through moods that might be musical. But I expect a number to be discarded or modified as your composition takes form.

By all means put the reed-warbler into the past tense. I am less certain whether the Eden poem can go into any but the present tense

220

since its very substance is nowness. But the Blackbird can certainly go. 'Bird in tree/Of white may' and 'With a bird's golden eye', or 'With bird's golden eye' if you like.

Meanwhile I shall go on working as time allows—my two grandchildren are being christened from here on Saturday at Chelsea Old Church, a point of neutrality where the various shades of belief and disbelief of the families, godparents and parents will rather uneasily converge, my own included. However, I shall have to feed them all on salmon and strawberries, an enormous piece of irrelevance, or so it seems, but the children and grandparents expect it of me.

Please give my regards to Lady Bliss, and tell her how very much I enjoyed meeting her.

Yours sincerely<br>KATHLEEN RAINE

P.S. As to putting 'The Child's Song' into the past tense, I would rather not do so unless you feel you must. The reason I am reluctant is that the poem describes precisely the state in which the world is experienced as 'here and now'—that is, as the present, without past or future, desire or regret. I would rather leave it so and let the hopes and fears of the sorrow of mankind come in the subsequent poems—as they will.

I have revised the poem, as you see, and think it is improved. The golden centres of life, the bird's eye, the sun, and the pollen grain seem to coincide better.

47 Paulton's Square,<br>S.W.3.

I am back and happy to know you are inspired. The 'bright bow' *is* the rainbow but a suggestion of the musical bow as well. This ties together ideas of the sun which makes the rainbow *and* inspires Orpheus who is Apollo's oracle and voice on earth. I would suggest 'Orphic Hymn' as a possible title for the whole series.

Next comes the evocation of Eurydice herself—music calling to the forgetful lost soul in Hades. That should, if it succeeds, be the last unless it seems to need yet one more poem.

After that I would like to see you and know if some poems will have to go, or others be written earlier in the series. I am beginning to enjoy this.

KATHLEEN RAINE

Kathleen Raine and I had some difficulty in finding a title for our Cantata, but when, finally, I proposed the name *Golden Cantata*, suggested by words of her own in the last poem of the cycle, she wrote to me agreeing.

(Undated)

*The Golden Cantata* is perfect. I wish the poems were *more* golden, but 'music is the golden form' they wear. I too am sorry about giving up 'Love's touch upon the vibrant seven-stringed lyre', but otherwise I approve all you have done, *but*—this is something I know so well, in altering and reshaping poems—'trace' now becomes a plural verb ruled by a singular noun ('harmony'). Since we had 'trace' to rhyme with 'face', could 'harmony' be made plural ('harmonies') or, failing that, the best thing will be to compose the grammar a little by putting a comma after 'flow'. If I print the poems later in book form I may still change the poem—meanwhile I am glad if they serve to be the bones of *The Golden Cantata*.

With all sincere wishes that the music may flow

Very sincerely

KATHLEEN RAINE

Could a composer have a more sympathetic or understanding collaborator?—or a more modest one, considering the poetic conception was all hers.

Two performances of the Cantata were given in the Guildhall at Cambridge in the third week of February 1964, and Kathleen Raine came to hear them. David Willcocks, the conductor of the Cambridge Musical Society, took over from me at the second performance. He had taken great pains with the young singers and players, and all I had to do was to enjoy myself, which I did, discovering yet again that a performance by young amateurs often has a vitality and exuberance that experienced professionals find it hard to recapture.

I hope the poet was equally pleased; at any rate at a later performance by the Huddersfield Choral Society, which she heard on the air, she generously wrote to me as follows:

*The Golden Cantata* was enchanting—full of beauty which only this time I was able to follow at all intelligently, appreciating the delicate turns of your musical phrases. The shocking violence and even ugliness forces itself on the attention, but resolution and harmony alone hold it, in the end: and nowadays *harmony* comes almost as a shock. Your music will last because it is real music, or simply *is* music. I was so glad to hear it again, with no longer a sense of being more than marginally involved in it, as a work. The words were like

222

tacking stitches in the sewing (useful while working), but the work
is all yours.

KATHLEEN

Gratitude to Kathleen Raine makes me end with another letter
from her, for there is no more heartening gift than appreciation from
another creative artist. She had been to a concert given by the Royal
Choral Society in the Albert Hall, where my piano concerto had
been given, followed by a performance of my setting of *The Beatitudes*.
After the concert she wrote to me:

*47 Paulton's Square,*
*S.W.3.*

I went last night to your *Beatitudes*, taking five friends with me;
for all of us it was a catharsis; in one way or another I was very
moved, especially by *The Beatitudes* though parts of the Concerto
also stirred some kind of indescribable recognition that, in your music,
you have understood, and imposed form and beauty upon our strange
time. Much reminded me of a world that seemed lost with the war—
a life with form and dignity and sweetness and magic. Then, some
of the great chaotic passages in *The Beatitudes* sent the images of
order shuddering like moonlight when a stone is thrown into a pond,
and then the forms reassembled and came back into harmony, and
then above those forms, the soaring beatitudes.

It was deeply moving, and I felt that a sensibility of an older
world, almost lost in this stark ignorant age, was experiencing the
present, and bringing to it something which hardly anyone seems
to have any more.

Seeing you there, conducting with such a diviner's wand was itself
quite overwhelming.

You said music has above all the power to move, and so it has,
and one becomes muted and frozen, and it is good to be told things
in sound, that no words can ever say. What a beautiful performance
it was! or, so at least I thought, and I hope you also did.

I felt the recent assassination of Kennedy as a kind of portent
and that from now on it is going to be darker and harder for all of us.

But blessed are those who hold such forms of beauty before us as
you gave last night.

KATHLEEN

As a coda to these letters I quote a final one, received after this book
of reminiscences had been finished. I had just read a beautiful poem
of hers 'By the River Eden' in, of all places, *The New Yorker*, and
in writing to her for permission to use her letters for publication,

I had expressed my admiration for it. Characteristically she makes no reference to this in the following reply:

*47 Paulton's Square,*
*S.W.3.*
*November 8th 1967*

Dear Arthur,

By all means make use of anything I wrote you that seems fitting. I was not at all satisfied with my share. I don't think I make a good collaborator, not from want of goodwill but because I am by nature (by the nature, that is, of my poetic daimon) a solitary. I have to feel the illusion of solitude, like a bird on its own tree.

That is not so of my outer personality. I like the company of my kind, and could very well have made a wild life of it for myself, if occasion had offered. I have it in me. But the poet is not like that at all,—which creates illusion and deception both for myself and others. They find me amenable in conversation, but that bears so little relation to the ensuing results. A musician must, obviously, be able *as* a musician to work with others. I wish it were so with me, but have by now come to see that it is not. I feel I failed you. If you quote me at all I would be glad if you'd say I was not satisfied.

Very sincerely yours,
KATHLEEN RAINE

As part of the quincentenary celebration honorary doctorates of music were conferred by the Vice-Chancellor on Michael Tippett and myself. After the ceremony the two new doctors stalked slowly in procession from the Senate House to St. John's College, resembling two tropical birds in search of food. We found it, in gracious abundance, in the hall of St. John's, following a beautiful Grace Anthem by William Byrd: and both Tippett and I were delighted to have a third composer, Rossini, figuring on the menu.

I have written earlier that I am not one of those who love to retrace their steps, but I make an exception of Cambridge, and felt singularly proud on this twentieth of February, 1964.

# Chapter XXIV

# 1964–1965

DURING THE YEAR 1964 the trip to Australia was finally planned. The visit to our family in Perth was to be combined with concert engagements arranged by the Australian Broadcasting Commission in Sydney and Brisbane, as well as in Perth. We were to have two months in Australia, and then fly to Japan to join the London Symphony Orchestra, who were scheduled to give concerts there in the course of their Eastern tour. It looked like being a wonderful experience, for neither Trudy nor I had yet been south of the equator.

We left London on Friday afternoon September 4th in one of the giant Qantas planes, stopping to refuel at Cairo, Karachi, Calcutta, Bangkok, Singapore, and finally reaching Perth in the early hours of Sunday the 6th. Chris met us and took us to a hotel where Trudy and I slept soundly till lunchtime. Soon afterwards our daughter Karen with the three small grand-daughters, Jill, Patricia, and Laura, each bearing a posy of flowers arrived, and we were taken to the house that had been rented for us just outside Perth, and within a quarter of a mile of their own home. On seeing it my wife was immediately reminded of America—one storey high and compactly built, with a garage alongside, it had a small garden behind, and a grass lawn in front that bordered the road. Each house down the quiet street was equipped in the same fashion, but with a different design: there were no dividing hedges, and the effect was of privacy and neighbourliness combined, very like America in fact. Our daughter and son-in-law had provided for us most generously, a hired car stood in the car porch, a piano had been imported into the living-room, and the refrigerator in the kitchen was well stocked with food and wine.

I must pause here to remark that Australian wine was one of the unexpected finds that I recall with particular pleasure. No wonder they do not export the best, or perhaps the best cannot withstand the long voyage. I remember later a dinner at the Australian Club in Sydney, where I was offered a claret that could vie with any French vintage. Compared with London, living conditions around Perth seemed very simple; we were staying in Ardross, one of the many suburbs that stretch along either side of the Swan River. Each suburb had its own complement of stores, and shopping in the car was a quick and easy matter—no difficulties about parking, no queues, no hurry, no strain.

Fortunately we had arrived at the most beautiful season in Western Australia, their spring. The sun had not yet shown what it could really do, nor for that matter had minor irritations like the flies. It was the time to see the wild flowers and shrubs, which are protected as a State asset; they bloomed everywhere, such as I had never yet seen—the blue leschenaultia, the Swan River daisies, fringed lilies, spider orchids, the grevillias and scarlet banksias, the bottle brushes and black boys, and the unique Kangaroo paws, of which the Mangles variety is the State flower emblem. In November, when we left, the Christmas trees were coming into bloom, with brilliant orange flowers against deep green leaves. Trudy, being the daughter of a botanist and orni-thologist, had always been interested and knowledgeable about plants and birds, and in middle age I succumbed, in an amateur fashion, to a similar enthusiasm. I found our yearly trips to the continent to be most rewarding when we could settle on some base in France or Italy or Spain or Portugal, stay there, and explore the surrounding terrain as thoroughly as possible in search of what could be found growing or spotted flying; each day brought its adventure with, at noon, a picnic lunch of local cheese, local wine, newly baked bread, fresh butter and chosen salami.

To be a holiday naturalist is to be free for the time being of the introspective self that can fret an artist so continuously. In Australia the excitement was enhanced, for what was to be found was relatively strange and exotic. Sometimes in Perth we would get up early and, equipped with bird glasses and bird book, motor to some lake or into the bush, and sit motionless awaiting the jewel in flight we could spot and identify. Bird watching has some kinship with gambling; you may strike lucky or, if you do not, there is always the future hope. Moreover there is the added pleasure of gradually absorbing the beauty of the setting where you wait, becoming yourself part of the natural surround—a satisfaction I imagine a fisherman derives, even when he has caught no fish.

We were lucky to make friends with an ornithologist and his wife. I remember the first bird that they showed us, on Bibra Lake, was a Musk Duck, making its way from bank to bank by throwing out jets of water on each side, using its feet to give a back kick. The brilliantly blue Wrens, the Willy Wagtails, the Mudlarks, the Honey-eaters, the Parrots, the Laughing Kookaburras, these and many others so familiar to the inhabitants were totally new to us in appearance—and in sound too. For the first two or three nights I had been worried by what sounded like the whining of a puppy coming from next door. As this house was shut up I made enquiries and learnt that the prolonged whimpering came from the common Western Magpies who used to perch on the telephone wires along the road.

Musical activity in Perth is mostly shared between the Broadcasting Station and the Music Department of the University. The latter is lucky, at the time I am writing, in having as its head, Professor Frank Callaway, a forceful and enthusiastic pioneer with a marked gift for organisation. I spent many hours of pleasure in that University rehearsing performances of my chamber and vocal works.

Two thousand miles away, in Sydney, a British Fortnight had been arranged, and in connection with this the British Council had planned four concerts. I had been invited to conduct the first (a chamber orchestral one) with the Sydney Little Symphony Orchestra.

As I sat in the plane, flying from Perth to Sydney, the extent and strangeness of this enormous country was dramatically made evident; below me hour after hour stretched the Nullarbor Plain, monotonously barren, bisected only by what looked like a rough dirt track. Accustomed in Europe to having engagements within easy reach, I had to accept here, as in Russia, a new yardstick of distance. The Australian is of course so used to it that moving from one city to another is to him no more than a bus ride.

At Sydney I was immediately immersed in rehearsals. I had put in the programme my own *Knot of Riddles* and *Music for Strings*, together with works by Purcell, Vaughan Williams and Britten. John Shirley-Quirk had flown out from England to sing the first of these pieces, and was later joined by the harpsichordist, George Malcolm, for subsequent recitals.

My concert duly took place in the Conservatorium, and I was much amused to read in one of the press notices that 'The Master of the Queen's Musick (as is only appropriate) prefaced the concert with one of the noblest performances of *God Save the Queen* that I have ever heard'.

My experiences in Sydney and events there are told through my letters back to Trudy in Perth.

*Australia Hotel, Sydney*
*September 23rd 1964—about drink time, 5.45 p.m.*
I had a very easy run to Adelaide—one more breakfast and lunch—pushing the watch on two hours.

At Adelaide the young members of the ABC staff, on the look out for a German pianist, collared me (they knew me from the pianist!) and saw me on to the plane for Sydney.

227

This hotel is a good one: my room is on the 9th (the top) floor, is air-conditioned and quiet, with an outsized bathroom. The first rehearsal this morning went well, and an atmosphere of friendliness secured. Social engagements pile up, but these are not onerous, and I shall insist on getting to bed early each night. It is a glorious day, bluest of skies and rather warmer than in Perth. I go to dinner this evening with Jack Woodbridge, the Manager of the Australasian Performing Right Association, and George Cooper, of Boosey & Hawkes, who sent us 'The floral mile' when we first arrived in Perth.

*Australia Hotel, Sydney*
*September 25th 1964*

The days are very full here. I've seen nothing of Sydney, which, except for the harbour and new Opera House (glimpsed from a car) seems like any big crowded city. I give this hotel full marks for efficiency. I found on the first night that my door rattled; next morning early a carpenter turned up and dealt with it. Handkerchiefs, socks, etc. sent to the hotel laundry this morning, turned up done, three hours later!

Every morning at 9.30 a car calls for me, whisks me away to the rehearsal room, an empty cinema some six miles away, and brings me back to lunch either here or with one of the ABC staff.

I slack about in the afternoon, except when I have a second rehearsal. Each evening I am a guest out somewhere.

The concert to-morrow should go well; Mrs. Mewton-Wood phoned me, and is coming to the final rehearsal to-morrow. On Sunday Jack Woodbridge is going to motor me to Canberra, where I shall stay the night, returning next morning. It will be good to get out of 'conditioned air' into the real thing. I envied you your bird vigil on Applecross Hill; I haven't seen a single thing with wings yet, but the glasses may show me something on Sunday.

*Australia Hotel, Sydney*
*September 26th 1964*

I came back from the final rehearsal this morning at the Conservatorium to find your telegram—most cheering! I also received 'best of luck' message from our London ex-mounted policeman friend. He has a Stall in the British Exhibition here, and has asked me to visit it.—Unfortunately, no time. Presently I shall have a bath, change, have my customary pre-concert omelette and half a bottle of white wine in my room, and proceed to the Conservatorium. It would be wonderful if you could pick up a few strains: I hope it is earlier in your evening, not later.

The concert last night was successful, all good performances from these excellent players. I await reviews, and as I shook hands with all the critics at a party afterwards, they should be pleasant ones!

Mr. & Mrs. Woodbridge motored me here this morning in their Chevrolet—some two hundred miles. He is a great big bluff Australian, who looks every inch a Senator, and I think is generally mistaken for one. His real enthusiasm is *his* farm and *his* breed of cattle, and he much amused me en route by his scathing remarks on all the cattle we saw, and the badly cared-for condition of the land, compared with his own.

We passed a huge lake, I think Lake George, which Woodbridge told me sprang up suddenly overnight and flooded the fields, drowning all the animals: telegraph posts and two windmills stick out of the water. He said the aborigines had predicted this would happen and say that in no distant future the water will all disappear again.

Another excellent hotel here; I have eaten a John Dory fish— delicious! I fly to Brisbane on Tuesday.


From Sydney I flew to Brisbane for two concerts. I had boldly suggested that the Queensland State and Municipal Choir with the Queensland Symphony Orchestra should rehearse the difficult *Beatitudes* for my visit. For months before I had been in communication with Alfred Grice, conductor of this chorus, and had realised how wholeheartedly he was working at my music, and what hours of practice his singers were putting in under his direction.

At the first concert I was to give my *Colour Symphony*, sharing the programme with the resident conductor, the Czech maestro Rudolph Pekarek, who had meticulously prepared my work; at the second *The Beatitudes* were to be performed. I was a trifle nervous about bringing this off successfully, but I need not have worried. All choruses are very much alike, a bit nervous and tentative at the first rehearsal when they meet a new conductor, especially if he is also the composer, and then at the second, when they have summed him up among themselves and agreed to feel confidence in him, sure and co-operative. I had no anxiety over my two soloists, Pearl Berridge and Ronald Dowd, both Australians, so it was an evening of pleasure for me, with Alfred Grice sharing the honours. Here are several of my letters home from Brisbane.

229

It was lovely to be greeted here by your letter posted Sunday—but where are *my* letters? This is the fifth that I have written to Money Road, and do want you to know that I am well and splendidly looked after. Of course it is a bit strenuous. I descended this morning from the air into a bevy of television and newspaper reporters, but as I glibly repeat all the old gags, it is fairly easy going. A third television unit has just left my bedroom, and another reporter comes at five o'clock! Well, it is the country for that, as Emmie Tillett said. I wish you could share these experiences, the local oysters, for instance, which appear in their dozens on every table. I would treat you handsomely to these!

I have had two good letters from you, one, last night, telling me of the baptism of the new bathing costume in the surf of the Indian Ocean, and the other of your jaunt with Jill. She will long remember going off with her grandmother.

I have now had two rehearsals with the orchestra. The first concert is a Youth Concert, and as in our London Children's Concerts I have been asked to talk to the audience and analyse excerpts first. I rather look forward to it.

Yesterday I was taken to the Lone Pine Koala Sanctuary run by 'the Peter Scott of Brisbane'. Here were some 120 Koala bears, male, female and young living together in the open—absolutely tame. I held two or three of the babies in my arms. Others were perched in the fork of trees sixty or so feet above the ground. These fascinating little marsupials are now preserved in Australia. When the population gets too big, the Director of the reserve takes them off and lets them free among the special gum trees, whose leaves provide both food and drink. It was extraordinary to see him walking among them, take a baby out of a pouch, say 'You know *that's* not your own mother', find the right one, and pop it in again!

I was motored yesterday to the nearest beach, about twenty miles away—not like the fine surf beaches fifty miles off, but a good sea nevertheless. I didn't bathe, but off with shoes and socks, and a walk-about in the water. I saw many ibises, a fairly common bird at this place, Sandgate. I enclose an emu's feather for the girls: I believe it is the only forked one among birds.

The paintings came in the post this morning. I laughed a lot (should I have?). I particularly like Laura's abandoned car, downright emphasising that hopeless outlook so necessary in the modern school of painting, and Patricia's sunflower so classical in feeling, an excellent poster for her later shows. As for Jill's darkly sinister piece —a good name, I think, would be lubra-cation.

The concert went off successfully on Saturday night, followed by a reception given by all the youngsters.

*Lennons,*
*Brisbane*
*October 7th 1964*

Last night I went 'as per protocol' to dinner at Government House: both host and hostess eminently likeable. He knows every foot of this vast state. To-morrow is *my* Civic Reception. What it is to have an old fashioned title!

This morning is like a beautiful English summer day. I put on my tropical suit, and trotted off to the Botanical Gardens—lots of unknown trees and shrubs in flower plus Kookaburras, Mynahs, wagtails, and a bird like a lapwing but with very long thin legs that croaked. I must look him up later.

*Lennons,*
*Brisbane*
*October 8th 1964*

I have just come back from the Civic Reception in the City Hall— a very cosy informal affair, with plenty of the right refreshment, and about a hundred people present. In his speech the Lord Mayor referred to 'the general regret that the gracious Lady Bliss could not be present too'. I applauded vigorously! I have just learnt that after the performance of *The Beatitudes* on the 10th, the sopranos and contraltos are going to give me a life-sized woolly Koala bear especially for Susan. You will know how touched I am by this gesture from the singers.*

On my return to Perth I had one more concert there, enjoyed a final week with my family, and then Trudy and I prepared to fly

* *The Beatitudes* is dedicated to my grand-daughter Susan.

231

to Japan. I relished every day in Australia; I liked the vast country and I liked the people, and I left it with regret. This was greatly mitigated for Trudy and myself by the knowledge that our family in Perth were planning to revisit England in 1966, and spend Christmas with us in London.

If I had been expecting a vision of Japan that corresponded to the description by Lafcadio Hearn, which I had avidly read in the 'twenties, the first glimpse of Tokyo would have disillusioned me straight away. If it is not already, it soon must become the largest and most densely populated of all huge cities, a super-Chicago, with immense push and drive and ruthlessness. Yet, in this seemingly Americanised capital one could still, if one sought it, find much of the traditional Japan of one's dreams. One morning, for instance, my wife and I found ourselves entering a small Shinto Shrine devoted to the worship of the Fox. It was only just off a busy thoroughfare but, in spirit, was many miles away. In the courtyard were numerous stone images of Foxes, each with a scarlet scarf round the neck (to denote divinity?). Worshippers were taking little sweetmeats, laying them in front of their particular image, clapping their hands to attract the Fox's attention, and then bowing and submitting their requests. As one of the attributes of the Fox is business acumen, I joined in a like ceremony, certainly in no derisory spirit, asking the sagacious animal-god to keep an eye on what investments I had, necessarily unwatched, so many thousands of miles away. With a final bow, I departed and it was with some chagrin that on returning to our room and opening the current copy of *The Times* I read that the Stock Exchange had suffered a bad fall. Understandably, the Fox had seen through my pretence and sensed the material go-getter beneath.

We had time to get one other glimpse, in Tokyo, of the Japanese character that persisted behind the façade of modern industrial life. Some private gardens in the heart of the city were opened for a day to visitors, in aid of a relief fund, and Trudy and I were taken on a tour of these. The Japanese are surely unique in their approach to landscape gardening; each of these was small, certainly no larger than the average Londoner's garden in St. John's Wood where we live, but they were so designed as to give the impression of a much larger space; there were small hills, miniature rivers with stepping stones, winding paths; the trees and flowering shrubs were shaped to scale, and there was invariably some surprise to greet us. One garden, for instance, in a high position was so sited as to allow, at one corner, on a clear day, a view of distant Fujiyama.

We found everywhere in Japan the garden treated as a work of art, and the gardeners aiming at perfection. In the magnificent Imperial Gardens at Kyoto we saw as we walked round the lake, overhung with conifers and weeping cherries, a gardener up a ladder, at work on an old pine tree. He was meticulously thinning out tufts of pine needles here and there, so as to realise the most artistic form of the tree. It would take hundreds of gardeners many months to achieve perfection in *all* the trees there; this lonely worker must have felt, as an artist, fully rewarded if he could bring one to its true perfection.

Most magical of all the gardens that we saw in Japan was the famous stone garden of Daisen-in in Kyoto, dating from the first years of the sixteenth century. It is constructed almost entirely of stone and sand. There are large upright rocks that represent steep mountains, from which springs a waterfall of white sand, soon to grow into a river which, flowing over a dam that cannot hold it back, widens into a great sea, a smooth stretch of meticulously raked white sand. At the end of this, in the furthest corner, is planted the only growing ornament, a flowering tree. As the sand river flows it passes many other stones. One group represents the turtle, the symbol to the Japanese of the depths to which the human can sink; another group depicts the crane in flight, the symbol of the aspiring soul. One conspicuous stone floated apart on the white sand, a ship weighty with the joys and sorrows of experience. We were guided through the garden by a monk. He was an ascetic-looking and impressive figure in his robes; in a deep-toned voice he explained how the three joined gardens conformed to the Zen philosophy, and how the forms in stone and sand showed the journey of the soul from birth to final purification, passing on its way through life's tragedies, doubts, dismays until at last it seeks rest at a tree similar to that under which The Buddha died.

If we could have visited the garden in mid-June, we should have seen this Sarasōzyu, the only growing feature in this abstract landscape, in its brief season of bloom. We sat for a long time in the tea-room in the Abbot's quarters looking out, in silence, on to this garden of meditation, feeling its power of refreshment to the spirit.

In Tokyo, the London Symphony Orchestra had already arrived, and were preparing for their eight concerts in Japan under the direction of Istvan Kertesz and Colin Davis: I was due to conduct my *Colour Symphony* and Dances from *Checkmate*.

Tokyo is now one of the busiest musical centres in the world; it has several fine resident orchestras, an enthusiastic young public, and shows an insatiable interest in records of Western music. The concerts were all crowded and at the end of each, a nice courtesy, flowers were presented to the conductor by girls in resplendent kimonos. In my own case, these were handed to me on the stage by two little girls, young enough to be my grandchildren; brilliant as little tropical birds, their solemn self-possession was enchanting.

The whole orchestra travelled to Kyoto in the wonder-train express, which moved smoothly along at a hundred miles an hour. We knew that we should have a view of Mount Fuji on our right, but were told that unless we were particularly fortunate we should not see the white cone which was usually begirt with cloud. But our luck held and, as we sped past, the mists all cleared, the summit was clear, and every camera in the long carriage clicked. I little thought, way back in 1924, when Trudy and I were engaged, and we sat one morning in the Metropolitan Museum of Art in New York looking at the Hokusai views of Fuji, that forty years later we should be seeing the mountain itself, of course through his eyes.

Before going on to Osaka for further concerts Trudy and I, with Colin Davis, had a chance in Kyoto to witness a ceremony of great beauty, the Festival of the Maple Leaf. It took place on the river, which was cut off on one side by a steep wooded wall of rock; the other bank was flat and lined with little booths selling refreshments, much patronised by the crowds waiting to see the procession. Soon distant music was heard (very similar in sound to the Court music of Japan which I heard so often on records in Henry Eichheim's studio in Santa Barbara during 1923) and round the bend in the river came a procession of large flat-bottomed boats, in each of which four young maple trees in leaf were planted. At bow and stern stood two men with long poles who punted the boats along, and seated or standing in each boat were groups of players and dancers. They were all robed in the Heian costumes of the early eleventh century, that is, contemporary with the novels of Murasaki. Indeed, one dignified figure in yellow and black, standing in the foremost boat, could have been Prince Genji himself. The boats passed and repassed to the continual twanging and percussive sounds of the instruments, making a gorgeous kaleidoscope of colours against the green background of the hill. There were diversions as well, comic wrestling on board, jugglers, or fights with dragons that brought ripples of laughter from the hundreds of children watching from the bank, when they could be induced to take the sugar floss, which all seemed to be clutching, from their mouths. Finally the players, dancers and actors came ashore, formed up into a long column, and made their way slowly over the bridge across the river, handing to the bystanders paper maple leaves as a souvenir of this Autumn Festival: we still have ours.

Another episode in Lady Murasaki's novel was called to mind as we drove up the slopes of Mount Hiei. Here at a temple in the trees—so she relates—Prince Genji stayed to worship, seeking solace from the sickness and sorrow that the death of his mistress Yugao had brought to him. What *we* saw that morning on the hill were the monkeys that countless Japanese paintings on silk make familiar; they were chattering in groups as they swung from tree to tree and with them, our Japanese companion told me, 'was their professor' i.e. the zoologist who was compiling a study of their habits.

Trudy and I became very attached to our escort, a member of the staff of the Osaka International Festival, a frail man of middle age whom we felt a day of tumultuous wind might blow away out of sight like a ginko leaf. He spoke excellent English and was widely informed on all the places we were fortunate enough to visit. He told us that his daughter loved playing the clarinet and I managed to send her a copy of my own quintet; in return, as we were leaving Tokyo airport, he suddenly appeared, breathless, clutching a large bottle of săké as a farewell present to us. The success of the Osaka International Festival is largely due to the beneficence of the Nagataka Murayama family, and it is their daughter Michi who acts as artistic director. This family gave the London Symphony Orchestra a lavish farewell luncheon party in their Tokyo garden. Arranged in a semi-circle were booths, behind each of which stood a chef noted for his artistry in the particular delicacies laid out there. These were served on little wooden platters, and were designed to delight the eye as well as the palate! Among them were such unaccustomed titbits as roasted quails on spits, Japanese 'fruits de mer', crab and rice wrapped in seaweed, raw fish of various kinds dipped in sᵛké, chrysanthemum leaves, and other unanalysable dainties. As a final courtesy each conductor was given a beautifully bound book containing candid shots of himself, taken while conducting at the concerts. I looked, shuddered, and resolved to profit by what I saw. I remember Stravinsky showing me pictures of famous conductors while they were conducting his music. 'Look at them,' he would exclaim, '*what* is he doing there?—why *that* gesture?—what does *that* anguished expression mean to an orchestra? He has *only* to ensure that my half notes, quarter notes, eighth notes have their *exact* value, indicate this clearly, and the players will play *what I have written*.' Some conductors, it is well known, have a third eye somewhere in the back of their heads, which keeps an unwinking gaze on the audience's attention and reactions. I just hope that I am not one of them.

Before returning to England Trudy and I determined to see something of Hong Kong and Ceylon; we had friends in both places, and this was an opportunity that was not likely to come again. It was a joy to have no official engagements, no set time-tables and, for the time being, no new people to meet. This was to be a restful holiday, a point of repose before the return to London and the dreaded encounter with three months' post and what that might entail.

As an example of quiet enjoyment, I recall especially a picnic lunch taken by an inlet of the sea in Hong Kong, which we shared with our friends. From where we sat we could see the barbed wire of the frontier and, beyond, the bare rolling hills of China. At that time it certainly looked very peaceful; only a few Chinese, in blue overalls and flat straw sun hats, working quietly in the fields under the limpid blue of the sky and, close at hand, the amah attending to our host's small son. This interlude of relaxation meant more to me than the dramatic scenes and colourful crowds in the streets of Hong Kong or the frenzied bustle of its great international port.

But it was in Ceylon that we got our deepest impression of beauty, beauty both of the people and of all that nature had lavished on this island. We ought to have stayed there for months to get all the new experiences to which we had looked forward. Our Sinhalese friend had, for instance, arranged a stay in the southern nature reserve at Yala, and visits to some of the ruined cities. Alas, we just did not have the time. We spent most of our week in Kandy, staying in a chalet overlooking the lake and Temple of the Tooth. Thanks to our friend we were able to see one of the festivals there, the Deepawali, which takes place during the full moon in November. It may not have been as magnificent as the famous Perahera held in August but it was, perhaps, more moving for not being a great tourist attraction. We were the only Europeans present, and watched in the crowd the gaily caparisoned elephants with gilded tusks, the torch-bearers and whip-crackers, the dancers and drummers and, inside the temple, families of worshippers, with their wreaths of marigolds. An added touch of beauty was provided by the hundreds of coconut oil lamps flickering in rows outside the houses throughout the night.

From Kandy we motored up to Nuwara Eliya, and spent a day among the hills with their gift of magnificent views. We returned late to our chalet, but before we were allowed home our driver wanted us to see—and indeed to see himself—the reflection of the full moon in the Sacred Lake. We halted there and waited until a cloud that obscured the moon should disperse. When it finally did our driver breathed a deep 'Ah', and remained as if transfixed admiring the beauty. This was just a free bonus he was giving his visitors, and I wondered in what other country one could find a corresponding sensitivity—in Ireland perhaps?

One day our Sinhalese friend took us to the wonderful Peredeniya Gardens, and introduced us to the director there. Trudy took many photos which show some of the beauties—the magnificent avenue of tall palms, the gigantic bamboo groves, the orchid houses, the ochre coloured river in which elephants were bathing, the flying foxes hanging like bunches of fruit from the trees. As the evening drew in they loosened themselves and could be seen flying across the disk of the moon, like so many messengers of Hecate.

Returning for one night in Colombo we were invited, thanks to the British Council representative there, to be present at a private dance ceremony at which the Diploma for Hindu Temple Dances was to be presented to a young Tamil girl. I gathered that this was the first occasion when such a Diploma had been given in Ceylon, all former aspirants having to undergo the long course at Madras. A theatre had been taken and filled with the girl's relatives and friends.

When I was told that I should have to see nearly two hours' dancing by a student, my first thought was that it might test my patience to the utmost. I need not have worried; it was an evening of great beauty. On one side of the stage was a lighted altar, and on the other sat a group of musicians with vínars or sitars, Indian flutes and oboes, and drums. Otherwise the stage was empty except for curtains at the back for the entry and exit of the dancer. I wish I had kept the programme of the sacred dances designed to test her powers. Throughout the evening she dressed in many magnificent saris, gleaming with jewels; the robes dropped to her ankles and her bare feet; every shade of drama was conveyed by movement of the head and eyes, and by expressive use of hands and, especially, fingers. A friend sat alongside us as we watched, and explained the religious myths that she enacted. It was a moving experience, and I felt gladdened and relieved when at the end of this exhausting test she knelt before her teacher and received her Diploma with honour. Though I know nothing of the intricacies of Hindu Temple Dancing, this girl was such an artist that I could not have endured a failure. Later that evening our friend from the British Council took us to dinner with the dancer and her parents. The late resplendent Hindu goddess sat beside me, now a young eager mortal, who prattled away happily about the dancers in our own Royal Ballet.

Trudy and I arrived in London from Colombo in the early hours of November 25th, and I immediately started to clear up the arrears of correspondence that had accumulated. Among the letters was an invitation from the National Book League to present a literary prize to John Masefield on the publication of his last book of poems *Old Raiger and Other Verse*. I had never before met Masefield, so I was able to tell him that I vividly remembered from my Cambridge days a performance of his *Tragedy of Nan*; Moreover I could tell him that as a student I had picked up in the Charing Cross Road a copy of *Reynard the Fox*, started reading it in the tube on the way to Hampstead, where I then had a room, and stood under a street lamp outside the station to finish it, as I could not bear to wait any longer for the denouement.

In his speech of thanks, Masefield used no notes in spite of his age and spoke fluently and eloquently of his past and of the writers he had known. He especially mentioned Hardy whom he particularly admired. At lunch afterwards the talk turned on Mark Twain. I was immediately interested, as my father used to speak of him and greatly enjoyed his dry humour, and I had myself received some years previous a mysterious document from the Clemens Society, appointing me a Knight of King Arthur's Round Table, in succession to Edward Elgar! What duties this entails or what its privileges, if any, amount to I have never been able to find out.

A few days after this meeting Masefield wrote in a short note:

*Barcote Brook,*
*Abingdon*
*December 9th 1964*
... Long ago, I was in the wilderness in Missouri, not far from where Mr. Clemens lived. I came out of a forest into grassy wilderness where two small tents had a big signboard.

> Good air. Good water. Good schools.
> Come and live with us!

My memory is less good than you did me the honour to think, or I should have told this at our lunch.

With my thanks, and all best wishes,

Yours sincerely
JOHN MASEFIELD

With this, came a signed copy of *Old Raiger*, with the inscription 'The days that make us happy make us wise'.

The intention of writing some kind of autobiography lodged in my mind as I was taking part, in 1965, in an hour's television programme devoted to my own life in music. The producer, John Drummond, was an indefatigable perfectionist. It was certainly a good preparation for writing this book. Old photographs had to be sorted out, the past probed in many quizzing interviews, television cameras invaded our house and garden, sessions were held in the BBC studios showing me conducting the London Symphony Orchestra. By the end of the ordeal, though John Drummond lightened it by his enthusiasm and gaiety, I felt years older, and indeed looked it, as the camera showed in the final shots of me as I walked down the little drive back into our house in St. John's Wood.

I admit to being a bad subject for the camera, as I am too for the portrait painter and the sculptor. My temperament demands activity, not a passive role: I only feel myself in action. When I have to sit still or pose, boredom at once creeps over me; an unnatural rigidity, I might say stupidity, settles on my features. This lack of ease may stem from childhood days when my father was insistent on his children being frequently photographed. It then involved posing, with the head held steady by some metallic construction, and enduring a long pause while the photographer counted the necessary seconds of exposure. Knowing how I automatically resist the discipline necessary for a television programme such as this, I think it a triumph for the producer to have got through it at all.

I knew that this autobiography would be a hard task if I had, as indeed was the case, to rely on my memory to recall the far distant past. For the events after my thirty-fourth year, when I married, I could turn for help to Trudy, who has a truly remarkable memory for incidents, places and people that we have met, but the earlier years might prove difficult, and I was determined not to see them through a haze of confused nostalgia. I have many pictures of myself as a child, a boy at school, a young man, and looking at these I cannot help feeling that there has been little real change in my personality, and by that I mean in my likes and dislikes, my admirations and prejudices. As I have written before, I have always been well aware of my own entity, and known how to preserve it, by a not particularly likeable self-assertion as a child and by encasing myself when a boy at school in an outward personality that very rarely gave my inner ideals away.

I soon learnt that preservation of my true self meant adopting for the time being the part that caused me the least expense of mental stress in the company that I was in. I am aware that this is far from the heroic role of the champion who wants to dominate his circle, but it served me well in the tough years at school, and in the tougher years in the Army. It enabled me, when I had endured these, to shake off the experiences that might have greatly affected me, and emerge again for my destined life in music as I truly was.

I suppose no one *really* knows what impression his personality makes on others: it is possible to live in a dream world, and greatly to exaggerate the respect and liking or, conversely, the boredom and dislike which you apparently cause in others. This doubt is magnified when it comes to the consideration of what one has created oneself, be it music, poetry or painting; even the estimate of one's own work varies with mood and time. In certain physical states of health, or happiness of mind, I have rejoiced in the musical work which I have been able to achieve; certain sections make me glow with pleasure; come another day, and a mood of dejection steals over me; those very moments in my music that had made me so happy now seem lifeless and commonplace.

How then is a true measurement to be found for judging what I am and what I have done? To keep a fair balance, then, this auto-biography aims at being mainly factual, showing the kind of life I have led from year to year, and offering a good many letters which, far better than narrative, can make up a composite picture of the writer. These letters are mostly to my wife. But I am an assiduous letter writer, and there must be many thousands of letters that in the course of the last fifty-five years have been despatched to others.

In the spring of 1965 Trudy and I were invited to stay in the island of Sark with the indomitable Dame of Sark. How indomitable she can be may be judged by reading her autobiography, *Sibyl Hathaway, Dame of Sark,* and pondering over the pages where she describes the German occupation of her tiny island during the Second World War, and her resistance to enemy oppression.

It was like returning to my childhood to find, when we landed at the quay, an open victoria drawn by a brown mare, Daisy, and driven by the Constable, awaiting us to take us to La Seigneurie. I had not ridden in such a carriage since the time my father used to go for afternoon rides in Hyde Park, in a brougham, if wet, and in just such a victoria, if fine.

As there was no urgent need for speed on this island, the pro-hibition of cars was no disadvantage whatsoever. The object of our visit was to discuss with the Dame of Sark appropriate music for the service to be given in August to commemorate the four hundredth anniversary of the granting of the Royal Charter to the Island; she had expressed the wish that I should write an Anthem for the occasion.

Many visitors have stayed at the sixteenth-century Seigneurie, and all must have been charmed by this remote little feudal outpost, for feudal it certainly is. Like a hereditary chief the Dame guards the right of the four hundred inhabitants to maintain their own parlia-ment, their own laws and customs. She has her own privileges, jealously preserved. She owns some beautiful white pigeons in her pigeon-cote, for she has the 'droit de Colombier'; she was also followed around by a handsome white poodle—only the Dame is allowed to keep a bitch. It was certainly a unique example of auto-cracy, beneficent, but even so I felt, as a visitor, that non-compliance might mean expulsion!

I could not get about much as I was suffering from a disabled shoulder, so I spent many hours in the grey-walled gardens, but Trudy,

After a concert with the London Symphony Orchestra in Tokyo, 1964

Trudy and myself outside our house in St. John's Wood, London, on my 75th birthday in 1966

*Godfrey MacDomnic*

Barry Glass

Taking a rehearsal, 1967

who loves nothing better than total independence, hired a bicycle and indefatigably toured the island during the four days we were there.

When the August celebration had taken place the Dame kindly sent me a tape-recording of the service. It was interesting to hear the sound of the spoken language, a variation, I believe, of the old Norman French.

During the year 1965 I gave two first performances of works in their completely revised versions, the *Hymn to Apollo* at the Cheltenham Festival in July, and *Discourse for Orchestra* with the London Symphony Orchestra in the Royal Festival Hall in September. It was a year too for 'Occasional Music': a funeral march as homage to Sir Winston Churchill at his death, a military march dedicated to the Scottish War Blinded, and a Ceremonial Prelude for the inauguration of the 900th Anniversary of Westminster Abbey.

But the real event of the year for us was the return of Karen and her family from Australia to spend Christmas at home here. They sailed in the *Oriana* from Fremantle in November, Chris following later by air. Trudy could not wait patiently until they docked at Southampton, but flew out to Naples to meet them and escort them home. The ship was due there early in the morning, and Trudy, too excited to sleep, saw from her bedroom window the lights of the boat as it approached Naples before dawn, and hastened down to the dock. By ill luck it was a pouring wet day and the problem was what to do with the three little girls during their hours on land. The question being put to *them*, they unanimously voted to go for a ride in the street cars. Right out to the suburbs they went in the rain, through far from inspiring streets, and having reached the terminus enjoyed the same long ride back in reverse, reaching the docks just in time to re-embark. I only mention this family outing to point out that for three young Australians, a Neapolitan tram was as novel an excitement as had been, for instance, Trudy's and my ride on an elephant's bare back the year before in Ceylon.

The family from Australia stayed with us till the end of January and they, with my elder daughter's family in London, made Christmas a uniquely festive and happy celebration. I was glad that Karen and Chris, while they were still here, could come to Westminster Abbey on December the twenty-eighth and witness the Service to inaugurate the 900th Anniversary Year.

Music was needed to accompany the Queen from her entry in procession from the Great West Door to the Chapel of Saint Edward, where she was to place upon the Altar of the Shrine her tribute of red roses, and thence to her Stall in Quire. The duration was

241

estimated at eight minutes, and the Dean had invited me to write a special Ceremonial Prelude for this, and conduct it myself. I used the organ and the brass choir of the New Philharmonia Orchestra, which was to play the rest of the music under the direction of Douglas Guest, the Organist and Master of the Choristers of Westminster Abbey. The timing and order of these great ceremonies in the Abbey are always perfectly carried out, and the pageantry was suitably impressive.

# Chapter XXV

# 1966

MY STORY DRAWS TO A close with my seventy-fifth year: a good place to insert the final cadence in the score of my life. I started these reminiscences in May 1966, when Trudy and I were on holiday in Brittany. We chose as our base 'Le Manoir de Stang', an ancient manor house in the small village of La Forêt-Fouesnant, a few miles from Beg-Meil, made famous in literature as the Balbec of Proust's novel. The manor house had a large and beautiful garden, and I sat out in a secluded summer house there, notebook and pencil in hand, waiting for the memories of my early life to flow in. The servants in this guest house wore the traditional 'coiffes'—those of Fouesnant and Pont-Aven are, I believe, the most elaborately devised—and as soon as I saw them, I felt a long-distant past rise up again, and I was back in my father's house in Holland Park. Through the years that we lived there my father had made a collection of etchings, lithographs and oil paintings by Alphonse Legros, and others of his French contemporaries. Among those hanging on the walls in our living-room was a painting of a Breton Pardon, with just such figures as I now saw every day in one village or another in our neighbourhood.

A stream of memories swept into my mind: of my father at his desk in his library, magnifying glass in hand, examining his cherished prints or working at the beautifully printed catalogue of his collection: of the concerts that we three brothers used to get up for him on birthdays or at Christmas time: of our first holidays abroad with him, to Paris, to Montreux, to Lugano, to Venice: of the London theatres he took us to, the vague figures of Sarah Bernhardt, Beerbohm Tree, Laurence Irving, Charles Hawtrey and many others dimly looming up: of the first concerts where I heard Ysaÿe and Carreño. My pencil began to move over the paper, and before I consciously realized it my story had started without further prompting—set going by the sight of the Breton 'coiffe'.

The thought of Beg-Meil and Proust leads me to mention those authors to whom I have for long been specially drawn, who from their wealth of experience or mastery of expression have influenced my thought and character as the years have passed—those whom I read and re-read. The first of these is Dostoevsky, whose *Crime and Punishment* I discovered during my years at Cambridge. I quickly read his three other great novels, *The Idiot*, *The Possessed* and *The Brothers Karamazov*. The impact of these guilt-ridden, demonic, schizophrenic beings on my youthful mind was bound to be tremendous. It was not the saintly figure of a Prince Myshkin or any Alyosha that excited me so much as the cold, ruthless, awe-inspiring personalities of a Rogozhin or Stavrogin; they must have touched hidden springs in my own nature.

From early years Dostoevsky gave me an intense curiosity and sympathetic liking for the Slav mind both in music and in literature; this fascination has never left me. Part of my being feels emotionally very much at home in Dostoevsky's world of luridly lit shadows, or rather has been revealed to me by him. I have often thought that if I had the gift of languages, and could converse fluently with whomsoever I pleased, I should have best enjoyed an evening's talk with a Russian of that time. It certainly would appear more easily possible with a Slav to throw off quickly the conventional covering of customary make-believe, and reach for the time being a more vital reality, whether in doing so we liked each other or not. An enormous slice of life can be swallowed up in chatter of absolutely no consequence, leaving in its wake only a dull depression. Perhaps my evening discussion with this imaginary Russian would have proved illusory, but I have discovered that there *do* exist living Dostoevsky characters, outside the pages of his books.

Most of us read books, unless for purely frivolous motives, for what we can learn about ourselves from their pages. Unconsciously, we say 'But for the Grace of God, there go I' or just, 'There go I'.

My second favourite author is Tchekov, and if I try to analyse why this is so, I find that it is largely due to his loving treatment of 'failures'. There is something boring in reading about the successful man, the man who gets to where he wants to be (by what means?), and is complacently aware of the fact. On the other hand, the lives of those who, through flaws in character, or ill health, or bad luck, or just lack of push, have failed in the ambitions with which they started, can be read with affectionate sympathy. I make no bones about implying that when I read some stories by Tchekov I think 'There go I'; that may be the reason why he is often my companion. I have always found difficulty in reconciling the two sides of my character: one, the wish to create, which I inherit from my mother, and two, the urge to undertake practical tasks, which I owe to my father's example. This dichotomy has never been satisfactorily resolved, and I have often wondered whether the many administrative posts that I have held have not trespassed dangerously on the private domain of the composer. I am aware that many of my musical dreams have never become realities.

It is possible to be cajoled by a friend's enthusiasm into admiring *his* specially admired author, though up to that moment one had felt no urgent wish to get acquainted. When I first met the poet, Robert Nichols, in Bath, in 1927, he was an avowed champion of Goethe, and by continually, in talk and letter, quoting him as the consummate guide to life, he persuaded me to start reading him. Unluckily, I could not read German, and the translation of Goethe's prose works that I got were in almost unrecognisable English; I tried *Werther*, *Wilhelm Meister*, *Dichtung und Wahrheit*, but in vain. Schnabel is said to have made the pronouncement 'An audience has a *right* to be bored'. This was, I fear, too germanically gnomic for me. I abandoned any thought of Goethe, until, on the eve of leaving for America in 1923, a friend gave me G. H. Lewes's biography of him, and for the first time I found myself absorbed in the growth of this man's life from his early years of genius to his maturity as an Olympian sage. There was one mystery in his long career that particularly fascinated me.

How did Goethe, the Privy Councillor, the President of the Chamber, the Administrator of the Ducal Estates and Finances of the Realm in Weimar manage to keep the poet in him intact and alive? Did he enjoy the burden of responsibility? Did the expenditure of time that it entailed even stimulate the poet by making those hours when he could work for himself seem more precious? I was not asking just an academic question, for the hint of the solution could help me in my own problems. There was obviously much to learn from Goethe's apparently serene command of his varied duties, though beneath this I think the real man spoke when he makes Wilhelm Meister bitterly exclaim 'How the man of the world longs, in his distracted life, to preserve the sensibility which the artist must never abandon, if his plans to achieve a lasting work of art are to come to anything!'

The last famous name in literature to whom I owe special gratitude is Henry James. I cannot identify myself with any of his characters as I can with those of Dostoevsky. I look at them, almost indifferently, from outside—nor have I learnt any particularly valuable lesson about how to conduct my own life from the way his men and women conduct theirs. My pleasure in his last great novels is purely an aesthetic one; I delight in his mastery of form. I do not know whether music meant anything to Henry James, or whether there is evidence that he ever went to a concert, but in *The Ambassadors*, *The Golden Bowl*, and *The Wings of the Dove* he achieves the architectural grandeur of great symphonies. And as in great symphonies, they have to be re-experienced again and again before that grandeur is fully realised. Little touches of imagery, minute symbols that appear early on in these novels are seen, like musical themes and phrases, to assume great significance as one reads on; they develop, modulate, throw out variations, grow in crescendos to the planned climax. These novels should especially appeal, I think, to composers, for a major difficulty is always to channel the fluid stuff of sound into a formal mould. Henry James appears to have chosen each word with precision. I like that. I am told by pupils of Nadia Boulanger that in her composition classes she insists on the importance of each note. I like that too.

Haphazard methods, whether an improvisation or the use of the aleatory method, do not for long interest me. I prefer the creed stated in a poem by Robert Frost—a whole aesthetic in eleven words.

> Let Chaos Storm!
> Let cloud shapes swarm!
> I wait for form.


I find it strange to realise that I have lived for seventy-five years. They have, in retrospect, passed so quickly, and time has a habit of accelerating as one grows older; old age is here before one is aware of its stealthy approach. Do I feel my full weight of years? I cannot say that I do, though I have to admit that there are adventurous invitations to conduct abroad, which I now hesitate to accept because of the strain involved; also, every night in London there are exciting concerts somewhere, many of which ten years ago I should have eagerly gone to hear, but nowadays miss by staying at home.

It is true too that I find my ability to concentrate is now less, and my joy in writing music on the wane. It is only natural, having lived a strenuous life, to feel the machine, which has upheld me so well, gradually slow down; but I certainly do not feel old age dragging at my heels. I felt indeed positively youthful on August 2nd 1966, when I celebrated my seventy-fifth birthday; perhaps that rejuvenation was accentuated by the exuberantly fine performance that John Ogdon gave of my Piano Concerto at the Promenade Concert that night, and by the kind reception of my birthday by friends both here and abroad.

As I have written in my Foreword, I feel that there is one damaging hiatus in these memoirs of mine, in that I have not paid any tribute to many close friends, both in the musical world and outside, who have made my life so varied and colourful. I knew when I started this book that I had a problem to solve here. I resolved to do without the clang of famous names, many of whom I was bound to encounter in my public life, since they were but passing figures, and would, when we parted, have no more regarded me than I them. But what about the musicians with whom I have made music or the staunch friends from early years? I beg their forgiveness for the omission, and can only plead in extenuation that this book started with the quite selfish intention of writing down what I wanted to say about *myself*, my intimate family and the few who, in one way or another, determined my musical future.

Enthusiasms felt in boyhood are apt to return with renewed force in later life. A short while ago I went to hear a performance of Beethoven's Ninth Symphony; I had not heard it for very many years and, as of old, I found myself wholly possessed by its power. Beethoven's vision of an ideal world proffers a ruthless yard-stick with which to judge the multiple impulses that lie behind the *isms* and *ologies* of our own musical era. Much of our contemporary music does indeed protest both against the obsessive weight of the musical past and against the conditions imprisoning humanity today, but only a few works seem to me to offer any panacea.

*All* Beethoven's music is a continual protest against the cruelty, misery and evil in this world, but he *does*, after a lifetime's struggle, supply an answer in the music of his last period, envisaging a world of compassion and serenity. I believe that through whatever changes and transformations music is passing it must unswervingly keep its idealistic aim; otherwise, it may cease to retain its mysterious power of healing and of giving joy, and just dwindle into an excitant aural sensation, and nothing more.

Tragic experiences in life are the lot of everyone, and our own family has not been spared. The odds against happiness can be so menacingly and terribly weighted that I doubt whether I would wish to be born again. But in this one life of mine—and I am conscious of speaking as one of a tiny minority of mankind—I have had much to be grateful for. I had the father that I could have wished, and I have the wife and two daughters that I could have wished. Grandchildren live to carry forward the link from me to the future, and fortune has permitted me to work at what I best love, music.

# Appendix A

*( see page 61 )*

# What Modern Composition Is Aiming At

*A paper read to the Society of Women Musicans
on July 2nd 1921
by Arthur Bliss*

At any given period in the course of musical history you can witness the spectacle of two distinct and antagonistic parties operating one against the other. Seldom has there been a time when there has not been a dispute worth contesting; if there has been a respite, it is only because there has been no music worth fighting about, and as soon as a new champion comes into the field the battle rages again with undiminished force, generally indulged in by musicians, and laymen alike. The fighters on each side have had the same banners, the same passwords, and the same weapons; they possess certain characteristics which serve to distinguish them. Ranged on the one side are those whose ideals and traditions have already passed safely into history; they may have had to contest them in their youth, but as soon as their views were accepted as established laws, all they had to do was to tighten their grasp on them with a view to developing them to their logical conclusion. Most of them were probably born at the end of an epoch, during which some new trend of thought had been sifted and probed, broadened and enlarged to the fullest possibility. Their sole aim now is to make use of that stable popularised structure as a prop for the expression of their own personalities They may not be old in years; in fact, there are many young folk among them.

Facing them in this Homeric struggle are those whose temperament reacts against well-worn formulas and existing traditions, and who descry in most of the music of the day the threadbare clichés of some dead master's achievements served up anew. They may not be very young; in fact, there is generally a sprinkling of grey hairs on this side.

It is always cheerful to think that the age in which we live scintillates above all others, towers in genius and talent over the years that have gone. We are, perhaps, too near the achievements of our own time to view them in their proper perspective, but assuredly this is an exceptional era, containing many great names on both sides, comprising those who are closing an epoch as well as those who are opening a new one. Both are equally important in the growth of sound, but as the subject of this paper restricts me to future developments in music, I will pass to a brief survey of the latter.

Gaze round Europe and cast a glance on those who are in the forefront of the new development; look not at America, for she brings in little. In Italy two potent forces have arisen, in the persons of Casella and Malipiero. Both are men whose thoughts soar futurewards. To those, who sickened under the fear that Italian opera is summed up in *The Girl of the Golden West*, the *Sette Canzoni* of Malipiero must come as a healing medicine. These bear the sub-title 'dramatic expressions' and are composed of seven alternately tragic and comic scenes, based on short dramatic incidents where the action is reduced to the mere element of contrast, contrast of environment, of character, of mood. They follow each other without interruption, with an easy change of scenery. Hating the operatic style of singing, he has expressed himself through a medium of absolute simplicity, and he is directly opposed to the commonplaces and paddings of the conventional drama.

Casella, some of whose works have been heard in England, notably *Le Couvent sur l'eau*, is an experimentalist in technique, daring and certain, who, along with Tommasini and Respighi, is a very active member of the Italian musical community. These latter two are chiefly known to the English public by their respective orchestral treatments of the Scarlatti and Rossini ballets.

In France Ravel stands apart by himself, the reincarnation of the seventeenth-century spirit under a modern habit, combining as he does an audacious harmonic scheme with classic clarity of style.

Behind him move the so-called 'Group of Six', who indeed, pretend to react against what they term Ravel's over-refinement, but who pay him often the compliment of imitation. They have been treated somewhat unjustly over here I think, being judged on their group output rather than on their several individual efforts. Personally, I think Milhaud and Honegger the most promising. Both have written much, both have healthy imagination and technical equipment, and both are too far removed temperamentally from the enervating Parisian Salon to deteriorate into fashionable jokers. But whatever be our personal opinion, the Six truly stand as a body for vitality and simplicity in music, and express hatred of the humbug and pomposity attributable to their neighbours across the Rhine.

In England many names shine forth, of which the most conspicuous are Vaughan Williams, Holst, Goossens, Bax, Ireland, and Berners. One of our national characteristics is the distrust of musical cliques; we do not band together mutually to protect common musical ideals, and in some ways this disunion is a healthy sign. Such an alliance as the invincible band of Russia or the Parisian Six is foreign to our nature, with the result that every side of musical progress is represented here. Vaughan Williams, with his strong adherence to modal counterpoint, and love of national folk song, is in direct communion with Purcell, as Ravel is with Couperin. Holst the mystic, Bax the romantic, Ireland the rugged, Goossens the exquisite, Berners, the satirist, all add their quota to the stream of national music that looks like flowing with nobler current than that of any other country.

In Spain we have de Falla, with his sincere portrayal of Andalusian melodies and rhythms, and his individual orchestral colouring, sufficient to grant him a special niche in the European movement.

In Budapest there is Bartók, in Amsterdam, Schoenberg. We have not had a chance to estimate the value of these two men; except for the *Five Orchestral Pieces* we know little of Schoenberg's later developments. These certainly made a deep impression by their almost brutal frankness, and raised him high above the composer of the Chamber Symphony and String Sextet, both of which works show only too plainly the intransigent professor.

Finally, we come to Russia, the birthplace of the most remarkable musician of the time, Stravinsky. The composer of *Petrouchka, Le Sacre du Printemps*, and *Rossignol* is too well-known over here to need any description from me, and keener pens than mine have written dissertations on his methods. I take my hat off to him and to the others whose names I have mentioned, not only for what they have created, but also for what they have killed, for their effective exposure of pretentious melodies, as well as for their contribution to the world's musical wealth.

Let us take toll of some of their victims.

1. The oratorio composed especially for the provincial festival on the lines laid down by the Dean and Chapter.

2. The symphonic poem à la Strauss, with a soul sorely perplexed, but finally achieving freedom, not without much perspiring pathos.

3. The pseudo-intellectuality of the Brahms' camp followers, with their classical sonatas and concertos, and variations, and other 'stock-in-trade'.

4. The overpowering grand opera with its frothing Wotans and stupid King Marks.

Give me such works as *Le Sacre du Printemps*, *L'Histoire du Soldat*, the *Sea Symphony* and *Savitri*, *The Eternal Rhythm* and *The Garden of Fand*, the Ravel Trio and de Falla's *Vida Breve*, *L'Heure Espagnole* and the *Five Pieces* of Schoenberg, and you can have all your Strauss *Domestic* and *Alpine* symphonies, your Scriabin poems of Earth, Fire and Water, your Schreker, your Bruckner, and your Mahler.

You may ask what constitutes this new development; is there any sign by which we can see it? And any criterion by which we can judge it? Tread softly! We are on dangerous ground; every composer has his own particular fetish, his own plan of attack and defence against the other side. I can but tentatively throw out some general hints; we can, for instance, say that the majority are continually striving towards a state of simplicity. It is not that the musical mind is becoming less subtle, but that, in translating thought into terms of sound, the mode of expression arrived at is a far more direct one.

There is abroad amongst them now a hatred of padding, a contempt of laborious super texture; they are, in other words, anti-Mahlerites. I fear I cannot say a good word of German music; it is to me anathema, not because it is Teutonic, but because to my mind it is at the same time ponderous and trivial, or, in the jargon of present-day science, boundless, yet finite.

This desire for simplicity assumes many forms; Vaughan Williams, for instance, prunes his work until it is reduced to the most concentrated essence of expression. He never makes a pompous remark, and he seldom utters a redundant statement. Holst, again, even with an imagination that likes a large canvas, in his mature work, avoids an over-elaboration. His score of *Savitri*, a drama on the great subject of love's triumph over Death, consists of three singing parts, an orchestra of twelve, reinforced by a small female chorus, and takes but half an hour to perform. He has painted a poignant scene with the fewest possible strokes, and the very simplicity carries with it an overwhelming conviction. So many contemporary composers, if they had the necessary breath, would preach 'Down with the type of music that Strauss upholds in his *Tod und Verklärung*, down with his doping of the uncultured with a mighty subject, and then feeding them with a sentimental and pretentious hymn-tune.' Rather would we have the other extreme, Milhaud's tangos in *Le Boeuf sur le toit*, and Stravinsky's three clarinets in *Les berceuses du chat*. Let the latter speak for himself and others on this subject of simplicity: 'I want neither to suggest situations nor emotions,' he says, 'but simply to manifest, to express them. Though I find it extremely hard to do so, I always aim at straightforward expression in its simplest form. I have no use

251

for working out in dramatic or lyric music. The one essential is to feel and to express one's feelings.' There you have in a nutshell the profession of faith of many on this subject of elimination of all but the essential—straightforward expression in its simplest form—feel and express your feelings!

With this clear inspired goal in view they do not bother with 'metaphysical preoccupations, with emotional hysteria, with pseudo-intellectual effusion'. They are determined to set a stern face against extra-musical associations. Stravinsky sums up his sound theories with one gigantic conception of *Le Sacre du Printemps*. Let it be judged as an aural sensation alone. Listen to it, if you can, unprejudiced. 'I appeal,' I am sure he would say, 'not to the professional, steeped in music, but to the man who can come to listen with his imagination awake, and his other faculties in subjection.' It is the child to whom the work makes the strongest appeal, who is attracted at once by the simplicity of its message, and the convincing sincerity with which that message is conveyed. I am afraid the fine ladies whom I see applauding it so vigorously have neither the one nor the other characteristic, but only find in it a sensation all the more delicious for being totally incomprehensible. While I am on the subject of this work, let me remind you it was written in 1912–13. It is, therefore, eight or nine years old. The magnitude of it will be more readily grasped if you can bring yourselves to reflect for a moment on most of the other works written at the same time by contemporaries. The other day, I believe, a learned professor actually hotly debated whether fifths should still be licensed or not, and often I hear the whole-tone scale discussed as if it were a pheno-menon remarkable and daring, whose continuance threatened the actual existence of composition. Poor Debussy, with whom alone that scale is to be associated, is dead, and to spend time on either of these two chestnuts is as reprehensible as to debate with Einstein as to whether Isaac Newton be not the most daring figure in contemporary science. The general mental attitude of the day, which, as I have said, is to condemn musical camouflage and dope, and to aim at sincerity and simplicity, reacts immediately on the technique of the composer.

The concentrated directness of thought is allied to an equally direct and forcible method of expression. There are several indications of this attitude. Firstly, with regard to the orchestra, there has arisen a keen desire to investigate more fully the individual timbre of each instrument, to explore its most extensive expressive capacity. Again, it is Stravinsky who has been the pioneer, although Holst and Goossens in England, and Milhaud in France, have explored the tendency. As an example of this 'particularisation' recall the opening of *Le Sacre*, where Stravinsky gives the long initial phrase to the bassoon, in spite of the extreme high register in which it has to be played. The peculiar timbre obtained plants one as immediately in the atmosphere intended, as does the opening sentence in *Hamlet*: 'Who's there?—Nay, answer me; stand and unfold yourself.' There is no preamble, you are in it, or, as his detractors affirm, *in for it*.

The custom of the moderns to make the instruments function in the most independent way possible has given rise in late years to the growth of the chamber orchestra, an orchestra of 10 or 12 players, shall we say, all soloists, in the texture of whose ensemble the particular timbres stand out like coloured threads in a variegated carpet. Great sonorities of tone can be obtained by the judicious use of a few instruments, and the concerted effort produces a richness and diversity impossible to obtain with the old method of treatment.

Stravinsky's *Ragtime*, which I performed several years ago at the Aeolian Hall, is scored for two violins, viola, bass, flute, clarinet, horn, cornet, trombone, percussion and cymbalum. His *Pribaoutki* is scored for voice and eight instruments, his suite from *L'Histoire du Soldat* for seven—violin, double-bass, clarinet, bassoon, cornet, trombone, and percussion. Both these works were presented by M. Ansermet last summer at the Wigmore Hall and the sonorities obtained were remarkable. Relatively speaking, Mahler's last symphony, with its required 1,000 performers, is a confused mezzo-forte. Of course, all those who are using the chamber orchestra do not make their various instruments balance, as, for instance, the four strings of a quartet. How can a trombone balance a violin? The idea of the instrumental groups in the classical orchestra is done away with, and the composer uses instruments that are widely incongruous in sound and dynamic value, just as Wyndham Lewis, Wadsworth, or the Nash Brothers create a picture with tones that are varying in density. This preoccupation with the timbre of instruments and the resulting mass-sonority obtained by the combination of them has brought two phenomena in its wake.

Our old friend 'abstract music' has cropped up again. We are tired of music that can only be appreciated by having a knowledge of the philosophic association which envelops it. Must I bring in Nietzsche to save the face of Strauss? Music has nothing in common with other arts. It stands aloof and mysterious. It can no more convey a philosophic truth or literary epigram than could Schopenhauer play the double-bass, or Wilde (Shaw, I almost said) deliver a musical criticism. Walter Pater was searchingly exact when he prefaced his essay, *The School of Giorgione*, with the words 'It is the mistake of much popular criticism to regard poetry, music and painting as but translations into different languages of one and the same fixed quantity of imaginative thought, supplemented by certain technical qualities of colour in painting, of sound in music, of rhythmical words in poetry. A clear appreciation of the opposite principle—that the sensuous material of each art brings with it a special phase or quality of beauty, untranslatable into the forms of any other, an order of impressions distinct in kind, is the beginning of all true aesthetic criticism.'

To the consequent ridding of sound of all its obligations to non-musical elements, this study of timbre and mass-sonority has largely contributed. We have been too long distracted with bygone associations. If we hear a phrase we are at once on the *qui vive* for its rhetorical development. We are so prejudiced that we cannot truly listen with the pure emotion evoked by sound alone. Debussy was right when he exclaimed 'Give me the note of the shepherd's pipe'. What is the use of sitting in a chair over a score and pretending that because you can inwardly hear the tune and general harmonic basis of it, being, thank God, an educated musician, you are realising the composer's intention, and extracting a more pleasurable excitement thereby than if you sit in a concert hall and actually drink in the resulting sound with your ears? With abstract music it is all tom-foolery. Crouch in front of a pêche Melba and see how far imagination and gastronomic associations carry you. Contemplation of still life is placidly pleasant, but ask Tantalus his feelings when the horn of plenty is actually within his reach. Similarly, perusal of non-abstract music like Max Reger's might conceivably while away ten minutes, but to study a Stravinsky score except from a technical curiosity is to display an abysmal ignorance of the very source of its inspiration. We are entering an age where emotion in music will be studied by the purely musical. When next Ansermet plays the Stravinsky symphony for wind instruments, I beg of you all to go with minds lightened of any past prejudices, and try to listen to the sound en masse, a symphony, in fact, as Leigh Henry puts it, conceived as an orchestral entity moulded in sound substance.

One more point and I have finished. I have tried to show that we are reaching an age of simplicity and vitality in expression, and that the very sincerity of our emotion has driven out all the tendencies culled from other arts, which serve only to obscure the issue of music—an issue wrapped in the word sound, and sound only.

Lastly, I want to dwell on an evolution in music that derives its source from these two movements—an evolution which emerges as a distrust of all existing sound combinations. If I am to judge by my ears alone—do I like the result obtained from a violin and a piano, from a piano and full orchestra, from two violins, viola and cello? Have we got so fixed, like flies in treacle, that we cannot revise our impressions in this direction? I ask you to bring this point, amongst others, to the forefront in the ensuing discussion. Do you not think that the Holst songs with violin alone, the proposed Quartet of Stravinsky for three violins and bass, Milhaud's Sonata for violins and piano, Bax's Trio for flute, viola, and harp, are not very definite steps in the required direction? The advent of the pianola, again, brings a most capable and original recruit into our army of sound. It is, of course, no converted or developed form of piano, but an entirely new sound-producing mechanism, more adapted for the unequal battle with full orchestra than any piano could be. We live in rapidly moving times—many mentalities are at work who are not afraid to experiment, who are desperately anxious for progress, as contrasted with growth, a subtle distinction that Edwin Evans has enlarged on. Do not be led away by vapid phrases like 'music of the future', 'ultra-modern developments', and such like. That talk springs from the fountain of fear. The progress I have described is a contemporary one, is bang in the midst of us. It is those who dub it futurist who are themselves clinging desperately to the past. Some musicians I meet are contemporaries of our Victorian grandfathers. It always remains a mystery to me why they will entrust themselves whole-heartedly to the taxi, the aeroplane, the tube, and the telephone—all products of our time—and yet in music shrink back.

# Appendix B

*Morning Heroes* was written as a tribute to my brother and all my other comrades-in-arms who fell in the Great War of 1914–18. Each of its five movements describes an aspect of war common to all ages and to all times.

The first movement, which is spoken by the orator against a background of music, portrays the poignancy of the farewell between husband and wife in wartime. For a famous example I have taken the passage from Homer's *Iliad*, in which Hector bids good-bye to his wife, Andromache, and to his little son. The three of them are on the ramparts of Troy, and Hector and Andromache speak their last words to each other before he goes down into the plains to fight Achilles and, as we know, to be killed by him.

In the second movement 'The City Arming' I have tried to recall the spirit of devotion and self-sacrifice in which in August 1914 the many thousands volunteered for active service. These were later to be known as 'The First Hundred Thousand'. The large majority belonged to my own generation. Few survived and hence the name 'The lost generation'. The nearest parallel I could find was in a poem by Walt Whitman describing the spirit of New York at the outbreak of the American Civil War in 1861.

The third movement is in two parts; the first depicts the thoughts and emotions of a young wife left alone, the second the thoughts and dreams of a young soldier far from home. Women's voices first sing of a Chinese girl embroidering her cushion of white silk. As she pricks her finger and a drop of blood falls on the silk, tears fill her eyes: she visualises her husband perhaps wounded on the icy battlefield. This poem is over 1,200 years old, but its emotion seems to me just as real and true today. The men then sing of the soldier on watch and how his thoughts stray to his home and those he loves there.

In the fourth movement the subject is heroism in battle, and I have chosen Achilles as the classical example of manly courage. He is pictured arming himself to avenge the death of his friend and comrade, Patroclus. At the end of this movement the chorus declaims a roll-call of heroes chosen from both sides, Greeks as well as Trojans. It would be easy for everyone to put contemporary names to these.

The last movement deals with the 1914–18 war and specifically with the Battle of the Somme in which my brother fell. The orator first speaks a poem by Wilfred Owen, which in moving words tells of the young soldier as he waits for the signal to advance into 'No man's land' against the enemy barrage. Finally the chorus sing a poem by Robert Nichols in which, as the sun rises over the 'scarred plateau' of the Somme, the words 'Morning Heroes' occur, from which this Symphony takes its title.

# Index

259

67, 71–2, 73–5, 78, 94, 145, 146, 229, 233; Concerto for pianoforte, tenor voice, strings, percussion, 66; *Conversations* (quintet), 60–1; Coventry Cathedral, opening of the new, *see Beatitudes*, above; Diaghilev, work scored for, 60; *Discourse for Orchestra*, 241; *Fanfares*, 161; Fanfare for Enid Bliss's own use, 193; *Fanfare for Heroes*, 159; Feeney Trust commission, *see Meditations on a Theme by John Blow*; *Golden Cantata*, 218–24; *Greetings to a City*, for American Wind Symphony Orchestra of Pittsburgh, 211–12; *Hymn to Apollo*, 90, 241; instrumental transcriptions of Sinding's *Fire Dance* for T. Karsavina, 67; *Introduction and Allegro*, 145, 146; dedicated to Stokowski, 90; *Kenilworth*, test piece for Crystal Palace Festival, 111; *Knot of Riddles*, song cycle, 213, 227; *Lady of Shalott* (ballet), 206, 207; Lyric, Hammersmith, chamber orchestral concerts for, 1919, 54; *Madam Noy*, 54, 55; *Mary of Magdala*, cantata, 93, 206, 213–14; *Meditations on a Theme by John Blow*, 194–5, 216; *Mêlée Fantasque*, 67, 68, 70; *Memorial Concert* (drama), with Trudy Bliss, 164; *Men of Two Worlds*, film music for, 168; *Miracle in the Gorbals* (ballet), 166; *Morning Heroes*, 17, 18, 19, 93, 96, 97, 157, 210, 256–7; *Music for Strings*, 108–9, 117, 227; Oboe quintet, written for Leon Goossens, 91–2, 143; *The Olympians*, opera, 152, 168, 170–82; *Pastoral*, dedicated to Elgar, 93–4; Piano concerto, for Solomon, 119–121, 169; Piano quartet, 23–4, 46–7, 53, 56–7; Piano sonata for Mewton-Wood: setting to elegiac sonnet for Mewton-Wood, 192; poems set to music: de la Mare's, 70; Hardy's, 85; Li-Po's, *see Woman of Yueh*; Kathleen Raine's, *see Golden Cantata*; *Music for Seven American poems*, 126, 145; *Rhapsody*, 54, 55–6, 66, 71; *Rout*, 59, 66, 72; *Scena* for Kathleen Ferrier, 191; *Serenade for Baritone and Orchestra*, 95–6; 'Street comes into the Room' (plans for a revue), 68; String quartet, 1915, 46–7, 53; String quartet, for Griller Quartet, 1950, 186; *Studies for Orchestra*, 65, 66; *Tempest, The*, music for, 63, 64, 71; *Things to Come*, film music, 137, 145, 157, 161; *Tobias and the Angel*, opera for television, 206, 207–8; Viola concerto, for Campoli, 193–194; Violin sonata, 101, 102, 146, 184; War Blinded, Scottish, military march dedicated to, 241; Westminster Abbey, 900th Anniversary, Ceremonial Prelude

for, 241; Sir Winston Churchill, funeral march as homage to, 241; *Woman of Yueh*, for voice and chamber ensemble (to poems of Li-Po), 78

Bliss, Barbara, A.B.'s elder daughter, 89, 133, 136, 137, 140, 141, 142, 144, 145, 147, 152, 153, 154, 155, 156, 160, 162, 193; at R.A.D.A., 165; in W.R.N.S., 165; marriage of, 165; *see* Gatehouse, Barbara and Richard

Bliss, Enid, A.B.'s half-sister, 76, 193

Bliss, Ethel, A.B.'s step-mother, 48, 193

Bliss, Francis Edward, A.B.'s father, 15, 16, 17; background of (New England), 17; learns of Kennard's death, 41; remarries, 48; moves to the U.S.A. in 1923, 76; as collector, 243; death of, March 1930, 100

Bliss, Howard, A.B.'s brother, 14, 16, 26–27, 32, 41, 51, 52, 54, 76, 79; friendship with Thomas Hardy, 85

Bliss, Eleanor Karen, A.B.'s younger daughter, 89, 100, 133, 136, 137, 140, 141, 142, 144, 147, 156, 158, 225, 241–2; ballet training, 152, 185; in Sadler's Wells Ballet Company, 165, 193; marriage of, birth of children, 212–13; in Australia, 212–13; visit to, in Australia, 225–32; holidaying in England, 1965, 241–2; *see* Sellick, Christopher

Bliss, Kennard, A.B.'s brother, 20, 210–11; acting in *The Tempest*, 30; as poet, painter, musician, 45; in the First World War, 32 seqq.; in 134th Brigade, R.F.A., 36; killed on 28th September 1916, 41, 257; A.B.'s last meeting with described, 42; letters from, to his brothers, 42–4

Bliss, Trudy, later Lady Bliss, A.B.'s first meeting with, *see* Hoffmann, Trudy; married in June 1925, 84; broadcasting by, 164; children's births, 89; first visit of, to N. Italy, 91–2; in England, November 1943, 164; in Russia in 1956, 196 seqq.; other principal references to, 95, 96, 97, 98, 102–3, 108, 109, 115, 126–8, 130–48, 154–61, 187, 193 225 seqq.; writings on Jane and Thomas Carlyle, 189–91; *see* other refs. *passim*, *see also* Bliss, Arthur

Bloch, Ernest, 124

Blow, John, *Coronation Anthems with Strings*, 194

Bohemian Grove (theatre) near San Francisco, 80

Bolshoi Ballet, 203

Boris Godounov, Tsar of Russia, 197

Boston Museum of Fine Arts, 122

Boston Symphony Orchestra, 78, 79, 90

263